KOREAN AIR WAR

OSPREY
PUBLISHING

MICHAEL NAPIER

KOREAN AIR WAR

SABRES, MiGS AND METEORS
1950–53

OSPREY PUBLISHING
Bloomsbury Publishing Plc
Kemp House, Chawley Park, Cumnor Hill, Oxford OX2 9PH, UK
29 Earlsfort Terrace, Dublin 2, Ireland
1385 Broadway, 5th Floor, New York, NY 10018, USA
E-mail: info@ospreypublishing.com
www.ospreypublishing.com

OSPREY is a trademark of Osprey Publishing Ltd

First published in Great Britain in 2021

A catalogue record for this book is available from the British Library.

ISBN: HB 9781472844446; eBook 9781472844415; ePDF 9781472844422; XML 9781472844439

21 22 23 24 25   10 9 8 7 6 5 4 3 2 1

Edited by Jasper Spencer-Smith
Assisted by Shaun Barrington
Cover design and art direction by Stewart Larking (Osprey)
Layout by Dave Ayres, creativebyte.co.uk
Index by Michael Napier
Produced for Bloomsbury Plc by Editworks Limited
Bournemouth, BH1 4RT, UK
Printed and bound in India by Replika Press Private Ltd.

Osprey Publishing supports the Woodland Trust, the UK's leading woodland conservation charity.

To find out more about our authors and books visit **www.ospreypublishing.com**. Here you will find extracts,
author interviews, details of forthcoming events and the option to sign up for our newsletter.

Title page: A flight of three Republic F-84E Thunderjets of the 27th FEG, which deployed to Korea
in late November 1950 to act as fighter escort to bomber aircraft. (USAFM)

This page: Vought F4U Corsairs being prepared for an airstrike on a North Korean position. (US Navy)

CONTENTS

AUTHOR'S NOTE

The Korean War is very much a forgotten conflict, but it holds a unique place in history for a number of reasons. Firstly, it was the first war involving large-scale jet-versus-jet combat, where the tactics of high-speed, high-altitude flight were tried and validated. Secondly, it was the first war fought by the newly independent United States Air Force (USAF), which came of age and finally broke free from meddling by the US Army commanders during the conflict. Thirdly, it was the baptism of fire of the recently formed *Zhōngguó Rénmín Jiěfàngjūn Kōngjūn* (CPLAAF – Chinese People's Liberation Army Air Force) and is still regarded in China as an important victory over neo-colonial forces. Fourthly, it was the first major conflict fought between the armed forces of the USA, the USSR and China, and military action was very much constrained by political considerations; the experience of Korea served as a template for the conduct of subsequent proxy wars between the super-powers over the next half century. During the Korean War, many lessons were learned about the organization and prosecution of modern aerial warfare and those lessons are still valid today.

Over the years a number of books have been written about the Korean War, but most appear to tell the story from just one perspective and none of them seem to be entirely objective. Furthermore, some of these works are difficult to follow because they do not keep to a chronological sequence. My aim has been to produce a comprehensive, logically ordered and impartial account of the air war over Korea, although I have also taken the opportunity to highlight the little-known British participation in the conflict by the Royal Air Force (RAF).

The war was fought by the air forces of nine countries (the USA, China, the USSR, North and South Korea, the UK, Australia, South Africa and Canada), so the primary source documents are scattered across four continents and are written in four languages. I have therefore relied to some extent on secondary sources, which are listed at the end of the book. However, I believe that I have found sufficient primary records in the UK National Archives and in the US to cross-check the accuracy of these secondary sources. RAF officers who flew the Douglas B-26 Invader, Gloster Meteor, Republic F-84 Thunderjet, North American F-86 Sabre, and the Douglas F3D Skyknight all wrote detailed reports of their experiences and Air Vice Marshal Cecil Bouchier sent daily reports to London from HQ US Far East Air Force throughout the conflict; in addition, resumés of USAF operations were circulated around front-line RAF units, as were periodic reports from 77 Squadron Royal Australian Air Force (RAAF).

Unfortunately, many accounts directly contradict others and some interpretation is needed in order to determine the actual circumstances. This is particularly the case with air-to-air combat, where, frequently, reports from either side of the same engagement differ markedly; on these occasions, I have used my own judgement based on my experience as a military fast jet pilot to propose the most likely course of events. Where this has been the case, I have indicated in the 'Reference Notes'. I have only reported 'kills' when they are confirmed in the records of both sides.

Narratives in four languages using four different alphabets present their own challenges, especially as the conventions for the romanization of East Asian languages have changed since the Korean War was fought. The McCune–Reischauer Romanization of Korean was replaced by the Revised Romanization system in 2000; the Wade–Giles system for Chinese has also been replaced by Pinyin Romanization and the picture is further complicated by the fact that may Chinese towns and cities have changed their names since 1953 (for example, Mukden/Shenyang). I have used the McCune–Reischauer system for Korean place names (for example, Pusan rather than the modern Busan) in order to retain commonality with contemporary documents, but I have also included the Revised Romanization in brackets after each first mention, so that readers can find those places using modern maps/documents if they so wish. I have used a similar convention with Chinese place names.

I have also used romanized abbreviations in the language of each country to designate the flying units of that country, so that the nationality of a unit is instantly recognisable. Thus the 5th JHY, the 10th FT, the 67th IAP, the 4th FIG can be distinguished easily as North Korean, Chinese, Soviet and US units respectively. USAF aircraft are referred to by their designations (for example, F-51 or B-29) but I have referred to US Navy (USN) and US Marine Corps (USMC) aircraft by their names (for example, Panther or Corsair); this reflects the practice of each service but also helps the reader to identify the service involved. Except where specified otherwise, I have used the term 'MiG-15' as a generic reference to both the MiG-15 and MiG-15bis, and similarly the term 'F-86' includes the F-86A, E and F variants.

CHAPTER I

THE KOREAN WAR

25 JUNE 1950–27 JULY 1953

Just before dawn on Sunday 25 June 1950, South Korean troops stationed along the demarcation line with North Korea were roused by an artillery barrage fired from across the border. Shortly afterwards, ten divisions of North Korean troops of the Korean People's Army (KPA), supported by tanks and aircraft, swarmed across the 38th Parallel near Kaesong and Chuncheon and advanced into South Korea. Simultaneously, a smaller force of North Korean marines carried out amphibious landings near Kangnung (Gangneung) and Samchok on the east coast. Taken completely by surprise, the poorly equipped South Korean forces of the Republic of Korea Army (ROKA) fought back bravely, but their units were swiftly overwhelmed by the North Korean assault.

Thus, began a war which would cover the whole length of the Korean Peninsula within the next few months; and rather than leading to the swift victory that the North Korean leadership had expected, the conflict followed its violent course for the next three years. The United States of America, the Soviet Union and China all became embroiled, as did many other countries which rallied under the auspices of the United Nations to support South Korea. In the skies over Korea, the newly independent USAF battled with the *Voyenno-Vozdushnye Sily* (VVS – Soviet Air Force) and the newly formed CPLAAF in the world's first aerial conflict fought predominantly by jet aircraft. The air war also involved the air forces of North and South Korea, the RAF, the Royal Canadian Air Force (RCAF), the Royal Australian Air Force (RAAF) and the South African Air Force (SAAF), as well as the USN, the Royal Navy (RN) and the Royal Australian Navy (RAN), and it included a diverse range of aircraft from jet fighters to wartime-vintage propeller-driven aircraft and early helicopters. Air combat over Korea brought its own lessons in tactics and organization, most of which remain valid today.

HISTORY AND GEOGRAPHY OF KOREA

Although it took the world by surprise, the outbreak of the Korean War was an almost inevitable result of the geopolitical influences in the region over the previous 50 years. The history of Korea reflects its geography, and over the centuries the country has

AD Skyraiders and F4U Corsairs are launched from the USS *Princeton* (CV-37) at dawn for attacks against the Chinese positions surrounding the US Marines at the Chosin Reservoir, December 1951. Air power was to play a decisive role during the Korean War. (CORBIS via Getty Images)

An aerial view of typical
Korean countryside - a
land of river valleys
cutting through high
hills. The lines of
communication generally
followed the lower
country. This view taken
in the winter shows
snow-covered terrain
under clear skies, but in
the summer monsoon,
the hills would often be
covered by thick cloud.
(State Library of Victoria)

periodically found itself caught in the midst of the struggles between its powerful neighbours. Korea lies on a peninsula that runs on a north-south axis extending southwards from north-eastern China (Manchuria) and is bounded by the Yellow Sea to the west and the Sea of Japan to the east. The northern border with China runs along the Yalu (Amnok) River in the northwest and the Tumen River in the northeast, but the lower reaches of the Tumen River also mark a short boundary with eastern Russia. To the south, the Korea Strait, just 150 miles wide at its narrowest point, separates the country from Japan. Thus, Korea lies at the focal point of the three major powers in the region: China, Japan and Russia. In the late 19th century, both China and Japan had begun to reassert themselves as regional powers after centuries of isolationism, while the Russian Empire sought to secure its far-eastern boundaries. After the Sino-Japanese War of 1894–5 and Russo-Japanese War of 1904–5, both of which were fought in and around Korea, Japan first assimilated Korea as a Japanese protectorate in 1905 and then annexed the country completely five years later. Over the next 35 years, the Japanese attempted to stamp out Korean culture completely, but there was strong resistance against their rule both within and outside the country. An independent government in exile, the pseudo-democratic Provisional Government of the Republic of Korea, was formed in Shanghai under the leadership of Syngman Rhee, and anti-Japanese guerilla groups operated in northern parts of Korea. These included the communist-inspired Northeast Anti-Japanese United Army, of which Kim Il-sung was a key member. During World War II many Koreans were conscripted into the Imperial Japanese forces, but others fought against the Japanese as members of the Korean Liberation Army (which formed part of the Chinese Nationalist Army), or the Korean Volunteer Army (which was aligned with the Chinese Communist movement).

Bridges over the major rivers in Korea were large robust structures. This photograph of the bridges over the Han River near Seoul shows the damage inflicted by UN air bombardment, but bridges were difficult targets to hit and a massive amount of effort was expended in trying to destroy them. (NARA)

FAR LEFT:
Map of Korea 1950. (NARA)

A Yakovlev Yak-17UTI
of the 29th GvIAP
(Guards Fighter Aviation
Regiment) at Dachang
airfield, Shanghai in 1950.
The Soviet unit had been
deployed to China to
help defend Shanghai
against Republican
bombing raids and to
train Chinese pilots.
(Krylov & Tepsurkaev)

A Yakovlev Yak-17UTI of the 29th GvIAP (Guards Fighter Aviation Regiment) at Dachang airfield, Shanghai in 1950. The Soviet unit had been deployed to China to help defend Shanghai against Republican bombing raids and to train Chinese pilots. (Krylov & Tepsurkaev)

At the end of World War II, the Soviet and US forces that had liberated Korea from the Japanese agreed to use the 38th Parallel as the demarcation line between their respective spheres of interest. Initially, Korea was governed by a US-Soviet joint commission, but each side manoeuvred to install their own client governments. In 1948, the Republic of Korea (ROK) was established in South Korea under Syngman Rhee, while North Korea became the communist-inspired Democratic People's Republic of Korea (DPRK) under the leadership of Kim Il-sung. Unfortunately, both governments proved to be autocratic dictatorships: in the DPRK the welfare of the population was sacrificed to communist ideology, while in the ROK the interests of the citizens were effaced by corruption. Neither of the Korean governments recognized the other as being legitimate and both claimed sovereignty over the other's territory. Border clashes were not infrequent, but Soviet forces left the country in 1948 and the following year US military forces were also withdrawn. A perception that, having left the country, the US forces would not return to intervene, led the North Koreans to believe that they could defeat the ROK in a swift pre-emptive strike and reunify Korea under the banner of the DPRK. This view was also shared by Josef Stalin and in early 1950 Kim Il-sung was given approval by Stalin to invade.

Just as Korea's geographic position defined its political history, so its internal geography shaped the course of the Korean War and its climate directly influenced the conduct of the air campaigns. With a length of approximately 550 miles and a width of some 250 miles, Korea is almost the same size as Great Britain. Most of the country

St Lt Dushin (credited with two B-26 kills over Korea) of the 351st IAP instructs a Chinese pilot before the flight, Kiangwan airfield, Shanghai in 1950. (Krylov & Tepsurkaev)

is mountainous, with terrain reaching around up to 6,000ft above sea level, but there is lower ground on the western and southern reaches of the peninsula. The weather itself in the region is dictated by the northerly and southerly monsoons. The former occurs in the winter months and is characterized by extremely cold, but very clear, air. Ground temperatures of -10°C are not unusual and there is frequently a strong northwesterly jet-stream of up to 200 knots at around 30,000ft. This jet-stream would provide a helpful tailwind for aircraft returning from operating over the north of the country to bases in the south. The period between October and March is, then, ideal flying weather. However, in the summer months the weather over the Korean Peninsula is affected by the southerly monsoon, which brings with it much warmer temperatures (20–30°C), but also thick clouds, heavy prolonged rainfall and thunderstorms, all of which limit aerial activity.

Because of the geographic position of Korea, local time on the peninsula is nine hours ahead of British Summer Time (BST) and 14 hours ahead of Eastern Standard Time (EST); thus at 04:00hrs on Sunday 25 June in Seoul it was 20:00hrs on Saturday 24 June in London and 14:00hrs on Saturday 24 June in New York. This difference in time means that simultaneous events in New York and in Korea may appear to have occurred on different dates. Military planning in Korea was complicated, too, by the dearth of mapping and the fact that, particularly in North Korea, a different grid datum had been used in different chart editions of the same area. On occasions, the US Navy, using one set of maps, and the US Army, using another, found that exactly

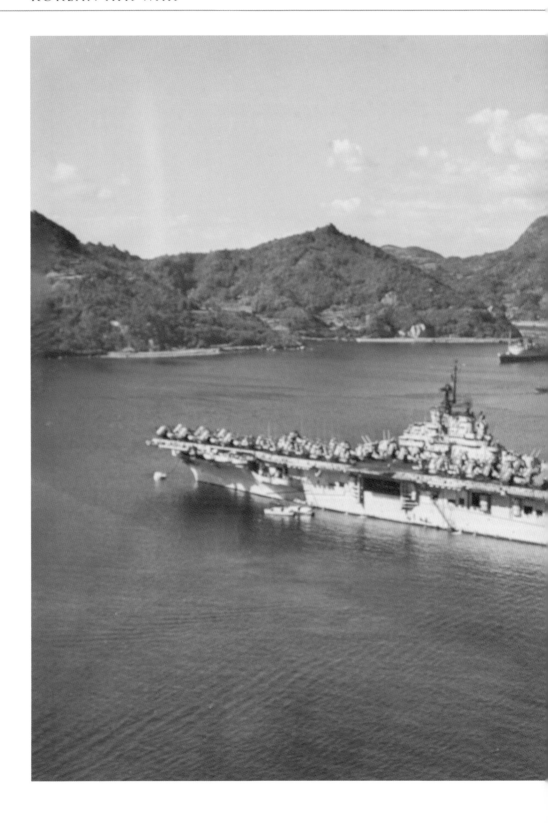

The US aircraft carriers USS *Valley Forge* (CV-45) and USS *Leyte* (CV-32) at anchor in Sasebo harbour, Japan, autumn 1950. (NARA)

the same co-ordinates on the respective maps described two different positions on the ground that were over a kilometre apart. This difference could have catastrophic consequences if, for example, the navy was providing fire support to the army. The maps were further complicated by the similarity of many Korean place names when transcribed into English. For example, Pyongyang is the capital city of North Korea, but Pyonggang is a small village in North Korea and Pyongyong is a village in South Korea; furthermore, many places were labelled with alternative names on different maps. To solve this problem, all airfields in Korea were given a 'K-number' to identify them: Pusan (Busan) became K-1 and Taegu (Daegu) K-2, and so on.

The lines of communication in the peninsula dictated the movement of ground forces during the conflict and therefore the interdiction targets for the air forces. The transport infrastructure in Korea was constructed by the Japanese during their occupation, primarily for the movement of military supplies and personnel. The railway network in the whole of Korea formed an 'X' with Seoul at the intersection, and the arms reaching out to Pusan in the southeast, Mokpo in the southwest, Sinuiju near the border with Manchuria in the northwest and Rajin near the border with Russia in the northeast. Because of its original strategic military purpose, the railway

system was designed to be more robust than a typical civilian network of the day. Embankments and cuttings were strongly reinforced and where bridges and tunnels were built for double track lines, they were often separate structures, sited far enough apart that an attack on one line would not compromise the other. The most vulnerable points of the rail system were the many bridges spanning numerous east–west flowing rivers. All these characteristics would become important factors in the air interdiction campaigns. In comparison to the railways, the roads in Korea were generally of poor quality but they followed almost the same pattern as the railway system. Again, the bridges were vulnerable, but the road bridges were not as critical as those on the railway lines: the rivers were shallow and since they had rocky beds, they could easily be forded in the summer months, while in the winter, the water froze and the ice was thick enough to support vehicles and pedestrians. A small number of airfields had been built in areas of low ground, but many of these were in valleys, where the close proximity of hilly terrain limited aircraft operations in poor weather. With the exception of Kimpo (Gimpo) – K-14 – and Suwon – K-13 – the runways at these airfields were generally quite short (around 1,100m), with gravel or compacted earth surfaces, so they were only suitable for use by light aircraft.

An AD-4N Skyraider of VF-194 traps aboard USS *Boxer* (CVA-21) after a mission over North Korea, early 1953. (US Navy)

OPPOSING AIR FORCES

During World War II, the air forces of the world had evolved into broadly similar organizational structures. The universal basic administrative formation was the wing or regiment, a unit based at a single airfield equipped with between 30 and 60 aircraft, depending on role and nationality. In the USAF, the wing was a self-contained entity that included all the functions necessary to support and carry out air operations. Within the wing, each function was carried out by a group, including, for example, a maintenance and supply group, a mission support group, and a medical group. The combat element of the wing was the operations group, which was designated by its role; for example, the operations group in the 4th Wing was the 4th Fighter Interceptor Group (FIG). The equivalent formations in the other air forces in the Korean conflict were the *Hang-gong Yeondae* (HY – Aviation Regiment) in North Korea, the *Fēixíng Tuán* (FT – Flight Regiment) in China and the *Aviatsionnyy Polk* (AP – Aviation Regiment) in the Soviet VVS and *Proti-Vovozdushnaya Oborona* (PVO – Air Defence Force). Each group/regiment-sized formation was typically further divided into three squadrons/brigades, each operating between ten and 20 aircraft, which constituted the basic combat units.

In North Korea, the *Joseon-inmingun Gong-gun*, (KPAAF – Korea People's Army Air Force) commanded by *Sojang* (Maj Gen) Wang Yong, had expanded rapidly between 1947 and 1950. In just three years, the Korean Aviation Society, which had operated a handful of ex-Japanese aircraft, had been transformed into a force of four regiments equipped with Soviet aircraft. By mid-1950, the KPAAF fielded some 40 Yakovlev Yak-9P fighters and a handful of two-seat Yak-11 combat trainers operated by the 56th *Jeontugi* (Fighter) HY based at Heijo near Pyongyang, and around 90 Ilyushin Il-10 attack aircraft operated by the 57th *Poghaeng* (Assault) HY based at Yonpo, near Hamhŭng on the east coast. Two more transport and training regiments completed the order of battle. Although the KPAAF had some 120 pilots in service and another 151 under training, only ten Yak-9 pilots and 22 Il-10 pilots were qualified as being combat-ready by mid-1950.

To the south, and in contrast to the corresponding air arm in the DPRK, the *Daehanmingug Gong-gun* ROK Air Force (ROKAF) was almost non-existent. In the summer of 1950, the ROKAF inventory comprised just eight Piper L-4 Grasshopper and five Stinson L-5 Sentinel light observation aircraft plus a further three North American T-6 Texan training aircraft. These were based near Seoul and flown by a cadre of 39 pilots. An earlier proposal to equip the ROKAF with a wing of North American F-51 Mustang fighters had been vetoed because the US government felt that it would increase tensions in the region.

After four years of civil war, the People's Republic of China (PRC) was proclaimed in September 1949. During their struggle, the People's Liberation Army (PLA) had not benefitted from air support and it was only in November 1949 that the CPLAAF was formed. This was largely a response to air raids on Shanghai carried out by the

A pair of North American F-51 Mustangs of 77 Sqn RAAF photographed over Japan in the late 1940s. The aircraft in the foreground crashed on a ferry flight in September 1950, while the Mustang in the background was shot down near Pyongyang on 22 December 1950. (RAAF Museum)

Nationalist *Koumintang* (KMT) bombers based in Taiwan. The USSR undertook to provide aircraft and training for the nascent air force, but when the Korean War broke out, the CPLAAF was still in the process of building an air force from scratch and there were no combat-ready Chinese pilots.

The nearest combat-ready air force to North Korea was the Soviet VVS, whose 83rd *Smeshannyy Aviatsionnyy Korpus* (SmAK – Composite Aviation Corps), commanded by *Generál-Leytenánt* (Lt Gen) I. D. Rykachev, was based on the Liaodong Peninsula, just across the Yellow Sea. This force, which comprised two fighter divisions, two bomber divisions and an assault division, provided the defence of Port Arthur (Dalian), which was leased from China by the USSR. The 83rd SmAK was equipped entirely with piston-engined aircraft, but Soviet jets arrived in China in March 1950 when the 106th *Istrebitel'naya Aviatsionnaya Diviziya* PVO (IAD PVO – Air Defence Fighter Division), commanded by Lt Gen P. F. Batitskiy, deployed to defend Shanghai from Chinese Nationalist air raids. This division included the 29th *Gvardeyskiy Istrebitel'nayy Aviatsionnyy Polk* (GvIAP – Guards Fighter Aviation Regiment) flying the

Four Lockheed F-80C Shooting Stars of the 36th FBS/8th FBG, each armed with two 1,000lb bombs, head for a target in Korea. The two aircraft in the background were both lost to anti-aircraft fire in late 1951. (USAFM)

Mikoyan-Gurevich MiG-15. The unit went into action against the KMT in late March 1950 and claimed its first air-to-air victory on 28 April. After seeing off the KMT air force, the 106th IAD was charged with training Chinese pilots in the new CPLAAF.

By far the largest air force in the Pacific region was the USAF. Formed in 1947, the newly independent USAF was a fraction of the size of its forebear, the wartime US Army Air Force (USAAF). Unfortunately, the USAF found itself under considerable political pressure from the leadership of the US Army, who felt that the air arm should remain subordinate to the army command. This friction was the cause of some poor decisions in the early days of the Korean War, when the desire to placate army commanders compromised the effective employment of air power. However, despite these difficulties and the post-war contraction, in mid-1950 there were still around 550 combat aircraft under the command of the US Far East Air Force (FEAF). The FEAF, comprising the 5th Air Force, 13th Air Force and 20th Air Force, was commanded by Lieutenant General (Lt Gen) G. E. Stratemeyer and had its headquarters in Japan; it covered a massive area stretching from the Philippines, Guam and Okinawa to Japan.

Pilot and crew chief shake hands through holes inflicted on an F-80 by anti-aircraft fire. Jet aircraft proved to be remarkably resilient to battle damage when compared to piston-engine aircraft, in which coolant systems were particularly vulnerable. This was one factor in the over-optimistic kill claims made by all sides during the conflict. (USAFM)

The FEAF was primarily responsible for the air defence of Japan, but it did have a strike force comprising the two squadrons of the 19th Bombardment Group (BG), part of the 13th Air Force, at Andersen Air Force Base (AFB) on Guam. These units were equipped with the Boeing B-29 Superfortress, which had been the most potent heavy bomber of World War II, but which was by 1950 obsolescent and had been reclassified as a 'medium bomber'. The 20th Air Force also included the 51st Fighter Interceptor Group (FIG), based at Okinawa, which operated the jet-powered Lockheed F-80C Shooting Star in the day-fighter role. Further to the southwest, at Clarke Field in the Philippines, the combat arm of the 13th Air Force was another F-80-equipped unit, the 18th Fighter Bomber Group (FBG).

In Japan, the 5th Air Force, commanded by Maj Gen E. E. Partridge, included two squadrons of North American B-26 Invaders of the 3rd BG based at Johnson AFB near Tokyo, and three fighter groups — the 8th FBG, 35th FIG and 49th FBG — which were based at Itazuki (Kyushu), Yokota (near Tokyo) and Misawa (Honshu) respectively and all of which were equipped with the F-80. Additionally, both the 8th FBG and 35th FIG included a squadron of piston-engined North American F-82G Twin Mustang night/all-weather fighters. All of the aircraft operated by the FEAF were

World War II vintage and even the newest type, the F-80, was obsolescent; its tactical capability was also limited by its short radius of action. Although the fighter groups had access to ground-attack weapons such as the 5-inch High Velocity Aircraft Rocket (HVAR), the emphasis was on training for the air-to-air role and their pilots had little practice in ground-attack profiles. Nor had they ever exercised with army units. Thus, the FEAF was singularly ill-prepared for an air-to-ground campaign to be fought some considerable distance from its bases, amongst mountainous terrain and during the summer monsoon.

US military air power in the region was also supplemented by the aircraft carriers of the US Pacific Fleet. In June 1950, USS *Valley Forge* (CV-45) was on station in the Pacific, with CVG-5 (Carrier Air Group 5) embarked. The air group included two fighter squadrons equipped with the Grumman F9F-2 Panther and one further fighter squadron with the Vought F4U Corsair, plus two attack squadrons with the Douglas AD-4 Skyraider. In the same month, the Royal Navy (RN) Far East Fleet carrier HMS *Triumph* (R-16) was completing a cruise to Japan. On board was the

A group of Republic F-84 Thunderjet pilots discuss their target. (NARA)

13th Carrier Air Group, comprising 800 Naval Air Squadron (NAS) with the Supermarine Seafire FR47 and 827 NAS with the Fairey Firefly FR1. The last vestige of the British Commonwealth Occupation Force in Japan still remained there, in the form of 77 Squadron of the RAAF. This unit, equipped with the F-51 Mustang, was based at Iwakuni, near Hiroshima, and was integrated into the US 5th Air Force. However, the rest of the British Commonwealth air power in the region was concentrated in Singapore and Malaya, where the RAF Far East Air Force (also abbreviated as FEAF) had been at full stretch since 1948 covering the Malayan Emergency. In mid-1950, the only British military aircraft available for deployment elsewhere in the Far East were the Short Sunderlands of the Far East Flying Boat Wing (FEFBW).

AIR COMBAT IN THE JET AGE

The air war over Korea was remarkable for being the first major conflict involving jet aircraft. Combat at high speeds and high altitude also emphasized the massive difference in performance between the first generation of straight-winged jet fighters, such as the F-80, the F-84 and the Meteor, and the subsequent generation of swept-wing aircraft such as the F-86 and the MiG-15. This difference in performance was essentially a function of aerodynamics and the effects of 'compressibility'.

The lift generated by a wing is dependent on two factors: its speed through the air and the density of that air. At high altitudes the air is much thinner (less dense) than it is at sea level, so the wing must travel faster to generate the same amount of lift. However, in doing so it becomes affected by a third factor, namely the local speed of sound. The relationship between the speed of the wing and the local speed

Conceived as a 'bomber destroyer' rather than an air superiority fighter, the Mikoyan-Gurevich MiG-15 nevertheless outperformed the Sabre, particularly at high altitudes. However, the slow firing cannon armament and the lack of 'G' protection for its pilots proved to be tactical weaknesses. (Sputnik)

of sound is expressed as its Mach number. Mach 1.0 represents the speed of sound: a Mach number greater than 1.0 is a supersonic speed and conversely a Mach number less than 1.0 (i.e. a fraction) is a subsonic speed. At high subsonic Mach numbers (approximately above Mach 0.85), the air surrounding a wing becomes 'compressible', which means that it forms into shock waves; these cause the normal airflow to break down which results in a loss of lift and a rise in drag forces. These shock waves form locally depending on the shape of the wing and if they form on control surfaces, they can cause loss of control. The effects of compressibility are most noticeable at high level because, just like the lift generated by the wing, the speed of sound is dependent on the density of the surrounding air, and it is reduced in the thin upper air. Thus, at high altitude a wing is affected by compressibility at a much slower speed than it would at low altitude.

Sweeping the wing backwards causes the air to behave as if it is travelling slower than it really is, which delays the onset of shock waves, thus delaying the onset of extra drag and possible controllability problems. For these reasons the MiG-15 and F-86 could operate easily in high subsonic Mach regimes at high altitude, whereas the earlier designs could not, and were therefore at a significant disadvantage.

The North American XP-86 prototype of the F-86 Sabre which proved to be a very effective fighter. The type was fast, manoeuvrable and robust, with excellent handling characteristics at high altitude and high speed. (NARA)

A typical scene at Itazuke Air Base, Japan, in mid-1950. On the right is a black-painted North American F-82 Twin Mustang night fighter of the 68th All Weather Fighter Squadron, while on the far side of the taxiway is a line-up of F-80s from the 8th FBG. (USAFM)

The inherent simplicity of the jet engine and the lack of vulnerable parts such as a cooling system made jet-powered aircraft far less susceptible to damage by small-calibre weaponry than previous generations of propeller-driven aircraft. The US-built fighter aircraft such as the F-80, F-84 and F-86 were armed with Browning 0.50 calibre machine guns and it was often possible for pilots to score numerous hits on a MiG-15 without causing major damage to that aircraft. Thus, there were many occasions were US/UN pilots claimed to have shot down MiGs, when, despite apparent confirmation

A flight of four bomb-carrying Republic F-84E Thunderjets of the 474th FBG heading towards a target in North Korea, late in 1952. (USAFM)

from gun camera footage, the aircraft had only been damaged and was able to return safely to its base. Indeed, the close proximity of the air bases in China to the combat areas over North Korea made it easy for Soviet, Chinese or North Korean pilots to disengage and land quickly if their aircraft was hit, but a near vertical dive by a MiG-15 towards the sanctuary of a nearby airfield was often misconstrued as the aircraft falling out of control. The MiG-15 was armed with more powerful weapons than its US-built types: a 37mm cannon and two 23mm cannons. These weapons were primarily

designed to bring down large bomber aircraft and although they had a much slower rate of fire than the Browning machine guns, their punch was much harder. However, while a MiG-15 might easily absorb a number of hits from 0.5-inch guns, a single hit from a 37mm shell could be enough to tear the wing off an F-86.

Air-to-air gunnery is a complex skill, requiring the co-ordination of three main variables: line, range and deflection. The trajectory of the shells must of course coincide with that of the moving target, so in general an attacking aeroplane must match the bank angle and flight path of its target; if it is flying to the left or right of the target plane of manoeuvre, the shells will miss. Gravity drop affects the shells, and if they are fired beyond a certain range, they will fall away from the target, so sighting is only accurate within that range. Finally, once the correct line has been established and the target is within range of the gun, sufficient deflection must be applied to ensure that the shells will fly to the same point that the target will reach as it continues to manoeuvre. Most air forces practise air-to-air gunnery by firing against a flag towed by another aircraft. Although well-practised gunnery instructors might achieve scores of 75 percent, most frontline pilots in the 1950s would have been pleased to achieve a success rate of ten to 20 percent. These scores were achieved against a non-manoeuvring target in an academic pattern, so the actual hit rate in high-G combat manoeuvring would undoubtedly have been far lower.

During the course of the Korean War, all of the air forces involved vastly overestimated the number of enemy aircraft that they had shot down in air combat. Such claims were probably made in good faith, based on the experiences of World War II, but they rarely reflected the real outcomes of aerial engagements. Indeed, the Soviets found that in Korea only 25 percent of gun camera films assessed as 'confirmed kills' had actually resulted in the destruction of the enemy aircraft. The gun cameras fitted to the MiG-15 had no 'overrun' and only filmed while the gun trigger was pressed, so the actual impact of shells was not actually recorded. In addition, during engagements with B-29s, Soviet pilots often opened fire well out of range because of the relative size of the large bomber (with a wingspan of 141ft) when compared with the fighters (wingspan typically 35–40ft) that they were more used to fighting.

An incident in the summer of 1953 illustrates one of the perennial problems faced by fighter pilots operating over Korea, namely the similarity in configuration between the F-86 and the MiG-15. Both aircraft types were almost the same size, with wings swept at a similar angle, and generally silver in colour. In a case of mistaken identity on 15 June, Major (Maj) J. Jabara, who was on his second combat tour over Korea and had already been credited with the destruction of eight MiG-15s, opened fire on his own wingman, Lieutenant (Lt) R.W. Frailey, and shot him down. Frailey ejected safely and was swiftly rescued, but the incident showed that even an experienced pilot could make such a mistake. In a similar incident on 4 August the previous year, *Mayor* (Mr) I.I. Rulakov of the 913rd IAP had fired on *Kapitan* (Kpt) M. P. Zhbanov of the 676th IAP, severely damaging his MiG-15. It seems likely, therefore, that other such incidents occurred during the course of the war and that inexperienced pilots remained unaware of their error. It follows that some of the victories and losses over Korea may have been due to unintentional fratricide.

In late 1952, Col Joseph Davis Jr, commanding the 474th FBG named his F-84G 'Four Queens' after his wife, Ann, and his three daughters. The four queen playing cards painted on the fuselage of his aircraft represent a poker 'four-of-kind' hand. The colours on the nose, tail, and wingtips of the aircraft represent the three squadrons of the 474th FBG (428th FBS, red; 429 FBS, blue; 430 FBS, yellow). (USAFM)

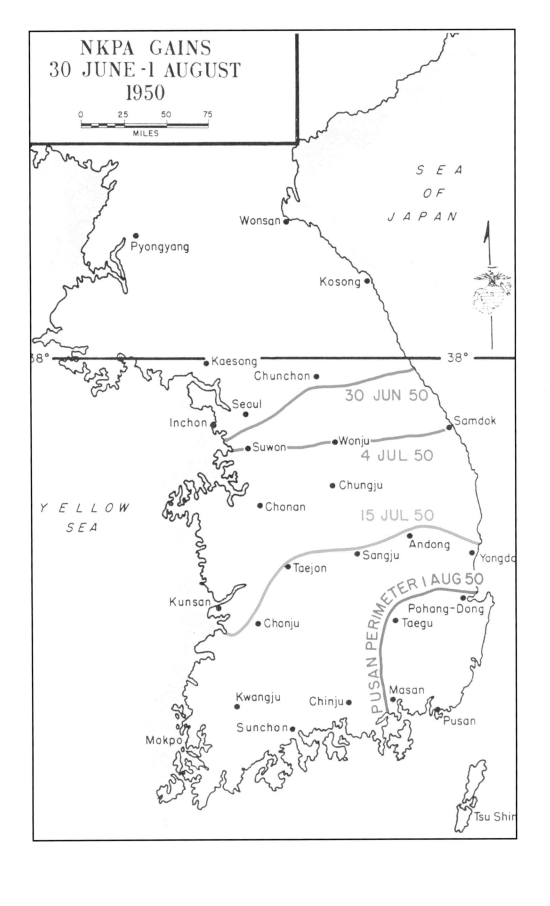

NKPA GAINS
30 JUNE -1 AUGUST
1950

0   25   50   75
MILES

SEA
OF
JAPAN

Wonsan

Pyongyang

Kosong

38°   38°
Kaesong
Chunchon
30 JUN 50
Seoul   Samdok
Inchon
Suwon   Wonju
4 JUL 50
Chungju
Chonan
15 JUL 50
YELLOW   Andong
SEA   Sangju   Yongdo
Taejon   PUSAN PERIMETER 1 AUG 50
Kunsan   Pohang-Dong
Chonju   Taegu

Kwangju   Chinju   Masan
Makpo   Sunchon   Pusan

Tsu Shin

CHAPTER 2

THE NORTH KOREAN INVASION

25 JUNE–31 JULY 1950

For Sqn Ldr J. F. Sach DFC AFC, sitting at the controls of a Boeing B-29 Superfortress, the flight on 24 June 1950 was something of a treat: he had escaped from his desk job at the US Far East Air Force (FEAF) for a week-long tour of inspection at Andersen Field, on Guam in the Mariana Islands. A wartime bomber pilot in the RAF, Jack Sach had flown the Vickers Wellington and Short Stirling over Germany. Now he was taking part with crews of the 19th Bomb Group (BG) in an 'operational exercise' from Guam to carry out a simulated strike at Okinawa, some 1,400 miles distant. The exercise proved to be remarkably prescient, for the very next day the North Korean invasion of the ROK marked the start of the Korean War and the bomber crews of the 19th BG would find themselves in action for real just days later.

THE FIRST FIVE DAYS

North Korean preparations for the forthcoming campaign started midway through June 1950 with field deployments of KPA combat units. The KPAAF also deployed to war stations, moving one of the two combat-ready Ilyushin Il-10 squadrons of the 57th PHY to join the Yak-9Ps of the 56th JHY at Pyongyang-Heijo (K-23) in support of the planned main advance against Seoul. Meanwhile, the other Il-10 squadron remained at Yonpo (K-27) to support a secondary thrust towards Choncheon in the centre of the country. In addition to these arrangements, four 'campaign airstrips' had been constructed closer to the 38th Parallel for use later in the campaign, when the relatively short-ranged KPAAF aircraft would need to reach further into South Korea. The KPA ground offensive started around 04:40hrs Korean time on Sunday 25 June with a heavy artillery barrage followed by infantry advancing forward behind a vanguard of Soviet-built T-34/85 tanks. But the southerly monsoon, bringing a low grey overcast and light rain, prevented the KPAAF from supporting the initial assault. By early afternoon, however, the weather had improved sufficiently for air operations

The KPA offensive, June to July 1950. (NARA)

and the Il-10s carried out successful strikes against fortified strongpoints on the ROKA lines.

The Yak-9Ps were also in action during the afternoon: four Yaks carried out strafing attacks at Seoul (Youi-do – K-16) airfield, where they destroyed seven of the ten ROKAF aircraft parked there. At the same time, two more Yaks attacked Kimpo Air Base (Gimpo – K-14), to the west of Seoul. Here they severely damaged a Douglas C-54D Skymaster belonging to the US Military Air Transport Service (MATS) which was parked there awaiting maintenance work. They also set fire to the airfield fuel storage. The next day, ten Yak-9Ps and a pair of Il-10s deployed to the forward operating base at Sinmak, some 70 miles northwest of Seoul, to keep pace with the advance. Once again, the weather limited operational flying, but during the morning the Il-10s, escorted by Yak-9Ps, carried out an airstrike against the railway station in Seoul. The two-seat Yak-11s of the 56th JHY were being used for tactical reconnaissance sorties and were sometimes flown in a 'pathfinder' role, leading formations of Il-10s or Yak-9Ps towards their targets.

This Ilyushin Il-10 Sturmovik is hidden in a damaged hangar at Kimpo (K-14). After capturing Kimpo, the KPAAF deployed its aircraft forward to give the relatively short-range types the ability to reach further into South Korea. (NARA)

US aircraft made their first sorties over Korea on 26 June. With no authority to conduct combat operations over Korea, the responsibility for the 5th Air Force in the event of hostilities on the peninsula was limited to ensuring the safe evacuation of US citizens. But despite the apparently powerful forces at their disposal, the planners at headquarters 5th Air Force had a problem as to how to carry out this task. The F-80-equipped fighter units would ordinarily have undertaken such a mission, but theirs were short-range aircraft. After a 298-mile transit from Japan to Seoul, an F-80 would only have only a few minutes of 'loiter time' in the operating area. The long-range F-51s of the RAAF contingent would have been ideally suited to the task, but they were still under national control and since the Australian government was not yet involved in the crisis, those aircraft could not be used. Instead, the F-82s of the all-weather fighter squadrons, whose crews were more used to night radar interceptions, were pressed into service as long-range day fighters. Relays of F-82s, drawn from both the 68th Fighter (All-Weather) Squadrons (F[AW]S) and 339th F(AW)S, mounted a continuous defensive patrol over Inchon (Incheon) from first light. During the course

of the day, nearly 700 non-essential personnel from MATS and the Korea Military Advisory Group (KMAG), as well as some 'friendly foreigners', boarded the Norwegian freighter SS *Reinholt* in Inchon harbour. The operation was uneventful until early that afternoon, when the first encounter between US and North Korean aircraft took place.

In the murky conditions, a pair of two-seat Yak-11s from the 56th JHY were carrying out an armed reconnaissance southward from Seoul. Nearing Inchon, the Yaks encountered two F-82s from the 68th F(AW)S, which were also patrolling just beneath the cloud base. Each pair saw the other at almost the same time. The Yaks split to attack the F-82s, which jettisoned their external fuel tanks and accelerated to combat speed, but the more manoeuvrable enemy aircraft quickly got behind the F-82s. One Yak pilot opened fire a long way out of range and missed his target, while the other never achieved a firing solution. After one turn, the Yaks disengaged and returned to the north.

The following morning, the KPA broke through the ROKA positions around Seoul and the KPAAF concentrated on targets in the ROKA rear areas. The Il-10s carried out airstrikes on Anyang rail station and military targets between Seoul and Suwon. The US military had already realized that Seoul would fall sooner rather than later and an emergency air evacuation had been quickly arranged for all remaining US and UN personnel. A fleet of two C-54 and 11 Douglas C-47 Skytrain transports was assembled together from disparate units in Japan to extract the remaining personnel from Kimpo Air Base, starting at dawn. The transport aircraft were heavily escorted by F-82s with a high cover of F-80s. The US mission was unimpeded during the morning, while the KPAAF concentrated on other objectives, but in the afternoon a Yak-11 led four Yak-9Ps to disrupt the evacuation airlift. In order to reach the transport aircraft, the

The F-82G Twin Mustang of the 68th F(AW)S flown by Lts W. G. Hudson and C. Fraser when they scored the first air-to-air kill of the Korean War against a Yak-11 on 27 June 1950. Trained in the night fighter role, the F-82 crews showed remarkable versatility in switching to long-range day fighter missions. (USAFM)

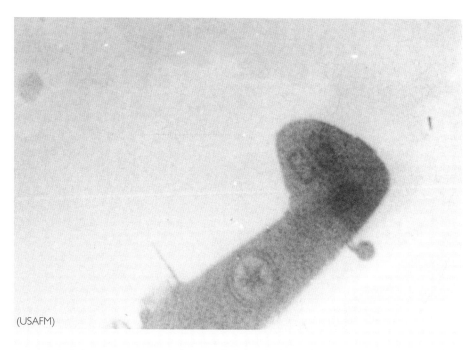

(USAFM)

Lt C. FRASER, USAF
F-82G, 68th F(AW)S, 27 June 1950

We were circling over Kimpo when two North Korean fighters came up out of some low clouds and started after Charlie Moran and Fred Larkins, who were flying the Number Four ship in our flight. The North Korean's shooting was a little better than yesterday and they shot up Charlie's tail. My pilot 'Skeeter' Hudson slipped around and got on the tail of their flight leader. When the guy realised that we were there, he pulled up into some clouds and tried to shake us off. Fortunately, we were so close that we could see him even in the middle of the clouds. Our first burst hit the rear of the fuselage and knocked some pieces off. The Yak pilot racked it over in a steep turn to the right and we gave him another burst along the right wing. This set the gas tank on fire and took the right flap and aileron off. By this time, we were so close that we nearly collided with him. I could clearly see the pilot turn around and say something to the observer. Then he pulled the canopy back and climbed onto the wing. Once again, he leaned in and said something to the observer. But he was either scared or wounded as he never attempted to jump. The Yak pilot pulled the ripcord and the chute dragged him off the wing, just before the ship rolled over and went in. The whole action took place below 1,000 ft. Later we found that Moran had evaded the Yak, but in doing so he had stalled out. When he recovered, he found himself dead astern of the other Yak and shot it down.

Two F-51D Mustangs, one from 12th FBS (foreground) and the other from 67th FBS (the two squadrons of the 18th FBG), are re-armed with rockets in late 1950. (USAFM)

KPAAF fighters first had to get through the F-82 Combat Air Patrol (CAP). Crossing Seoul at 10,000ft, they dived onto the four F-82s of the 68th F(AW)S, which formed the low CAP at 4,000ft. Although the USAF crews were taken by surprise and took some hits, they were able to turn the tables. Moments later, the Yak-11 became the first air-to-air casualty of the Korean War when it was shot down by 1st Lt W. G. Hudson and 1st Lt C. Fraser. At almost the same time, Lt C. B. Moran and Lt F. Larkins shot down a Yak-9P, but their F-82 was badly damaged by another KPAAF fighter and they had to carry out a forced landing at Suwon (K-13). Reinforcements from the 339th F(AW)S on a nearby patrol joined the fray and accounted for another Yak-9P. An hour later, another attack on Kimpo airfield was mounted by a formation of nine Il-10s from Yonpo. However, as they approached their target, they were intercepted by four F-80s from the 35th Fighter Bomber Squadron (FBS), which shot down four of the Il-10s and severely damaged another. The rest of the formation scattered into the clouds and returned home.

Seoul finally fell to the North Koreans on 28 June, and while the KPA consolidated its position, the KPAAF continued its offensive operations in an attempt to cut off the US resupply efforts into the airfield at Suwon (K-13). The previous evening, US President Harry S. Truman had authorized combat operations by US forces, and that morning, 12 B-26 Invaders from the 3rd BG flying under a low cloud base carried out a bombing raid on the rail yards at Munsan, some 25 miles north of Seoul on the banks of the Imjin River. This first operation behind the North Korean lines was not without loss: one B-26 crashed into the Yellow Sea when the pilot lost control while descending through the clouds and another diverted into Suwon after anti-aircraft fire disabled an engine. A third Invader crashed on recovery from the raid while making an approach to Ashiya, possibly as a result of battle damage. A follow-up raid by nine B-26s later in the day targeted traffic on the road and rail networks to the north of Seoul. In mid-morning and again in the mid-afternoon, the 8th FBG launched six waves, each of four F-80s, from Itazuke, tasked with strafing targets of opportunity in the vicinity of Seoul. The pilots reported heavy enemy road activity, which they attacked successfully. Meanwhile, the first KPAAF strike against Suwon was carried out in the early afternoon by four Yak-9Ps. The Yaks evaded the USAF defensive patrols and strafed the aircraft parked on the airfield, destroying an F-82G which had diverted there the previous day and the B-26B which had landed that morning. A second attack by six Yak-9Ps five hours later, caught one C-54D on the ground and another in the landing pattern. The aircraft on the ground was destroyed, but the C-54D in the circuit, belonging to the 6th Troop Carrier Squadron (TCS), managed to escape and despite the aircraft being badly shot up, the crew made a successful emergency landing at Ashiya.

The B-29 Superfortress bombers of the 19th BG made their operational debut that evening. The unit had deployed forward to Kadena Air Base on Okinawa for operations over Korea and in the late afternoon of 28 June four aircraft set out for an armed reconnaissance sortie over the area to the north and east of Seoul. The bombers split into two pairs: one pair followed the railway northwards from Seoul to Kapyong while the other pair followed the line eastwards towards Uijongbu, attacking

targets of opportunity on the roads and railways. The B-29s were in action again the following morning: bombing from just 3,000ft, nine B-29s targeted the buildings at Kimpo airfield, which was now in KPAAF hands, while two more aircraft bombed the railway station in Seoul. Two Yak-9Ps scrambled from their new forward base at Kimpo to intercept the bombers but the B-29 gunners claimed to have shot down one Yak and damaged the other. During the course of the day, the KPAAF was active over Inchon, attacking the railway station and shipping in the harbour. KPAAF aircraft also continued to harass US operations at Suwon, mounting six attacks on the airfield. Five of these were repulsed by USAF CAPs, which shot down an Il-10 and a Yak-11, but during the afternoon a flight of three Il-10s escorted by six Yak-9P fighters broke through the defences and delivered their bombs onto the terminal building.

Despite efforts made by US forces to stem the progress of the KPA, their advance continued throughout the afternoon. A force of B-26s from the 13th BS attacked the bridges over the Han River, losing one of their number, but wreaking havoc amongst troops and vehicles jammed on the bridges. The F-82s of the 68th F(AW)S also demonstrated their flexibility by changing role once again, this time to provide Close Air Support (CAS) to ROKA troops. This was the first time that napalm was used in

After the long transit from Japan, the F-80C Shooting Star had only a few minutes of loiter time over the target areas. This aircraft crashed near Taegu (K-2) after an engine failure in June 1951. (USAFM)

the conflict. The F-80s were tasked with operating CAPs at 10,000ft above the Han River to prevent the KPAAF from intervening. If they had not engaged enemy aircraft after their allotted time on task, the F-80s were encouraged to strafe road traffic in Seoul before recovering to Itazuke.

Soon after the KPA invasion of South Korea, the US administration had agreed to release ten North American F-51 Mustangs to the ROKAF under the supervision of USAF officers. The aircraft were tired airframes that had been used for target towing duties and had recently been declared surplus to US requirements. The Mustangs were to be based at Taegu (K-2), in the southeast of the country, where they would be used to train ROKAF pilots in combat procedures. The project, known as 'Bout One', was commanded by Maj D. E. Hess and included some experienced US fighter pilots as well as a number of Korean pilots who had seen wartime service with the Imperial Japanese Army Air Force (IJAAF). Eight of the F-51s were due to be delivered by pilots from the 8th FBG to Taegu on 29 June. On the same day Gen D. MacArthur, US Commander-in-Chief (CinC), decided to visit Suwon to see the ground for himself. Although MacArthur's personal Douglas C-54 Skymaster 'Bataan' was scheduled to be escorted by a screen of F-80s, the Bout One F-51s were also appropriated to fly as a close escort to the aircraft. While MacArthur held a conference in the local schoolhouse, the Mustangs established a CAP over Suwon, and when a formation of KPAAF strike aircraft appeared overhead, the Mustangs engaged them. The ensuing battle took place at low level over the airfield and was a one-sided affair during which three Il-10s and

An F-51 of the ROKAF operating from an abandoned hangar. The unit started as 'Bout One' under the command of Maj D.E. Hess, mainly with USAF volunteer pilots until sufficient Korean pilots could be trained to combat-ready standard. (NARA)

a Yak-11 were shot down. MacArthur himself witnessed the proceedings and was instantly convinced of the pressing need to establish air superiority over the peninsula. On his orders that evening, 18 B-26s ventured north of the 38th Parallel and carried out a dusk attack on Pyongyang airfield (K-23). The Invaders caught a large number of KPAAF aircraft on the ground and destroyed a total of 19. Of five KPAAF fighters which scrambled to intercept the raiders, three were destroyed by fragmentation bombs during their take-off run, but the other two engaged the B-26s. One Yak-9 was shot down by defensive fire from the bombers, but one B-26 also failed to return from the mission.

The Yak-9Ps of the 56th JHY, which had deployed forward to Kimpo, spent much of the last day of June flying CAS sorties in support of the KPA offensive across the Han River. Meanwhile, USAF aircraft attempted to bolster the ROKA defences. Bombing missions by 15 B-29s in the course of the morning against KPA troop concentrations to the north of the Han River were ineffective, but 18 B-26s that attacked traffic on the bridges over the Han met with more success. The F-80s also continued their tactic of strafing targets of opportunity at the end of their CAP before recovering to Japan. It was during one such attack that a pair of KPAAF Yak-9Ps flown by Jung-wi (Lt) Lee Dong-Gyu and Maj Tae Kuk-Sung bounced two F-80s of the 8th FBG flown by Lt J. B. Thomas and Lt C. A. Wurster. During the engagement at low-level, Lee Dong-Gyu realized that his wingman was threatened by four more F-80s and came to his rescue, firing on an F-80, although his own aeroplane was under attack

In 1950, the Grumman F9F-2 Panther was the prime air-defence fighter in the US Navy. The first arrived over Korea aboard USS *Valley Forge* (CV-45), although this particular aircraft is from VF-721 from USS *Boxer* (CV-21) and is taking part in an attack on Hungnam in 1951. (US Navy)

by Wurster. The Yak flown by Lee was shot down but he bailed out successfully and although the other Yak-9 was damaged, Tae managed to return to Kimpo. The North Koreans claimed to have shot down one F-80, although US sources claim variously that the F-80 flown by Lt E. T. Johnson which was lost on that day was either hit by anti-aircraft fire or flew into power cables.

The first days of the aerial conflict demonstrated on the one hand the flexibility of USAF aircrews, but on the other hand the shortcomings of their equipment. The F-82s had proven adequate as stop-gap escort fighters, but the aircraft was neither designed nor suitable for close air-to-air combat. The B-26s, too, were little better, being elderly airframes, which were poorly maintained because of a shortage of spare parts.

The main problem, however, in a conflict that had rapidly become a long-range ground-attack campaign, was the F-80C. Unfortunately, its many advantages, such as its speed, the good forward view afforded to the pilot and its reduced vulnerability to ground fire, were more than offset by its short range and the lack of hardpoints for bombs. Its pilots, too, were unpractised in ground-attack profiles. Furthermore, the F-80 could not be based forward in Korea because the remaining airfields there, such as Taegu, were only rough strips that were completely unsuitable for use by jet aircraft. Apart from being too short, the runway surfaces could not support the high-pressure tyres of jet aircraft, whose engines were also susceptible to damage if they ingested debris such as gravel or stones. There was a fix of sorts for the issue of inadequate range by modifying the fuel drop-tanks of the F-80. By cutting the standard tank in half and inserting the centre section of a Fletcher tank, each could carry an extra 100 gallons. The idea was pioneered by the 49th FBW at Misawa Air Base and attaching two of the modified 'Misawa tanks' generated an extra 30 minutes of flying time at medium altitude. However, the Misawa tanks were no panacea: they did not have baffles, as fitted in normal fuel tanks, to stop fuel from surging from one end to the other, so in dynamic manoeuvres, such as pulling out from a dive attack, the aircraft could be subject to extreme and rapid changes in its centre of gravity. A further problem was that the runways in Japan were relatively short, so despite the ability to carry extra fuel, the aircraft take-off weight (fuel plus weapon load) was still the limiting factor. The ultimate solution to the shortcomings of the F-80 was to replace the type in the inventory with the F-51. But the Mustang was hardly an ideal ground-attack aircraft – the liquid-cooled engine was vulnerable to small arms fire, also it obscured the forward view and its noise and vibrations made the aeroplane more fatiguing to fly than a jet – but the type had a long range, making it ideal for operations over Korea. Most of the FEAF F-80 pilots had previously flown the F-51, so type conversion would not be a problem; but consequently, they were all aware, too, of the shortcomings of the type

An F-80C Shooting Star of the 49th FBG taking off from Misawa in the early days of the war. As well as underwing HVARs, it carries the large 265-gallon 'Misawa' wingtip fuel tanks, which were improvised by Lt E.R. Johnson and Lt R. Eckman of the 49th FBG from the centre sections of the standard 165-gallon Sergeant Fletcher tanks. (USAF)

and they were not necessarily enthusiastic at the prospect of flying the Mustang again in the ground-attack role.

The KPAAF had also demonstrated its determination during its combat debut. North Korean aircraft had been effective in supporting the KPA offensive and had carried out successful attacks on ROKA rear areas. However, the small size of the KPAAF meant that its tactical effectiveness was limited. The inexperience of KPAAF pilots in air-to-air combat was also telling: for although they had claimed to have shot down several US aircraft, the kill ratio still favoured the USAF and KPAAF aircraft inevitably came off worse when they encountered US fighters.

THE CONFLICT WIDENS

The day after the North Korean invasion, the US had convened a meeting of the United Nations (UN) Security Council to debate the crisis. At that time China was represented at the UN by the Nationalist KMT government, rather than the PRC and as a result of this arrangement the USSR had chosen to boycott the UN Security Council in protest. Thus, neither the USSR nor the PRC were in a position to challenge the perspective of the US and its major ally, the UK. UN Security Council Resolutions issued on 25 and 27 June demanded the withdrawal of KPA troops from South Korea and called upon UN member states to 'furnish such assistance to the Republic of Korea as may be necessary to repel the armed attack'. In the next few days, two aircraft carriers, USS *Valley Forge* and HMS *Triumph*, were despatched to the area to form Task Force 77 Striking Force (later renamed the TF77 Fast Carrier Force) for operations over Korea.

US ground forces were also committed to Korea. Initially it was thought that a small number of US troops could rally the ROKA and a battalion of the US 21st Infantry Regiment was deployed by air to Korea on 1 July. The unit, known as 'Task Force Smith' after its commanding officer Lt Col C. B. Smith, was tasked with stopping the KPA advance as far north as possible. The rest of the 24th Infantry Division was also transported by air and sea across the Straits of Japan to Korea in the following days. Air transport movements were hampered by bad weather and the poor state of the runway at Pusan (Busan – K-1), but the division was deployed in the Pusan area by 4 July. Meanwhile, Task Force Smith travelled by rail to Taejŏn (Daejon) and then, accompanied by rain and low cloud, it continued by road towards Suwon, moving through a tide of refugees travelling in the opposite direction.

The Prime Minister of Australia, Robert G. Menzies, had authorized 77 Sqn RAAF to participate in combat operations on 30 July, but weather conditions kept the unit grounded for the next two days. The squadron flew its first sorties of the conflict on 2 July, escorting a formation of B-26s to bomb the bridges over the Han River and a formation of B-29s from the 19th BG to bomb the airfield at Yonpo. The latter mission had been planned on the basis of reconnaissance photographs taken two days earlier, which showed over 60 KPAAF Il-10s at the airfield. However, the KPAAF had subsequently moved most of those aircraft to Wonsan (K-25), Kimpo and the forward operating strip at Pyonggang (K-21), leaving only 15 aircraft at Yonpo. Despite all of the bombs being delivered accurately within the airfield perimeter, the KPAAF aircraft

(State Library of Victoria)

Lt H.C. JOHNSON, USAF
F-51, 51st FS, July 1950

We had two cans of napalm and plenty of ammunition and were looking for a fight as our UN ground forces were being pushed down into the Pusan Perimeter. It didn't look too good! We flew past the Naktong River at 1,500 ft and started to look for something to hit. When the KPA started taking a lot of hits during the day, it quickly moved to advancing at night – troops learnt how to camouflage their tanks, trucks and artillery by day. If you strafed a haystack and sparks flew from it, you knew that there was something inside other than hay. Sometimes they would drive their tanks into houses to hide them. On this mission the first thing that attracted us while flying over a village was when we spotted some dark-green painted military vehicles parked around a building. We gave them a burst from our 0.50-cals and then all hell broke loose. We took a lot of them out, destroying their vehicles and the building. It seems that the KPA was using it as some kind of headquarters. We still had most of our ordnance on board, so we moved over to a sand dune in the riverbed. Closer scrutiny revealed that there were six pieces of KPA artillery all lined up on it, firing away at our guys on the other side of the Naktong. I led our flight in and we each dropped our cans of napalm on them. Our napalm did not ignite, however, and we could see signs of relief on their faces. This was short-lived! Bad fuses on our napalm was not unusual, as we had experienced it before. Every third round in our 0.50-cals were incendiaries, so we made another pass on the non-ignited napalm. The rounds set the cans off and the entire area went up in flames, completely enveloping the bad guys and their cannon.

An F-51 Mustang of 77 Sqn takes off from Iwakuni on the first RAAF mission of the conflict, escorting a C-47 casualty evacuation flight on 3 July 1950. (State Library Victoria)

parked there remained unscathed. When darkness fell across the peninsula, the F-82s carried out their first night-intruder operations, searching for KPA convoys on the roads around Seoul.

Just before dawn on the following morning, the aircraft carriers of TF77 launched their first airstrikes on North Korea. Rocket-armed Seafires and Fireflies from HMS *Triumph* attacked the KPAAF airfield facilities at Haeju (K-19), while USS *Valley Forge* dispatched 16 Corsairs and 12 Skyraiders, escorted by eight Panthers, to bomb the airfield at Pyongyang (K-23). With no early warning facilities, the KPAAF did not respond to the British attack and in any case, there were no aircraft at Heiju. In contrast, as soon the US fighter sweep appeared over Pyongyang airfield, a number of Yak-9Ps took off to intercept the attackers; the two Yak-9s were swiftly shot down by Panther pilots Ensign (Ens) E. W. Brown and Lt L. H. Plog from VF-51, after which the other Yaks did not interfere with the US aircraft. Both of the KPAAF pilots (Maj Ki Hi-Kiung and Maj Tae Kuk-Sung) bailed out successfully and were able to rejoin their unit. That afternoon, the aircraft of CVG-5 mounted another mission against the rail facilities at Pyongyang, destroying a number of locomotives. This time they were unopposed by fighters.

The same day saw USAF F-80s armed with the HVAR for the first time, but employing the weapon operationally proved to be far from straightforward. First of all, the extra drag caused by the external stores had a more limiting effect on the aircraft's range than had been anticipated, and secondly, the few pilots who had previously fired practice rounds discovered that the ballistics of the live rounds were completely different. These problems were exacerbated by the low cloud base prevailing over the battle area: it forced pilots to fire the rockets from close range on a flat trajectory, which made aiming inaccurate and also caused the warheads to ricochet off their targets. Firing from close range also meant that aircraft were at risk of flying through the debris caused by their attack, exposing them to self-damage. As the situation on the ground became critical, pairs of F-80s, each armed with two HVARs and guns, were launched from Japan every 15 minutes during daylight hours. The aircraft had sufficient fuel to fly to the target area, quickly find a target to attack and then recover to Japan.

By 3 July the KPA had crossed the Han River in force, having ferried its armoured units across the water when the bridges were denied to them. The KPA 3rd Division was fighting to the southeast of Seoul, while the 4th Division fought its way through Yeongdeungpo to the south. The ROKA was trying to hold back the tide but sheer weight of numbers made a North Korean breakthrough only a matter of time. USAF aircraft attempted to intervene where they could, but the ground situation was far from clear and low clouds hampered air operations. By now the 56th JHY had seven Yak-9Ps operating from Kimpo and over the next few days these aircraft ranged between Seoul and Osan, strafing targets of opportunity. On 4 July, three Yaks jumped a newly arrived US Army artillery spotting aircraft, which was directing fire for US infantry south of Osan. The artillery spotter was agile enough to evade its attackers, so the Yaks left it and pressed on to Pyongtaek airfield (K-6), where they strafed US Army Piper L-4 Grasshopper and Stinson L-5 Sentinel aircraft, which had arrived that morning.

Vought F4U-4B Corsairs of VF-113 (Naval Fighter Squadron 113) prepare for launch from USS *Philippine Sea* (CV-47) for a strike mission over Korea in the Wonsan area, October 1950. (US Navy)

KPAAF aircraft were active on the east coast as well. That evening, two Il-10s bombed targets near Chumunchin (Jumunjin), after which one aircraft attacked the British naval sloop HMS *Black Swan* (L-57), which was offshore nearby. The Il-10 carried out two strafing passes, raking the upper deck of the ship with cannon and machine gun fire.

As the situation was becoming desperate for the ROKA, Bout One was pressed into action despite being nominally a training unit. At first, the South Korean pilots were included on operations from Taegu, but their inexperience in the role was soon apparent. On 4 July, the senior Korean pilot Junglyeong (Lt Col) Lee Geun Seok crashed while attacking KPA tanks near Siheung: it appears that he was attempting a manoeuvre that might have been appropriate in the IJAAF types he had flown during World War II, but which proved to be fatal in the heavier Mustang. As a result, the Korean pilots in 'Bout One' were withdrawn from operational flying. However, over the next week, the 'Bout One' Mustangs flew several sorties each day, mounting 2-to-3-hour patrols over the battle lines to provide CAS for the ROKA troops. The Mustangs of 77 Squadron RAAF were also in action again on that day when they

were tasked to attack road and rail traffic in the area between Suwon and Pyongtaek. The squadron commander, Wg Cdr L. T. Spence DFC, queried the orders as the target position seemed to be a long way behind the battle line, but he was assured that the details were correct. Leading eight Mustangs armed with British-manufactured RP-3 60lb rockets, Spence found a train and military convoy just outside Pyongtaek and attacked them. The attack was carried out with thorough efficiency, leaving the train derailed and wrecked vehicles burning. Unfortunately, when they landed, the Australian pilots discovered that the target position that they had been given was several miles in error and they had just destroyed a ROKA troop convoy, killing a large number of South Korean troops.

On the same day, the US and British naval aircraft carried out another airstrike against a railway bridge between Haeju and Yonan. KPA anti-aircraft fire damaged one Skyraider, which managed to recover to USS *Valley Forge*, but it crashed on the deck while landing, destroying two Corsairs and damaging another, as well as three Skyraiders and two Panthers. Having been diverted in mid-cruise to Korea, USS *Valley*

Light aircraft were used both for artillery observation and for airborne Forward Air Controller (FAC) duties. This Stinson L-5 Sentinel is flown by Maj V.J. Gottschalk USMC of the 1st Marine Air Wing. This particular aircraft was destroyed in a mid-air collision with a Corsair on 24 April 1951, killing the crew Capt R.F. Good and T Sgt R.J. Monteith. (NARA)

Forge now needed to replenish and re-arm, so after just two days of operations, the carriers were withdrawn from the Korean station and proceeded to the US naval base at Buckner Bay, Okinawa.

The early naval air operations had highlighted the limitations of the British aircraft: although both the Seafire and the Firefly were effective in their roles, neither type had enough range for long-distance missions over Korea. It was therefore decided that during future TF77 operations, the role of the Seafires from HMS *Triumph* would be to establish a defensive CAP over the task force while the Fireflies carried out anti-submarine patrols during the hours of daylight.

THE ADVANCE TO PUSAN

Late in the evening of 4 July, the KPA broke through the ROKA lines and started to push southwards. Early the following morning, as it advanced through pouring rain near Osan, the KPA 4th Infantry Division encountered Task Force Smith. The US troops were dug into a strong defensive position, but they had no weapons to counter to the T-34 tanks leading the KPA forces and the weather precluded any support from the air. Completely out-gunned and outnumbered by a well-trained and disciplined adversary, Task Force Smith managed to hold up the KPA advance for six hours before they were inevitably overrun. The poor weather continued into the morning of 6 July, when the KPA column ran into a second roadblock set up by the US Army 24th Infantry Division at Pyongtaek. This time the US troops were quickly routed by the superior North Korean force and the KPA continued its relentless march southwards.

By late morning, the weather had improved sufficiently for limited aircraft operations to resume over Korea. The KPAAF was active and during the early afternoon four KPAAF Il-10s operating from Kimpo strafed and bombed the communications relay station in Osan. Earlier, a flight of B-26s, escorted by the Mustangs of 77 Squadron, had found breaks in the cloud to the north of Pyongtaek. Descending through these they came across a concentration of tanks and vehicles, which they strafed and bombed. A follow-up attack on the convoy later in the day by three more B-26s was also successful, but one B-26 was shot down by ground fire. An F-82G was also lost during an armed reconnaissance mission that day. Meanwhile, three more Mustangs from 77 Squadron RAAF carrying out an armed reconnaissance to the south of Pyongtaek were called by an airborne Forward Air Controller (FAC) to attack a road bridge between Pyongtaek and Chonan (Cheonan), but their rockets had little effect on the structure. The Mustangs subsequently landed at Taejŏn (K-5) to refuel and re-arm overnight.

Elements of the US 24th Division fought another delaying action over the next two days at Chonan. Once again, the weather conditions were poor, but USAF aircraft continued to harass KPA forces wherever they could. F-80 pilots stayed over Korea for as long as they dared, looking for targets, and occasionally they ran themselves short of fuel. On 7 July, two F-80s carried out 'dead stick' landings in Japan after running out of fuel and a third pilot was forced to abandon his aircraft over the sea for the same reason. Although the main KPA thrust was from Seoul towards Taejŏn, the secondary advance down the eastern side of the country was steadily gaining ground. On that day, four Mustangs from 77 Squadron were tasked with an armed reconnaissance near

A Boeing B-29 Superfortress of the 307th BG dropping its weapon load over North Korea in late 1950. The Group deployed from MacDill AFB, Florida to Kadena AB, on Okinawa in August 1950. (USAFM)

The Douglas B-26C Invader (not to be confused with the Martin B-26 Marauder of World War II) was the main night interdictor. This aircraft is from the 8th BS (3rd BG Light) which operated initially from Japanese bases but began to operate from Taegu (K-2) from November 1950. (USAFM)

Samchok (Samcheok) on the eastern side of the country. During an attack on the railway station there, Sqn Ldr G. Strout was shot down by anti-aircraft fire, becoming the first Australian casualty of the war.

After a hard fight, the might of the KPA 3rd and 4th Divisions eventually overwhelmed the US force at Chonan on the morning of 8 July, forcing them to retreat once again to a new defensive line on the Kum River near Taejŏn. Regardless of the inclement weather, USAF aircraft were launched regularly from the Japanese bases to seek out and attack KPA convoys and troop concentrations. In three days, from 7 to 9 July, almost 200 trucks and nearly 50 tanks were destroyed by US aircraft on the roads between Seoul and Pyongtaek. Reinforcements, in the shape of two wings of B-29s, had begun to arrive in theatre, too. The 22nd BG deployed from its base at March AFB, California, to Kadena on 8 July, while the 92nd BG from Spokane, Washington, deployed to Yokota. The aircraft from the US mainland were equipped with the AN/APG-13 radar, which gave them a capability to bomb targets 'blind' through cloud, whereas the 19th BG aircraft had to find their targets visually. The arrival of aircraft with an all-weather capability was a major benefit to the FEAF bomber force in the midst of the summer monsoon.

Less dramatic, perhaps, but arguably of greater significance, was the arrival at Taejŏn on the next day of two L-5G liaison aircraft equipped with VHF radios. These were to be used by FACs to control airstrikes more closely. The airborne FAC was to become one of the major factors in the success of CAS sorties during the conflict.

Unfortunately, on 9 July the radios did not work in the field, but undaunted, the FACs 'borrowed' two Ryan L-17 Navions from the artillery aviation flight of 24th Division and during the course of the day they directed the airstrikes of some ten sections of F-80s onto suitable targets. The TACPs were also busy on 9 July, calling for airstrikes on a concentration of KPA armour and vehicles near Chonui (Jeonui) which was threatening US positions. The first aircraft on the scene were F-51s from 'Bout One', which struck the front and rear vehicles to immobilize the column. Subsequent waves of F-80s, F-82s and B-26s, as well as the continued attention of the 'Bout One' aircraft destroyed most of the tanks and other vehicles.

As the frontlines moved southwards, the KPAAF had also deployed aircraft forwards, moving five Yak-9Ps to operate from Suwon. Just as USAF aircraft roamed the rear KPA areas in search of targets, so the KPAAF aircraft ranged over the ROKA lines. Two Yaks caught the airborne FAC working between Ichon (Icheon) and Umsong (Eumseong), to the northeast of Chonan, but once again the more manoeuvrable L-17 was able to evade its attackers. By now the KPAAF had worked out how long US jet fighters could remain on station and they timed their patrols to coincide with the departure of F-80s from the battle area. On 10 July, four Il-10s strafed US troops at Cheongju during a gap in their air cover and the next day three Yaks bounced a flight of F-80s just as they were leaving the same area but did not achieve any kills.

During this second week of July, B-29 sorties included armed reconnaissance missions against targets of opportunity on the roads between Chonan and Suwon. It was a role for which the large bomber was singularly unsuitable, and the crews had little success against small targets, but they were very effective against well-defined static targets, such as bridges. In the afternoon of 10 July, a flight of F-80s located a concentration of North Korean armour and vehicles that had halted short of a destroyed bridge near Pyongtaek. Throughout the rest of the afternoon, all available aircraft were launched from Japan to attack this valuable target. In the course of the afternoon, and despite thick clouds in the area, US aircraft claimed the destruction of over 100 soft-skinned vehicles and some 40 tanks.

B-29 raids against bridges in the rear area continued through the next day and on 12 July a force of ten B-29s attacked KPA lines of communication near Seoul. This latter raid was intercepted by two Yak-9Ps and a two-seat Yak-9V flown by Lt Lee Dong-Gyu set one of the B-29s ablaze with cannon fire. The bomber crew bailed out over the sea and were subsequently rescued. The next day, fifty B-29s from the 22nd and 92nd BGs carried out a radar-aimed bombing raid through the clouds against the oil refinery and railway marshalling yards at Wonsan.

As the KPA divisions advanced southwards, they encountered another defensive line manned by the US Army 24th Infantry Division along the line of the Kum River, almost ten miles to the northwest of Taejŏn. The KPA 3rd Infantry Division opened its attacks on US positions on the morning of 14 July and the battle raged around Taejŏn over the next six days. Once again, air support to the battle area was greatly limited by the weather and the Mustangs of 77 Squadron RAAF managed only two successful missions during the battle, on 14 and 16 July, against bridges and ferries

An F-51 Mustang of the 12th FBS parked in its dispersal in Korea, while surplus stores are burnt in the background. The 12th FBS deployed as far north as Pyongyang East (K-24) in November 1950 before withdrawing to Suwon (K-13) in the face of the Chinese Offensive. (State Library of Victoria)

crossing the Kum River. However, USAF aircraft continued to mount around 200 combat sorties each day over Korea, attacking the KPA resupply and reinforcements lines wherever the weather permitted. B-29s attacked targets near Seoul, including airfields, as well as railway facilities nearer to the combat area. Engagements between USAF and KPAAF aircraft became more frequent over the next few days, resulting in losses on both sides. However, it was the KPAAF that suffered the higher losses and the rate of attrition had a much greater effect on the smaller North Korean force.

The system of airborne FACs became more established in the first few weeks of July. A trial using a North American T-6 Texan for FAC work had proved successful: the aircraft was faster and more rugged than the light aircraft used by the US Army units and it proved to be an ideal platform for the FAC. Initially, the FACs used a number of insect-related callsigns such as 'Dragonfly' and 'Mosquito', but they soon

The RN aircraft carrier HMS *Triumph* seen near the Philippines in March 1950. The Seafire FR47s of No.800 NAS are visible on the forward deck, while the Fairey Firefly F1s of No.827 NAS are on the aft deck. (US Naval)

adopted the universal callsign 'Mosquito', which also became the generic term for the T-6 aircraft. Lessons had been learned, too, from various unfortunate incidents of friendly fire where US and Australian aircraft had attacked US or ROKA troops in error: a realistic 'bomb line' was established beyond which aircraft had freedom to attack any ground targets, but inside which attacks had to be approved or controlled by a FAC or a Tactical Air Control Party (TACP). In theory, requests for air support were routed through the army headquarters units to the Joint Operations Center (JOC), which had originally been established at Taejŏn but had by now moved to Taegu (and would later re-locate to Pusan). If the JOC in turn approved the request, it sent it to the co-located Tactical Air Control Center (TACC), which then tasked aircraft to launch from the bases in Japan to respond to the army requirements. Once they arrived on the scene, the aircraft contacted the TACP or FAC for detailed instructions.

A damaged Supermarine Seafire FR47, of 800 NAS, after engaging the safety barrier on HMS *Triumph* in late 1950. (Thomas)

However, the unwieldy communication chain and the swiftly changing tactical situation often made the system unworkable: at best the aircraft might respond in approximately 40 minutes, by which time it could be too late. Sometimes the most pragmatic solution was for the FAC or TACP to re-direct fighter-bombers on pre-planned missions and divert them to more urgent tasks.

Meanwhile, more F-51 units were deployed to Korea. Raised from volunteers serving with the 12th FBS in the Philippines, a unit code-named 'Dallas' had been issued with ten surplus F-51s which had been in storage in Japan. Arriving at Taegu on 11 July, Dallas was renamed the 51st FBS and also absorbed most of the F-51s used by 'Bout One'. The 51st FBS flew its first operational mission on 15 July. Enough surplus aircraft were also obtained from storage for the 40th FIS, normally based at Yokota, to convert back to the F-51. Work had started on 12 July to improve and extend the runways at Pohang (K-3), on the coast 48 miles to the east of Taegu, which would become the new home of the 40th FIS. Hard standings were built for aircraft dispersals and the runways were strengthened and overlaid with Pierced Steel Planking (PSP). The 40th FIS deployed to Pohang on 16 July and over the next few days the pilots flew CAS sorties under a 150ft cloud base. Operating in these marginal weather conditions amongst the hilly terrain of Korea was an impressive feat of airmanship. Because of the difficulties in employing the HVAR successfully in such conditions, napalm became the preferred weapon against KPA targets.

Unfortunately, inter-service politics between the US Army and the USAAF marred some of the tasking decisions for the B-29 force. The US Army commanders made no secret of their belief that all close air support functions should be directly controlled by the army rather than the USAF; as a result, air force commanders felt that they could not refuse any request for air support, or the USAF would be seen to be failing in its responsibilities. The B-29, with its huge bomb load, seemed to army planners to be the ideal machine for CAS missions, even though the aeroplane was designed as a strategic bomber and its crews were trained accordingly; nevertheless, eight of the aircraft were employed for CAS on 16 July. This came as a great surprise on the day to the airborne FAC when he asked for details of the aircraft armament, expecting perhaps two 500lb bombs and HVAR, but was astonished to be told that each aircraft carried no less than 48 500lb bombs. Two days later, Gen Stratemeyer insisted that the B-29s be used correctly. However, targeting had become the responsibility of the US Army GHQ Targeting Group from 14 July. The result of such specialist decisions being made by laymen was perhaps inevitable: the first target list produced on 19 July included bridges and other targets which did not actually exist. The ill-considered GHQ Targeting Group was superseded by the joint service Far East Command (FEC) Target Selection Committee on 24 July, which went a long way to ensuring the correct use of USAF strategic assets. One continued shortcoming, however, was the lack of any proper mechanism to co-ordinate USN aircraft into the daily tasking.

The only RAF flying units committed to UN air forces arrived in mid-July in the form of three Sunderland flying boats from 88 Squadron, normally based in Singapore. The aircraft were to supplement Lockheed P-2V Neptune, Consolidated PB4Y-2 Privateer, and Martin PBM-5A Mariner maritime patrol aircraft operated by the USN to enforce the blockade of North Korean ports and carry out anti-shipping, anti-submarine and anti-mine patrols. Sunderland operations started on 18 July with a daylight anti-submarine patrol over the Yellow Sea.

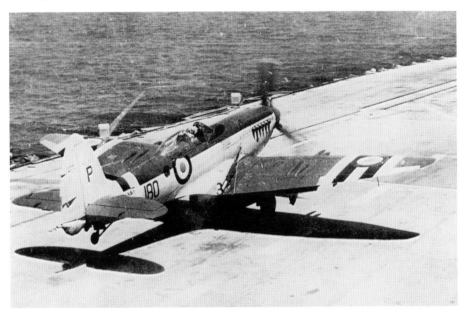

A Supermarine Seafire FR47 of No.800 NAS taking off from HMS *Triumph* in September 1950. On a crowded flight deck, there was insufficient room to use the catapult for the first aircraft, so the aircraft is using Rocket Assisted Take-Off Gear (RATOG): the jettisonable rocket packs are visible above the inner wings. (Thomas)

The aircraft carriers of TF77 arrived in Korean waters once again on 18 July, this time stationing themselves in the Sea of Japan almost 60 miles northeast of Pohang in order to support amphibious operations there. The US 1st Cavalry Division (in fact an infantry division) landed at Pohang that day in order to secure the northern flank of US and ROK forces. The landings at dawn were unopposed and USN aircraft jettisoned their unused weapons in the sea prior to landing back onto the USS *Valley Forge*. Meanwhile, the aircraft from HMS *Triumph* flew defensive CAPs and anti-submarine patrols. Later that morning, USS *Valley Forge* launched her air wing for operations against rail and road targets along the eastern coast between Kosong and Wonsan and the airfield at Pyonggang (K-21). Two formations of Panthers and one of Corsairs found some 25 KPAAF aircraft in two rows at Pyonggang and left most of them either wrecked or damaged. In another strike that evening, Skyraiders and Corsairs attacked the oil refinery at Wonsan, which was apparently undamaged by the

B-29 attack five days previously. The naval aircraft left the facility wrecked and aflame. At dawn the following morning, USS *Valley Forge* launched 13 Skyraiders, 19 Corsairs and 24 Panthers against targets in North Korea. The primary target for the Skyraiders and Corsairs was the chemical plant at Hamhŭng, while the Panthers attacked the airfields at Hamhŭng West (K-28), Sondok (K-26) and Yonpo (K-27). There were no aircraft at Hamhŭng West, but the Panthers found 15 KPAAF aircraft on the ground at Sondok and another 12 at Yonpo; at each base they left behind around six burning aircraft. Another strike by aircraft from *Valley Forge* later that afternoon against Hungnam (Heungnam) was less successful owing to thick cloud cover over the peninsula, but the Skyraiders found 9 KPAAF aircraft on the ground at Sondok and attacked them.

Pyonggang airfield was also visited on the afternoon of 19 July by seven F-80s of the 8th FBG. The pilots reported seeing approximately 20 aircraft parked along the

Shorts Sunderland GR5 flying boats of 205 Sqn and 209 Sqn of the RAF FEFBW on their moorings at Iwakuni in autumn 1950. The aircraft supplemented US Navy Martin PBM-5 Mariners patrolling the Yellow Sea and the Sea of Japan flying as far north as Vladivostok. (Thomas)

western side of the airstrip, camouflaged under tree branches. After strafing passes by the F-80s, almost all of the KPAAF aircraft there had been destroyed or damaged. Continuing the pressure on the KPAAF bases, the airfields at Pyongyang Heijo (K-23) and Pyongyang East (K-24) were also visited the next day by 14 B-29s. The losses inflicted upon the KPAAF during the airfield attacks on 18 and 19 July, as well as those incurred during air-to-air combat in the previous few days left it with only a handful of aircraft and pilots.

Nevertheless, KPAAF aircraft continued the fight: on 19 July three Yak-9Ps severely damaged a B-29 over the west railway bridge at Seoul. The same day, four Yak-9Ps escorted two Il-10s which bombed the railway bridge just north of Okchon (Okcheon), to the southeast of Taejŏn, in an attempt to cut off the US Army retreat. The Yak-9Ps then strafed the US Army command post and airfield at Taejŏn, although two of their number were subsequently shot down. KPAAF losses were mounting and so too were the logistic and tactical challenges facing it. The KPA frontlines were stretching towards the range limits of the aircraft at the same time that US aircraft, now operating closer to their own bases, were filling the airspace over the battle area, while naval and longer-range USAF aircraft actively sought out the KPAAF operating bases. In response, the KPAAF changed its tactics, instead choosing to operate in pairs, carrying out guerrilla-style hit-and-run attacks on targets of opportunity.

Although the KPAAF played little part in the North Korean offensive after mid-July, the KPA continued its victorious advance, having cleared the last US

A crowd greets Fg Off W.C. Horsman of 77 Sqn RAAF on his return from his first mission over enemy territory. (State Library of Victoria)

resistance from Taejŏn on 20 July. The North Korean progress towards Pusan was held up briefly by troops from the newly arrived US 25th Division near Yeongdong, but over the next ten days the frontline moved steadily south-westwards to the Naktong River, some 60 miles to the west of Pusan. By 31 July, the Pusan Perimeter had been established, extending from the south coast northwards along the Naktong River to Taegu, thence eastwards to Pohang on the coast. As the frontlines moved closer to the air bases in Japan, the F-80s could spend longer on station either finding their own targets of opportunity or being directed towards KPA positions by Mosquito FACs. Improved weather also meant that F-80s could deliver the HVAR from a dive attack, which greatly improved the accuracy and effectiveness of the weapon.

UNSCR 84, issued on 7 July, had directed the establishment of 'a unified command under the USA' for all UN forces in Korea. The United Nations Command (UNC) was inaugurated on 24 July with Gen MacArthur as the Commander-in-Chief. By then it was obvious that only UNC air power could stop the momentum of the KPA.

Over the next days, sections of F-80s and B-26s continued to launch at regular intervals from their bases in Japan, as did F-51s operating from Taegu (K-2) and Pohang (K-3), to attack KPA troops and stem their advance. Over Korea, each formation was assigned to a Mosquito FAC or ground-based TACP to be directed against a suitable target. USN aircraft also played an important role in blunting the KPA progress, although the first attempt to operate with Mosquitoes on 22 July, when TF77 was 100 miles off the west coast of Korea, was unsuccessful because of communications difficulties. Unable to support the ground forces directly on this occasion, the naval aircraft attacked secondary targets near Seoul instead. Three days later, the carriers were sailing off the east coast near Pohang; a 'free naval opportunity area' was established in the centre of the peninsula in which the air group could operate autonomously. On each of the next two days, four waves, each of 25 aircraft, from USS *Valley Forge* ranged over the area, engaging targets of opportunity such as railway and road traffic. The weather intervened on 27 July, but on 28 July the carriers had returned to the Yellow Sea and were able once more to fly four combat waves during the day. This time the naval aircraft were able to contact the Mosquitoes. Some of the Skyraiders were also used for FAC work to ease the burden from the hard-pressed Mosquito pilots. An unfortunate incident occurred on 28 July when a B-29 strayed near the task force and was investigated by two Seafires from the defensive CAP: The B-29 crew were convinced that the unfamiliar aircraft were KPAAF Yak-9Ps and shot down one of them.

With a chaotic situation on the ground and aircraft operating in often difficult conditions, it was inevitable that mistakes would also be made with ground targets. The situation was exacerbated by a KPA tactic of infiltration by small groups of soldiers in civilian dress. On 20 July two sections of F-80s from the 8th FBG rocketed personnel at No Gun Ri on the instructions of the FAC, inadvertently killing a number of refugee civilians. Four days later, naval aircraft strafed a building they believed was a military installation but was in fact a pottery factory that had become a refuge for a large number of women and children.

The Douglas C-124 Globemaster, which entered USAF service in 1950, marked a step-change in load capacity and played a vital role in the reinforcement and resupply of UN forces in Korea. (USAFM)

The carrier USS *Boxer* (CV-21) had arrived in Japan on 23 July with a load of 145 F-51s, which had been collected from Air National Guard (ANG) units across the US in order to re-equip some of the fighter-bomber units operating over Korea. After bringing the two F-51 squadrons in Korea up to full strength, these aircraft were used to re-equip the F-80 units in Japan, starting with the 67th FBS of the 18th FBG on 30 July. This unit was due to deploy to Taegu to join the 12th FBS (the 51st FBS there had returned to its original unit designation), but like the airfield at Pohang (K-3), the strip at Taegu (K-2) airfield needed improvement. US Army engineers had started the job on 18 July, but the work would not be completed for some weeks, so the 67th FBS remained in Japan. The 39th FIS converted to the F-51 on 8 August and moved to join the 40th FIS at Pohang, thus making up the 35th FBG once more. Finally, the squadrons of the 8th FBG (35th FBS and 36th FBS) swapped their F-80s for F-51s on 11 August and moved to Tsuiki, Japan, as there was no space for them at Taegu or Pohang.

One of the critical problems suffered by the US Army during the first weeks of the Korean War was a lack of artillery. As a result, tactical aircraft were being used as a substitute, being called on to attack enemy troop concentrations and vehicles close to UNC ground forces. Although this employment of aircraft was successful in slowing the KPA advance and relieving the pressure on the army, it prevented the use of air power to isolate the battlefield through a concerted air interdiction campaign. UNC air operations throughout the first month of the conflict had been those of short-term crisis management, and as a result, the KPA was able to move significant amounts of men and materiel into South Korea, where an extensive road and rail network permitted the swift transfer of reinforcements and supplies to the battlefield. Despite having lost any protection from its air force, the KPA had been subjected only to harassment rather than properly focussed and coordinated attacks. Furthermore, the KPA was able to move freely at nighttime and it used this opportunity to develop its night-infiltration tactics and to keep its front-line forces re-supplied.

UNC troops inspect the wreckage of a KPAAF Il-10 (NARA)

CHAPTER 3

UNITED NATIONS OFFENSIVE

1 AUGUST–25 OCTOBER 1950

After the decisive thrust southwards in the first month of its campaign, the KPA advance began to run out of momentum as it came up against increasing resistance from re-equipped and reinforced ROKA and US Army troops. By early August, the UN ground forces consisted of five divisions of ROKA troops holding the northern front running from Taegu to Pohang and three divisions from the US 8th Army holding the western front along the Naktong river between Taegu and Masan. The UNC naval forces were also reinforced: the aircraft carrier USS *Philippine Sea* (CV-47), carrying the five squadrons of CVG-11 joined the USS *Valley Forge* off the west coast of Korea on 5 August. This left HMS *Triumph* free to carry out autonomous operations against coastal targets as part of the British Commonwealth naval task force TF91. Two days previously, the light escort carrier USS *Sicily* (CVE-118) had taken up station off the southern coast carrying VMF-214, the first of the two F4U Corsair squadrons making up Marine Aircraft Group 33 (MAG-33). The second squadron, VMF-323, arrived a few days later onboard USS *Baedong Strait* (CVE-116), a Commencement Bay-class escort carrier. The two ships would take turns in replenishing so that at any time there was at least one USMC squadron on station to support Marine troops. All USMC units and groups deployed to Korea were under the command of the 1st Marine Aircraft Wing (MAW).

The role of the USMC Corsair squadrons was to provide CAS to the troops of the 1st Marine Provisional Brigade, which deployed to the Masan area on 7 August. Unlike USAF aircraft supporting the UN troops, the USMC air squadrons were an integral part of the USMC land operations. Pilots had infantry experience and USMC TACPs were embedded within each unit; during ground operations, USMC aircraft orbited overhead the battlefield, ready to carry out immediate attacks against enemy forces in contact with the Marines on the ground. During early August, the Corsairs provided support to the Marine brigade as it battled with the KPA 6th Division in the area of Chinju (Jinju).

Armed with napalm cannisters and fragmentation bombs, Douglas AD-4 Skyraiders of VA-35 set out from USS *Leyte* (CV-32) in late 1950. (John Dominis/ The TIME LIFE Picture Collection via Getty Images)

THE PUSAN PERIMETER

While July 1950 had been characterized by a mobile and fast-moving campaign, August was a month of relatively stable frontlines. The KPA continued its efforts to break through UNC lines, but the increasingly confident UN troops were able to hold their positions. Air power played a major part in the success of UNC forces: tactical aircraft continued to provide CAS to ground forces, while the FEAF bomber force was able to conduct an interdiction campaign designed to destroy the North Korean industrial base and to cut off the KPA resupply lines. Factories and railway facilities around Hungnam were bombed between 30 July and 3 August, before the B-29s switched to the marshalling yards near Seoul on 4 and 5 August. Two more B-29 groups, the 98th BG from Spokane and 307th BG based at MacDill AFB in Florida, deployed from the US to Japan in early August, bringing the number of B-29s in theatre to around 130. From then onwards, three B-29 groups concentrated on industrial targets in North Korea, while the other two groups attacked interdiction targets and in particular the road and railway bridges. By now, the KPAAF fighter force was ineffective and the bombers enjoyed the security of US air superiority over the peninsula. Industrial targets at Pyongyang, Wonsan and Rashin (Rason) were all bombed during the second week of August.

During interdiction sorties against bridges in North Korea, the B-29s were able to attack from as low as 10,000ft, making as many bomb-runs as they needed to without fear of interruption from enemy fighters. From 23 August, the aircraft of the 19th BG also used precision guided weapons in the shape of the 1,000lb radio-controlled VB-3 Razon (Range and AZimuth ONly) bomb. Initial results with this weapon were poor,

During the first year of the war, the L-5 Sentinel was used by the USAF for forward air controller (FAC) duties, but it was quickly superseded by the more suitable North American T-6 Texan. (Carl Mydens/ The TIME LIFE Picture Collection via Getty Images)

A F9F-2 Panther of VF-111 is moved on the busy flight deck of USS *Philippine Sea* (CV-47) during operations off the north east coast of Korea in autumn 1950. Despite being air defence aircraft, the Panthers were used in Korea primarily for strafing ground targets. (US Navy)

but once guidance issues had been resolved, it proved to be accurate and of nearly 500 Razons dropped, approximately two-thirds scored direct hits on their targets. The bridges were difficult to destroy, having been sturdily built by the Japanese and the FEAF estimated that each bridge had taken an average of 13 bombing runs before it was finally demolished. By the end of the month, some 140 bridges between Seoul and the Pusan Perimeter had been knocked down.

Meanwhile, US naval aircraft also conducted interdiction operations: between 5 and 7 August the two carrier air groups attacked bridges, warehouses and moving vehicles between the bomb line and the 38th Parallel. Each day the carriers typically launched four strike waves, each made up of 12 to 24 Skyraiders and Corsairs armed with rockets and bombs, plus another four waves of eight Panthers. Although they were equipped to carry HVARs, the Panthers were unable to do so because the high summer temperatures reduced their engine performance: the problem was exacerbated by seasonally light winds, which reduced the wind speed over the deck for launching, so the jets were generally armed only with their guns. Attempts to provide CAS for army units on 5 August were unsuccessful because of overloaded radio frequencies and a lack of planning to integrate USN aircraft into the air support system; but these problems were later rectified and aircraft from the USS *Valley Forge* flew CAS missions

With a full load of bombs, US Navy AD-4N Skyraiders, probably from USS *Valley Forge* (CV-45) start up for a mission after refuelling and rearming at Kimpo (K-14). (State Library of Victoria)

(NARA)

Capt W.H. HAZLETT, USMC
F4U Corsair, VMF(N)-513, 20 August 1950

Night flights are launched at 23:00 and 01:00hrs. Pre-dawn strikes get off at 04:30hrs and dusk hops take off at 1900. Flights average four hours in duration. It takes one hour to get to the target area and an average of an hour and 45 minutes to spend over the target area. Night flights carry bombs and ammo; pre-dawn and dusk flights are armed with rockets, a 500lb GP bomb and a napalm bomb... Marines are doing the bulk of night work at the present time. F-82s are all grounded (except one plane) for maintenance. B-26s conduct deep night intruder missions... Pilots fly in pairs with the lead plane showing running lights and the wingman blacked out. This system was initiated to avoid mid-air collision with Air Force aircraft after several near-misses. But it was soon discovered that the system was more effective against the enemy. When a target is located the lead aircraft orbits away from it, while the wingman attacks. Since the enemy only turns his lights out when he believes he's under attack, this procedure sometimes catches him with his all his lights on. On clear nights navigation is no problem – rivers and mountains provide definite landmarks. During unfavourable weather, pilots find it extremely difficult to orientate themselves.

A rare photo of a KPAAF Polikarpov Po-2. These aircraft were used to carry out 'night heckler' bombing raids against UN airfields. The slow speed and small radar signature of the Po-2 made it a difficult target to engage. (Cooper/ Grandolini)

on 6 and 7 August. The following week, the carriers of TF77 moved farther north to engage targets near Seoul and Inchon. The carriers left the theatre on 14 August, their place in the Yellow Sea taken by HMS *Triumph*. Six Seafires and six Fireflies attacked shipping near the naval base at Chinnampo (Nampo) on 14 August and over the next five days aircraft from *Triumph* engaged targets of opportunity in the vicinity of Kunsan (Gunsan). The main purpose of these operations was to fool the KPA leadership into expecting amphibious landings at Kunsan, rather than farther north.

Approximately 66 percent of the air effort over Korea during August was taken up with CAS missions. Even during periods with little action, around 400 CAS sorties were flown each day by F-80s and F-51s, on a front just 120 miles long. Mosquito FACs in T-6s constantly patrolled the length of the frontline at 1,500–3,000ft, looking for suitable targets. Despite overflying KPA units they were relatively safe from ground fire as the well-disciplined North Korean troops did not want to reveal their positions. When CAS missions contacted the Mosquito, they would be directed very precisely onto their target, with the Mosquito continuing to give instructions over the radio even while the attack aircraft were diving onto their target. The Mosquito corrected their weapon aiming on each pass. In the view of some observers this system was 'nursing the fighter-bombers to the extent where they were losing the power to find

An F-80C Shooting Star of the 8th FBG taking off armed with two napalm tanks. Napalm was the weapon of choice against enemy troops and armour. This photo of an aeroplane from the 36th FBS/ 8th FBG actually dates from November 1951. (USAFM)

their own targets', but it worked in practice. The F-51 pilots operating from bases both in Korea and Japan might fly four or five CAS missions per day, with the Japan-based aircraft re-arming and refuelling at Taegu between sorties, before returning to Japan at the end of the day.

Napalm continued to be the prime weapon against ground targets unless friendly troops were nearby. The napalm tanks were produced locally, using a standard 110-gallon drop tank as a container for gasoline mixed with a thickening agent comprising aluminium naphthenate and aluminium palmitate. Within the tank, two fuses were attached to white phosphorous grenades; designed for dropping bombs from 300ft, the arming vane required 17 turns to arm, but as pilots dropped napalm from around 100ft, they tended to pre-arm each tank by turning the vanes manually before getting airborne, a technique that was not without risk. Dropping napalm was described as being 'similar to throwing a bucket of water over the floor, as fluid runs and spreads in all directions... napalm will destroy any vehicle within 75ft of the point of impact... this "spread" factor is one of napalm's greatest assets, for the rocket must secure a direct hit whereas a near-miss with napalm is often effective.' An improved anti-tank rocket also appeared from early August to replace the HVAR. The new

A line-up of Vought F4U Corsairs from VMF-214. The US Marine Corps (USMC) units supported UN troops during the battle for Seoul. After the capture of Seoul, VMF-214 embarked on USS *Sicily* (CVE-118) and deployed on the east coast of Korea. (NARA)

B-29 Superfortress of the 30th BS/ 19th BG on a daytime strike over North Korea in late 1950. The aircraft was severely damaged by a MiG-15 on 12 April 1951 while bombing the railway bridge over Yalu River at Sinuiju. (USAFM)

6.5-inch Anti-tank Aerial Rocket (ATAR) had an improved shaped-charge warhead, which was far more effective against armoured targets than had been the HVAR, although its accuracy remained questionable. Interestingly, while USAF pilots claimed to have destroyed three times as many tanks with rockets as they had with napalm, study of the knocked-out tanks by ground forces indicated that three times as many of them had been killed by napalm as had been by rockets.

The second week of August saw vicious fighting between the KPA 6th Div and the 1st Provisional Marine Brigade at the southernmost point of the Pusan Perimeter, near Chinju. On 11 August, four Corsairs from VMF-323 supporting the Marines spotted the KPA 83rd Motorized Regiment, which was attempting to withdraw from Kosong in a 100-vehicle convoy. In what later became known as the 'Kosong Turkey Shoot', the aircraft managed to destroy 40 vehicles, leaving them ablaze, although at the cost of two Corsairs shot down by ground fire. The job was finished off by another flight of USMC Corsairs and by USAF F-51s. One of the Corsairs ditched at sea and the pilot was rescued by a Sikorsky HO3S helicopter operated by Marine Observation Squadron 6 (VMO-6).

At the same time as the battles in the south, the KPA also attempted to break through UNC positions on the northern and western fronts. KPA divisions threw themselves against ROKA troops in the Pohang sector and at Waegwan, some 12 miles northwest of Taegu. On 9 August F-51s destroyed six tanks attacking ROKA positions near Yongchon (Yeongcheong), but the KPA 5th Div slowly pushed the ROKA lines southwards. Two days later, F-51s were effective in halting KPA forces just north of

Pohang airfield. The pilots operating from Pohang commented that they hardly had their wheels in the wells before they started their first strafing pass. However, their success was at the cost of four aircraft shot down by ground fire. Because the enemy forces were so close to the airfield, the 35th FBG was withdrawn from Pohang to Japan on 13 August.

At Waegwan, the KPA 3rd Div had constructed an underwater bridge across the Naktong River and established a bridgehead on the eastern bank during the night of 6/7 August. B-26s attacked troops and tanks as the main body crossed the river on the night of 10 August. Five days later, rocket-firing aircraft destroyed tanks leading an advance and later that day an estimated 300 KPA troops were also killed in airstrikes. Nevertheless, the KPA continued to take ground and on 17 August US Cavalry troops were surrounded on Hill 303. A well-aimed airstrike caused the KPA troops to be routed, but not before they had executed a number of US prisoners of war.

A little farther south, approximately seven miles southwest of Changnyeong, the KPA 4th Division had crossed the Naktong River during the night of 10/11 August into a salient defined by a meander in the river known as the Naktong Bulge. Once again, the KPA established underwater bridges that were virtually undetectable from the air, enabling them to cross armour and heavy weapons into the salient under cover of darkness. A planned airstrike by 100 USAF aircraft had to be cancelled because of the weather. Having dealt with the KPA 6th Division in the south, the 1st Provisional Marine Brigade was redeployed to the Naktong Bulge to bolster the defences. Here, the

A fully armed F-80C Shooting Star of the 80th FBS/ 8th FBG, carrying two 1,000lb bombs. bombs. The bombs were used against targets like bridges or buildings. Note the pierced steel planking (PSP) which was a feature of most airfields in Korea. (USAFM)

Corsairs of MAG-33 were able to support the Marines during actions on the Obong-ni Ridge on 17 and 18 August; one Corsair scored a direct hit on a machine gun post that was pinning down troops on 18 August. The USMC observation unit VMO-6 also used its HO3S helicopters to evacuate casualties from the battlefield.

Three days later, the B-29s were once again employed against tactical targets: a force of 98 B-29s bombed an area close to the frontlines at Waegwan, where 40,000 North Korean troops were reported to be assembling to renew their offensive. Over a period of 30 minutes, the bombers delivered over 3,000 500lb bombs into an area some four miles by 19 miles. Subsequent reconnaissance showed no evidence of any enemy troops having been in the area, but the spectacle was said to have lifted the morale of the US Army and ROKA personnel who witnessed it. On the same day, all available aircraft, including those of TF77 which was now steaming off the east coast, were committed to CAS missions in support of the ROKA 3rd Div fighting the KPA 5th Div near Yongdok (Yeongdeok) just north of Pohang.

Despite the successes of the B-29 interdiction campaign against bridges, one structure, the West Bridge over the Han River at Seoul, seemed to be indestructible. Another strike against it was carried out by naval aircraft on 20 August, but it, too, appeared to have done little damage. In fact, the hits obtained by the USN had indeed caused major damage and two spans subsequently collapsed overnight. Another B-29 raid by the 19th BG completed the work and dropped a third span later that day.

F-51 Mustangs of 77 Sqn RAAF under maintenance at Iwakuni, 1950. (USAFM)

A 'solid nose' B-26B Invader of the 13th BS/3rd BG at Iwakuni. The aircraft was armed with eight .50-inch machine guns in the nose, which were very effective, but the muzzle flashes blinded the pilot at night. (State Library Victoria)

While the campaign continued against the bridges, the naval forces in the Yellow Sea enforced a blockade of the North Korean ports. In this they were supported from mid-August by the Sunderlands of the RAF FEFBW, which carried out nightly anti-shipping patrols in the Yellow Sea. These 11-hour sorties were vital but unglamorous, taking off at dusk and landing the following dawn.

Meanwhile, despite the increased KPA traffic in the hours of darkness, night operations accounted for only 4 percent of FEAF sorties. Aware of the shortcomings of its night-intruder operations, the FEAF staff sought expert advice from the RAF. Accordingly, the distinguished wartime RAF fighter pilot Wg Cdr P. G. Wykeham-Barnes DSO, OBE, DFC, AFC, who was the chief test pilot at the Aircraft and Armament Experimental Establishment (A&AEE), arrived in Japan on 20 August. The following day, he visited Gen Partridge, commanding the 5th Air Force at his headquarters in Taegu, which was close to the headquarters of the 8th Army. Wykeham-Barnes noted that the command chain was complicated by the fact that although Gen Partridge was in Taegu, the advanced headquarters of the 5th Air Force was 70 miles distant in Pusan and its main headquarters was 300 miles away in Nagoya, Japan. Every morning, Gen Partridge would fly over the frontlines in a North American T-6 Texan to assess the fighting in progress, before flying to Pusan to discuss the day's tasking with his staff. After noting that the result of this unconventional command structure was that close air support missions were taking priority over all other tasks, Wykeham-Barnes joined the 3rd BG at Itazuke, where he flew several B-26 sorties. The main burden of night-intruder missions at that time was borne by the B-26s of the 3rd BG; each of the two squadrons alternated a week of night flying, changing over each Sunday. Approximately 20 missions were flown by B-26s each night, with a further ten flown by the F4U-5N Corsairs of VMF(N)-513, which had been operating from Itazuke from 7 August. A small number of night sorties were also flown by the F-82s of the 68th F(AW)S. The main problem with the night-intruder sorties was that they were

FAR RIGHT:
A pair of F-80C Shooting Stars from the 49th FBW using Jet-Assisted Take Off (JATO) rockets to improve their take-off performance while carrying a heavy bomb load from Taegu (K-2) in late 1950. (USAFM)

BELOW:
A flight of four F-80C Shooting Stars from the 36th FBS/ 8th FBG over Korea in late 1950 or early 1951. The aircraft nearest the camera was shot down in November 1951, while the one furthest away was shot down in January 1953. (USAFM)

improvized in a haphazard manner. Mission planning was not co-ordinated, and it was not unusual for different aircraft to arrive over the same target at the same time. The terrain and weather conditions in Korea also made night attack difficult: high ground surrounded deep and tortuous valleys, while line squalls and violent electrical storms were commonplace. Nor was the B-26 particularly suited to night operations. The aircraft was slow and could only zoom climb by about 2,000ft, amongst hills reaching up to 5,000ft. Cockpit lighting was poor and the muzzle flashes from the nose-mounted guns blinded the pilot. Fortunately for night-intruder crews, the KPA always kept their headlights on at night, so convoys were relatively easy to find. Even so, night-intruder operations were of a harassing nature, rather than a properly planned interdiction campaign. After flying night-intruder sorties between 22 August and 1 September, Wykeham-Barnes wrote a detailed report and a draft concept of operations for night interdiction. Grateful for this expert opinion, HQ 5th AF fully accepted the recommendations made by Wykeham-Barnes.

Early on the morning of 22 August, two Il-10s from the 57th PHY carried out a hit-and-run attack on the RN destroyer HMS *Comus* (D20) in the Yellow Sea, some 80 miles west of Kunsan. Flying at 1,000ft, Lt Ahn Hon-Zhu led the pair to attack the ship. The Il-10s dived to 100ft and each one dropped four 50kg bombs on the ship. The lead aircraft dropped its bombs close to the ship, causing major damage, but the second aircraft missed when the destroyer took evasive action. The leader then made

a second strafing attack on the ship, after which both aircraft disappeared into the clouds. Lt Cdr R. A. M. Hennessy, commanding HMS *Comus*, described the attack as having been 'carried out with skill and determination'. KPAAF aircraft also claimed successful attacks on other UN coastal vessels over the next few days.

The British 27th Infantry Bde arrived in Korea on 27 August but it did not take its place in the frontline on the Naktong River until 5 September. Although the only RAF aircraft in theatre were the Sunderlands of the FEFBW, RAF personnel participated in combat operations with US forces: on 29 August Wg Cdr A. H. C. Boxer DSO, DFC (the assistant operations officer of the 92nd BG) completed his ninth operational B-29 mission, as the deputy leader for the 326th BS during the mission against Seishin.

At the beginning of September, the KPA opened a major offensive to break the UN army. In the assault, known as the Great Naktong Offensive, 13 KPA divisions

A Boeing 377 Stratocruiser of Pan American World Airways is chartered to transport US Marine Corps reinforcements to Japan, 21 August 1950. (NARA)

simultaneously attacked the Pusan Perimeter in five places: Kyongju in the northeast, Yongchon in the north centre, Taegu in the northwest, the Naktong Bulge in the west centre and Masan in the southwest. All available aircraft were called in for CAS missions, including aircraft from the fast carriers. One perennial problem with naval aircraft was the procedure of deck launches: the carriers could not launch and recover aircraft simultaneously, so they would each launch some 30 aircraft in quick succession. From two carriers, potentially 60 aircraft might arrive on task at the same time. The effect was to swamp out radio channels and overload the Mosquitoes who were equipped to manage flights of two or four aircraft arriving at discrete intervals.

Once again, B-29s were called in on 2 and 3 September to attack towns close behind the KPA lines. Over the first two weeks of September the efforts of the 5th AF and of TF77 were concentrated on providing CAS for UNC forces, although naval aircraft

were also involved in 'softening up' attacks around the Inchon area, in preparation for the planned amphibious landing. It was during this time that an unfortunate diplomatic incident occurred when a Soviet Douglas A-20 Havoc torpedo bomber of the 36th MTAP approached the task force. It was intercepted by four Corsairs from VF-53 and after the A-20 apparently fired upon the US fighters, they returned fire and shot it down into the Yellow Sea.

In the second week of September, air operations were badly affected by the weather associated with Typhoon Kezia, which was approaching Japan. Two F-51 groups were moved forward from Japan to mainland Korea: the 18th FBG deployed to Pusan East (K-9) on 7 September and the 8th FBG operated from Taegu (K-2) from 12 September. Heavy rainstorms on 8 and 9 September raised water levels on the rivers, so that the underwater bridges could no longer be used by the KPA, but the same weather prevented aircraft from reaching many areas of the battlefield. After a slight improvement in the weather conditions on 11 September, a record 683 sorties were flown and by the next day the KPA forces had exhausted their efforts. During this period of fighting, UN air forces suffered a number of casualties to KPA ground fire: between 1 and 12 September combat losses were five F-80s, one B-26, two B-29s and nine F-51s, including that of Wg Cdr L. T. Spence, commanding 77 Sqn RAAF, who was killed during a mission near Pohang in marginal weather on 9 September.

By early September 1950, the North Korean advance had ground to a halt along the Pusan Perimeter. The Great Naktong Offensive had failed, leaving an exhausted KPA whose strength had been badly depleted by air attacks. Facing it was an increasingly well-equipped UNC army supported by progressively well-organized air forces.

Gen MacArthur judged that the time was right for a counterstrike and in a bold initiative he decided to carry out amphibious landings, code-named Operation *Chromite*, at Inchon, 180 miles behind the KPA frontlines. It was a particularly daring move as the tidal conditions at Inchon were hardly ideal for amphibious operations: the tidal range of around 30ft is amongst the largest in the world and it causes strong currents in a wide but shallow bay. The landings would be synchronized with a breakout by the 8th Army from Pusan, thus forcing the KPA to fight on two fronts.

INCHON

Since charts of the coastline and tide tables were not thought to be accurate, RF-80s of the 8th TRS were tasked to provide photographs of the approaches and the waterfront at high and low tides. The 8th TRS had been the only tactical reconnaissance asset in the 5th Air Force at the start of hostilities and it had done its best to carry out its missions but, despite the challenges of the weather over Korea and the logistical problems for the aircraft based at Itazuke, the photo-processing laboratory was at Yokota, 500 miles distant. There was also a shortage of photographic interpreters within HQ 5th Air Force at Nagoya, which was another 150 miles from Yokota. Nevertheless, photographs taken for an urgent reconnaissance task might be delivered 12 hours after the order had been given. While the 8th TRS covered the tactical requirements, the

Armourers from 77 Sqn RAAF clean one of the guns from a Mustang, while their colleagues work on the engine. Conditions were harsh for maintenance personnel who had to work outdoors on Korean airfields in the winter. (State Library of Victoria)

31st SRS operated the RB-29 to provide pre-strike target images and post-strike bomb damage assessment for the B-29 force. The tactical reconnaissance force was expanded at the end of August when the 162nd TRS, which operated the RB-26, moved from the US to Japan.

Armed with accurate photographs of their objectives, the 230 ships of the landing force sailed into the Yellow Sea, just as Typhoon Kezia struck. Thanks to their superior speed, the fast carriers USS *Valley Forge* and USS *Philippine Sea* were able to remain in the shelter of Sasebo harbour for a little longer, departing on 11 September. The following day they joined the USS *Badoeng Strait* and USS *Sicily* on station off North Korea, launching airstrikes on the North Korean defences on and around the landing areas. The USMC fighter bombers had used napalm to clear trees and overgrowth from possible defences on Wolmido Island. USAF fighters also carried out sweeps over the KPAAF airfields that might interfere with the landings, destroying a Yak-9 at Sinmak (K-20) on 11 September and another four Yaks at Pyongyang the following day.

At dawn on 15 September, the Marines of X Corps began landing on Green Beach at Wolmido Island. The naval bombardment ceased at 06:00hrs and under a high

A US Marine Corps F4U Corsair makes an attack during a close air support mission in October 1950. The Marine Corsair units worked closely with ground forces. (NARA)

This damaged KPAAF Il-10 shows how the KPAAF camouflaged their aircraft with tree branches while they were dispersed on the ground. The North Korean and Chinese forces became the masters of camouflage, hiding their equipment from UN aircraft during daylight hours. (NARA)

overcast, Corsairs from USS *Badoeng Strait* and USS *Sicily* took over, strafing the areas just 45m ahead of the Marines as they advanced. Further air support came from USS *Valley Forge* and USS *Philippine Sea*, as well as USS *Boxer*, which had arrived that day carrying four more squadrons of Corsairs and one of Skyraiders. HMS *Triumph* was also on station, but with few of her aircraft still serviceable, her participation in the assault was limited to providing two Fireflies to direct the gunfire of the RN cruisers, HMS *Jamaica* (C-44) and HMS *Kenya* (C-14). After Wolmido had been secured, the next wave of Marines began to land on Red Beach on the western edge of Inchon at 17:30hrs. A little later another wave landed on Blue Beach, to the south. By nightfall there were 13,000 US troops ashore at Inchon. CAS by naval and Marine aircraft had been a major factor in the success of the landings, but the aviators paid a high price: two Panthers, nine Corsairs and one Skyraider were shot down by KPA anti-aircraft fire, along with a HOS3 helicopter.

The next day, as the Marines pushed out from the beachhead towards Kansong-ni (Ganseok), six KPA T-34 tanks advanced to block their way. An airstrike was called in and eight Corsairs from VMF-214 attacked them with napalm and rockets, immobilising most of the tanks but losing one Corsair in the action. Shortly afterwards, an airstrike by a second flight of Corsairs eliminared the remaining vehicles.

In the southeast of the country, the 8th Army started its breakout from the Pusan Perimeter on 16 September. Heavy clouds still persisted and a 'carpet bombing' raid by 82 B-29s intended to clear a path through KPA positions near Waegwan was cancelled because of the weather; instead, the aircraft attacked their secondary targets near Pyongyang and Wonsan. However, there were enough gaps in the clouds for the more manoeuvrable fighter-bombers to find their way to low level over the battlefield and F-51s and F-80s were soon in action. The breakout had not met with great success because in some parts of the line the KPA had already launched attacks on UN positions, but around Taegu the 1st ROK Div made some ground. Further to the south, opposite Changnyeong, the US 2nd Division also made good progress, thanks in no small part to a flight of F-51s that cleared the way ahead of the advance with rockets, napalm and guns. Unfortunately, the clouds closed in during the afternoon and even the F-51s could not get through them, leaving the army to fight without air cover. The CAS efforts continued the following day when UNC aircraft dropped 260 napalm cannisters in this area, but once more air operations were limited by low clouds.

Dawn on 18 September brought an improvement in the weather and 286 CAS sorties were flown on that day. At Waegwan, 42 B-29s from the 92nd and 98th BGs bombed two areas on either side of the road and rail bridges over the Naktong River, saturating their targets with 1,600 500lb bombs. To the south in the US 2 Div area, the strong KPA positions on Hill 409 were bypassed by the ground troops, while air attacks isolated and neutralized them. The following day was busier still, with 361 CAS sorties flown over the battlefield. The advance of the US 1st Cavalry Div was helped by three flights of F-51s, which dropped napalm to clear enemy log-covered bunkers on Hill 268. The 8th Army had now crossed the Naktong River in two places: near Waegwan and near Changnyeong. As KPA troops began to fall back across open country, they became vulnerable to UNC aircraft, which made the most of the opportunity. Even so, the 8th Army managed only slow progress against a determined enemy.

An F-80C Shooting Star of the 8th FBG serves as a comfortable seat for one of the maintenance crew, 'somewhere in Korea' in late 1950. It is fitted with 'Misawa' tip tanks. (USAFM)

On 17 September, the KPAAF had launched a mission against the naval forces, which were still standing off Inchon to provide gunfire support to troops of X Corps as they advanced towards Kimpo and Seoul. Just after dawn, two Il-10s took off from Kimpo and approached the line of cruisers off Wolmido Island. The aircraft attacked the US flagship USS *Rochester* (CA-124), but all four of their bombs missed their target. They then wheeled around to strafe HMS *Jamaica*. As they manoeuvred to attack, the Il-10s were engaged by the anti-aircraft guns on HMS *Jamaica* and the lead aircraft disengaged to the south; however, the number 2 continued to strafe the British cruiser, killing one sailor before it was shot down. Meanwhile, X Corps had recaptured Kimpo airfield and that evening the Grumman F7F-3N Tigercats of VMF(N)-542 arrived. They were joined the next day by the Corsairs of VMF-212 and VMF-312. The Tigercats started ground-attack operations straight away and proved themselves to be very effective in the hours of darkness or the half-light of dawn and dusk; however, during daylight missions their size made them easy targets for KPA anti-aircraft gunners. The opening of Kimpo meant that X Corps could now be re-supplied by air and the first C-54 arrived at the airfield on 19 September. A round-the-clock operation now commenced, with C-54s and Fairchild C-119 Flying Boxcar transports bringing in aviation fuel for the USMC air group and evacuating casualties on the return leg.

A flight of four rocket-armed F4U Corsairs of VMF-312 prepare for take-off from Kimpo (K-14) in late 1950. (NARA)

While X Corps closed in on the city of Seoul supported by USN and USMC aircraft, the 8th Army in the southeast of the country found that far from collapsing, the KPA was still fighting hard. A slow withdrawal was defended by fierce and effective rearguard actions. However, the employment of KPA armour was severely hampered by UNC air action. The Mosquito aircraft were now equipped with SCR-300 'walkie-talkie' radios, which enabled their crews to speak directly to forward troops and tank commanders. On 21 September Mosquitoes observed a force of 30 T-34 tanks advancing towards the US 24th Div. They were able to co-ordinate artillery fire with attacks by F-51s and F-80s, destroying nearly half of the tanks and putting the rest to flight. Night-interdiction missions now took on more urgency, since much of the movement of North Korean troops and materiel was carried out in the hours of darkness. A very successful tactic had been introduced using a B-29 working with a flight of B-26s. The B-29 illuminated critical road and rail chokepoints with parachute flares and B-26s then attacked any targets under the light of the flares. On 22 September, a B-29 illuminated a section of the main road and railway line connecting Kumchon (Gimcheon) to Suwon and the accompanying B-26s destroyed an ammunition train near Taejŏn, severely damaged another train near Yongdong (Yeongdong) and strafed troop concentrations. An attempt to extend the tactic using one B-29 to bomb under the flares of another proved unsuccessful, as the large bomber was not manoeuvrable

Locally recruited labourers prepare to clear the airfield at Pohang on 20 October 1950. In the foreground are the wrecks of three KPAAF Il-10s, and Vought F4U Corsairs of VMF-312 are parked in the background. (NARA)

enough for the profile. B-29 daylight missions continued, including a bombing raid on 21 September on Wonju, which was a chokepoint on the main escape route to the north. Some aircraft dropped leaflets on KPA troops encouraging surrender, while other aircraft continued to attack the few remaining strategic targets. During one such mission on 22 September, a B-29 attacked a railway marshalling yard close to the Yalu River; the crew were to discover later that they had bombed Antung in Manchuria, north of the Yalu.

Also on 22 September, Mosquito pilot Lt G.W. Nelson located some 200 KPA troops near Kunsan and dropped a handwritten note signed 'MacArthur' instructing them to surrender. The North Koreans complied and were captured by UNC patrols, which Nelson directed towards them. The next day the main KPA resistance broke in the south, as the North Koreans attempted to withdraw before they were cut off completely by X Corps at Seoul. However, they did not give up easily: when two companies of the Argyll and Sutherland Highlanders cleared enemy forces from Hill 282 near Songju (Seongju), they were almost immediately counterattacked. Faced with a desperate situation, the Argylls called for air support and shortly afterwards a Mosquito led three F-51s overhead. The aircraft had been given the positions of friendly and enemy forces by the ground-based TACP, but the Mosquito could see correctly displayed ground-air identification panels at the co-ordinates given for

A Vought F4U-4B Corsair, of VF-113 from USS *Philippine Sea* (CV-47) on patrol over the USS *Missouri* (BB-63) and other UN shipping at Inchon on 2 October 1950. The large hill, just right of centre, is Wolmido Island, the site of the initial landings by UN forces on 15 September. (US Navy)

the enemy positions. After ten minutes spent trying to resolve the discrepancy, the Mosquito was overruled by the TACP and the F-51s attacked the hilltop with napalm and cannon fire. The hill was still in British hands and 60 British soldiers were killed or wounded.

A more successful use of air power took place that afternoon a little farther south, after UNC troops drove two KPA battalions from Hypochon (Hapcheon). Two flights of F-51s caught the retreating troops in the open, killing most. Another 53 fighter-bomber sorties were flown in the area the following day, and in the afternoon of 25 September, UN aircraft bombed and rocketed the village of Kochang (Geochang) where KPA troops had taken refuge. To the northeast, the towns of Yechon (Yecheon), Hamchang, Andong and Tanyang (Danyang), where KPA forces were retreating ahead of the ROKA divisions, were also bombed by B-29s. Over the next two days, the speed of the UN advance quickened as the US 24th Div drove to link up with X Corps in the northwest and as ROKA forces gained ground along the eastern seaboard. Daylight CAS sorties and night-interdiction missions continued apace, harrying the retreating KPA troops.

Fire crews spray an F9F-2 Panther from VF-51 or VF-52 after it overran the runway, possibly at Taegu. Naval aircraft that ran short of fuel would often divert to USAF forward bases to refuel before returning to the carrier. (NARA)

In the northwest, X Corps had crossed the Han River on 20 September and four days later the Marines were fighting on the outskirts of Seoul. The Corsairs of VMF-214, VMF-323 and VMF-212 launched flights of four to five aircraft at two-hourly intervals throughout the day in support of the Marine infantry. The action continued into the next day when, in the space of two hours, the squadron commanders of VMF-212, VMF-214 and VMF(N)-542 were all shot down. Lt Col W. E. Lischeid of VMF-214 was killed but the other two officers were uninjured. That evening USS *Sicily* left Inchon, taking VMF-214 with it, but by then the battle for Seoul had almost been won; the KPA began to withdraw from the city overnight, but once again, its rearguards fought fiercely. By 27 September, Seoul was in UNC hands.

Leading elements of the 8th Army linked up with X Corps near Osan on 26 September, although Taejŏn was not recaptured until two days later. On the same day, the B-29s had started a campaign against the North Korean hydro-electric installations. But the first raid, against the Fusen (Bujeon) generating plant 30 miles north of Hungnam, was also the last. With the possibility of operations north of the 38th Parallel, it was decided not to continue the destruction of strategic industrial targets. On the same day that Taejŏn finally fell to UNC forces, air support played a vital role in clearing up operations by 1st Cavalry Div in the Pyongtaek area, where five enemy T-34 tanks in a group of ten were destroyed by airstrikes. As the KPA was

A Grumman F7F-3N Tigercat of VMF(N)-513 pulls up from a weapon delivery pass during a close air support mission. The Tigercat night fighter was employed for offensive support missions in autumn of 1950, but its large size made it vulnerable to ground fire; it was, however, extremely effective in the night interdiction role. (NARA)

ejected from South Korea, the need for CAS sorties diminished and the F-51s began to range farther afield, carrying out armed reconnaissance missions over North Korea. The ROKA divisions continued their advance northwards, crossing the 38th Parallel on 28 September, but the non-Korean UNC forces paused while MacArthur secured political support for a counter-invasion of North Korea and while the logistics caught up with the fast-moving advance.

It was an opportunity, too, for some of the combat elements of the UNC air forces to deploy into Korea. The 51st FIG, equipped with the F-80, moved from Okinawa to Japan for operations over Korea on 22 September and most of the Japan-based units prepared to move to forward bases on the peninsula. By 7 October, the F-51s of the 35th FBG were back at Pohang (K-3), where they were joined by 77 Sqn RAAF, while those of the 8th FBG had started to operate from Suwon (K-13). Despite the apparent pause in the ground war, air operations continued apace with armed reconnaissance sorties mounted by F-51s, F-80s and B-26s across North Korea to find and attack enemy troops, military installations and traffic.

The F-80s of the 49th FBG had deployed to Taegu on 28 September, taking advantage of the new runway, made of PSP strips laid over reclaimed paddy fields. While the 5,700ft runway was just long enough to permit jet take-offs using water-methanol injection or Jet Assisted Take-Off (JATO) packs, the surface was uneven and prone to rippling during the take-off run. On landing, sharp edges of the undulating steel surface damaged tyres, and in the first months of operation, F-80 mainwheel tyres typically lasted for just seven landings. Nevertheless, the cost of tyres

A Soviet-built T-34 tank of the KPA which had been disabled by napalm during an airstrike. Air attacks proved to be the most effective way of stopping KPA armoured assaults. (NARA)

Mustang pilots
Capt W. Evans and
Maj G. Brown, talk to a
group of the US Marines
who recaptured Kimpo
airfield in October 1950.
(Bettmann/CORBIS/
Bettmann Archive via
Getty Images)

(US Navy)

CARRIER AIR GROUP 2, USN
USS *Boxer*, 16 September 1950

The second flight... commenced at 0600I with the launching of six AD [Skyraiders] for deep support, two F4U [Corsairs] for Naval Gunfire (NGF) spot I, seven F4Us for TARCAP and eight F4Us for deep support, for a total of 17 offensive and eight defensive sorties. The planes carried 500lb GP bombs, HVARs and Napalm. The six ADs on deep support hit a railroad yard adjacent to Yongduri with rockets and left railways cars and a warehouse burning fiercely. No hits were recorded as they dive bombed a railway at Suishoki-ri. Moderate flak was observed over Seoul at 6-8,000 ft and it was apparently 3- or 5-inch [calibre]; though inaccurate, the altitude was correct... The two F4Us scheduled for NGF spotting were not used by the controller. The eight F4Us scheduled for deep support were released to search for targets of opportunity. Altogether nine railroad cars were destroyed by direct bomb hits; one bomb hit a railroad junction two miles west of Suwon; eight railroad cars were left burning at Uijongbu after being hit with napalm and rockets. One railroad car, located at Jo-To, was ignited by napalm.

was but a small price to pay in order to base the jet fighter-bombers 200 miles nearer to the frontlines. The F-80s could also now reach as far north as the Yalu River. One consequence, however, occurred on 8 October, when two F-80s of the 49th FBG flown by Lt A. H. Quanbeck and Lt A. J. Diefendorf were tasked to carry out an armed reconnaissance sortie over Chongjin airfield. As they flew outbound above the cloud tops at 37,000ft, they were completely unaware that a 200mph jetstream was blowing from the south and as a result, they broke cloud considerably further north than they realized. As they flew southeast at low-level, they located a coastal airfield as they expected, and they strafed two lines of P-63 Kingcobra fighters. Unfortunately, these were aircraft of the 821th IAP at the Soviet airfield of Sukhaia Rechka, near Vladivostok, some 60 miles over the border from Korea.

TF77 had withdrawn from the Yellow Sea at the end of September, and on 10 October, the aircraft carriers USS *Valley Forge*, USS *Philippine Sea* and USS *Leyte* (CV-32) commenced operations in the Sea of Japan to prepare for another amphibious landing by X Corps at Wonsan. They were joined by USS *Boxer* four days later. Naval aircraft carried out airstrikes, fighter sweeps, reconnaissance and naval gunfire spotting

F-51 Mustangs of 1 Sqn ROKAF being refuelled in the skeleton of a warehouse or hangar. (NARA)

sorties against targets in an arc between Wonsan and Chongjin, extending 20 miles inland from the coast. Targets for the airstrikes included communications installations and the transport infrastructure, often hitting the same targets again a few days later, after the North Koreans had repaired them. Naval strike aircraft were also diverted to provide CAS for the ROKA 3rd Div, which was advancing along the east coast.

The amphibious landing at Wonsan was intended as a repeat of the Inchon landing, but it did not go according to plan. Firstly, Wonsan was in fact captured by the ROKA 3rd Div on 10 October, ten days before the date of the planned landing, and secondly, Wonsan harbour was found to be heavily mined and had to be cleared before it could be used. The main aircraft tasked with mine clearance were the PBM-5s of VP-47, which flew mine reconnaissance sorties throughout the month. On spotting mines, their crews attempted to detonate them by dropping depth charges nearby, or by firing the waist guns mounted in the aircraft. However, these methods did not always meet with success, and clearing the minefields was a long and hazardous task. In an experiment on 12 October, aircraft from USS *Philippine Sea* dropped 50 1,000lb bombs with hydro-static fuses into the minefield in an attempt to explode the mines, but this method was unsuccessful.

In the Yellow Sea, the British aircraft carrier HMS *Theseus* (R-64) arrived off the west coast of Korea on 10 October, replacing HMS *Triumph* in TF95. Like *Triumph*, HMS *Theseus* carried a squadron of Fairey Firefly fighters (810 NAS), but it also carried 807 NAS equipped with the Hawker Sea Fury. HMS *Theseus* launched her first missions against Korea that day, with an airstrike by Fireflies on the bridges at Changyon (Jangyeon) and one by Sea Furies on a storage depot near Chinnampo. During the latter sortie, Lt S. Leonard was shot down by ground fire and force-landed

An AD Skyraider of VF-115 ready for launching from USS *Philippine Sea* (CV-47) on a daylight strike mission in October 1950. The aircraft is armed with bombs, probably indicating an interdiction task. (US Navy)

nearby. While the rest of the flight maintained top cover, driving off KPA troops, an H-5 helicopter from the 3rd RS flown by Lt D. C. McDaniels and carrying doctor Capt J. C. Shumate set out from Kimpo, 125 miles away. The H-5 was escorted by USMC Tigercats, which took over from the Sea Furies when they arrived over the crash site. With the Tigercats providing top cover, the helicopter crew picked up the seriously injured pilot while under fire from KPA troops, thus completing a daring long-range rescue. For the next few days, aircraft from *Theseus* continued to attack targets in the Chinnampo area.

The KPAAF commenced a new phase of operations on 14 October. Using two Polikarpov Po-2 biplanes, the *Honhab Hang-gong Yeondae* (HHY – Mixed Aviation Regiment) carried out a night-bombing attack on Kimpo airfield in the early hours.

When HMS *Theseus* (R-64) took over from HMS *Triumph* in October, it brought the Hawker Sea Fury FB11s of No.807 NAS. Here, a Sea Fury dives to attack a road convoy in Korea. (Thomas)

A similar raid followed that evening. No physical damage was done by either attack, but the value of these 'night hecklers' was in the irritation they caused and their effect on morale. Night raids continued sporadically over the next few months, although the cost to the KPAAF was high: nine Po-2s had been lost by 1 November, either through take-off and landing accidents, or simply not returning from nocturnal missions.

Declarations by the Chinese Premier Mau Zedong that any advance into North Korea by non-Korean troops would trigger an armed response were disregarded by the US and UK governments and the UNC commanders as mere bluff and the first non-Korean UN troops crossed the 38th Parallel on 8 October. Air support for UNC ground forces continued to target KPA artillery, armour and strongpoints, although Mosquitoes also began to range ahead of the frontlines, seeking targets for aircraft. On 17 October a Mosquito located a North Korean troop train 20 miles south of Pyongyang and called in a flight of F-80s to destroy it. Nine days later, an RB-26 patrolling a few miles south of Kanggye discovered five North Korean freight trains. Unable to report the target to a TACP or Mosquito, the pilot managed to call in a pair of F-51s and another of F-80s, which diverted to the scene. The F-80s were only armed with guns and they strafed the locomotives, after which the F-51s followed up with Napalm and 5-inch HVAR, destroying the engines and most of the freight cars.

Pyongyang was captured by British, Australian and US troops on 19 October. The next day brought rain and low cloud, but the weather had cleared sufficiently by 14:00hrs for a fleet of 71 C-119s and 40 C-47s to deliver the US Army 187th Regimental Combat Team in a mass parachute drop on two drop zones at Sukchon and Sunchon, both some 120 miles north of Pyongyang. These troops were intended to cut off the escape routes of the retreating KPA. The airborne assault was supported by waves of F-51s, F-80s and B-26s, which continued to attack KPA

Groundcrew work on an F-80C Shooting Star of the 16th FIS/ 51st FIG, while another F-80 takes off using JATO. The aircraft in the foreground, which is armed with napalm cannisters under the wings and a single bomb on the centreline, was shot down by anti-aircraft fire near Sunan on 11 August 1951. (USAFM)

positions throughout the afternoon. Over the next few days, the paratroops were resupplied by C-47s and C-119s. By now HMS *Theseus* was on station off the western coast of North Korea and for the next week her rocket-armed Sea Furies and Fireflies carried out armed reconnaissance patrols between the bomb line and the Yalu River. At the end of the month, *Theseus* left the Yellow Sea to replenish in Japan. USS *Boxer* also departed from TF77 and headed homewards.

   Having switched from strategic industrial targets, FEAF B-29s concentrated instead on known KPA training camps, such as Hungnam, which was bombed on 12 October, and also on bridges. By 20 October, 108 Razon bombs had been dropped on bridges,

Ordnance men carry out final checks on the rocket armament of a US Marine Corps F4U-4B Corsair just before it is catapulted from the deck of USS *Sicily* (CVE-118) for a night strike over Korea, in the autumn of 1950. (US Navy)

destroying spans on six of them. However, such was the paucity of targets that the FEAF bomber force reduced its sortie rate to just 25 each day and two B-29 groups, the 22nd BG and 92nd BG, returned to the US on 22 October. It was on that day that UNC forces crossed the Chongchon (Cheongcheon) River, buoyed with a sense of impending victory. Reflecting this mood of optimism, the British liaison officer to Gen Stratemeyer, Air Vice Marshal C. A. Bouchier, reported in his daily dispatch to London on 23 October that there was 'still no sign whatever that the Chinese intend to intervene in this conflict, which is now to all intents and purpose from a fighting point of view all over.'

CHAPTER 4

THE CHINESE OFFENSIVES

25 OCTOBER 1950–10 FEBRUARY 1951

The optimism of the UNC commanders was misplaced. The threats made by Mau Zedong were serious and Chinese ground forces had started to infiltrate North Korea in mid-October. In order not to escalate the conflict into a direct war with the US, the units earmarked for deployment to Korea were nominally part of the *Zhōngguó Rénmín Zhìyuànjūn* (CPVA – Chinese People's Volunteer Army) rather than the PLA. These soldiers had supposedly volunteered for duty in Korea out of loyalty to their communist comrades across the border, although they were, in fact, regular PLA troops. Led by Yuan Shuai (Marshal) Peng Dehuai, they were well disciplined and well trained, especially in the arts of camouflage and of night fighting and their presence went undetected by aerial reconnaissance. By late October, over 200,000 Chinese troops had entered into Korea.

CHINESE AND SOVIET INTERVENTION

The CPVA launched its first attack on UNC forces on 25 October. The main thrust of this offensive was aimed at the leading elements of the UNC forces, which were advancing from Sinanju on the Chongchon River towards Sinuiju on the Yalu River. Breaking through the ROKA II Corps on the east of the UN advance, the CPVA troops were able to hook round almost as far as Anju, nearly cutting off all the UN forces north of the Chongchon River. The Chinese offensive was held temporarily at Unsan by the ROKA 1st Div and US 8th Cavalry Div. On 27 October, while other forward troops hastily fell back to the Chongchon River, ten C-119s dropped supplies to the UNC forces holding the line at Unsan. However, one ROKA regiment, the 7th Regt, was caught well north of the UNC lines, having reached Chosan on the Yalu River. After being resupplied by an air drop on 28 October, it attempted to retreat southwards, but was caught at a CPVA roadblock at Kojang, where despite strong supporting airstrikes during the following day, it eventually capitulated.

Pilots of 2 Sqn SAAF strapping into their cockpits for a mission. The F-51D Mustangs are armed with napalm cannisters. The aircraft nearest the camera was lost on 11 May 1951 when Cmdt J.P.D. Blaauw crash landed to aid another downed pilot. (SAKWVA)

MiG-15s of the 29th GvIAP at Dachang airfield in April 1950, well before the deployment of Soviet fighter regiments to Korea. The introduction of the MiG-15 over Korea signalled the end of UN air supremacy over North Korea. (Krylov & Tepsurkaev)

On 1 November, numerous airstrikes were launched, throughout the day, in support of the US 8th Cavalry Division as it attempted a fighting withdrawal from Unsan. UN fighter-bombers also operated in strength between the Chongchon and Yalu Rivers, providing CAS for UNC troops and also carrying out armed reconnaissance missions, attacking KPA and CPVA transport where they could find it. By now UN pilots were used to complete freedom of operation, thanks to complete air superiority over the peninsula. Their only threat, apart from the hazards of terrain and weather, was North Korean anti-aircraft fire. But the situation was about to change dramatically.

Firstly, the KPAAF 56th JHY had deployed its strength to Sinuiji in the last days of October and was ready to enter the fray, and secondly, the USSR had undertaken to defend Chinese airspace and the bridges across the Yalu River until the CPLAAF was able to do so itself. The 56th JHY had been re-equipped with a full complement of 22 Yak-9P fighters and reinforced with fresh pilots who had just graduated from training schools in China. Meanwhile, during early October, Soviet VVS fighter units had arrived in China in great secrecy to form the 64th *Istrebitel'naya Aviatsionnaya Korpus* (IAK – Fighter Aviation Corps). Their aircraft carried KPAAF markings and the pilots were dressed in Chinese uniforms. Furthermore, the pilots had been instructed to use Korean phrases on the radio in order to disguise their true identity. Like the Chinese, the Soviets were keen not to provoke a direct war with the US and had gone to great lengths to cover up their involvement in the Korean conflict. By the end of October, the 151st Gvardeyskiy (Guards – Gv) IAD, comprising the 28th GvIAP, 72nd GvIAP and 139th GvIAP, each of which was equipped with the MiG-15, was deployed on the airfields at Anshan, Mukden-East and Liaoyang. All three airfields were close to Mukden (Shenyang) and were approximately 100 miles distant from the Yalu River.

On 1 November, both the 28th GvIAP and 72nd GvIAP mounted patrols over the Antung (Dandong)-Sinuiji bridges and they had authority to cross into Korea if necessary. Because of the range involved, the MiGs carried under-wing fuel drop tanks. On the same day, eight Yak-9Ps flying in two four-ship formations were also

launched by the KPAAF to intercept UNC fighter-bombers. The Yaks engaged a
Mosquito which was working with a B-26 but were driven off by a nearby flight of
F-51s, which subsequently claimed to have shot down all of the Yaks. At almost the
same time, six MiG-15s attacked a flight of four F-51s, but the more manoeuvrable
F-51s were able to evade them. Later, another MiG-15 patrol from the 28th GvIAP
engaged three F-51s and claimed to have shot down one of them. However, no
F-51 losses were recorded on this day. At midday, an RF-80 had reported sighting
15 Yak-9Ps in revetments on Sinuiji airfield and 12 F-80s were scrambled to attack
them. The problem facing the F-80 pilots was that the revetments faced north and
therefore had to be attacked on a southerly heading, but the F-80s were not permitted
to cross the Yalu River in order to run in on that heading. As a result, they had to bomb
from curved approaches, which reduced their accuracy at the same time that it exposed
them to anti-aircraft fire from the Chinese on the north bank of the river. Four MiG-
15s from the 72nd GvIAP were also patrolling over Antung at the time, and having
seen a flight of ten F-80s below him, *Starshiy Leytenant* (St Lt – Senior Lieutenant)
S.F. Khomich dived to make a high-speed firing pass, pulling up sharply after shooting
at one of the F-80s. One F-80 from the 51st FBG, flown by Capt F. L. Van Sickle, was
lost during the mission. Although the loss was recorded by the USAF as having been
due to anti-aircraft fire, it is plausible that a high-speed slashing attack by a fighter
might have gone unseen by the other aircraft in the formation, so perhaps Khomich
scored the first jet-versus-jet kill during the Korean War. The raid had destroyed one

A MiG-15 pilot from the
29th GvIAP returns the
salute from his ground
crew, Shanghai 1950.
(Krylov & Tepsurkaev)

Yak and damaged three others and the remaining aircraft were quickly withdrawn to the safety of Antung airfield. Later in the afternoon another formation of F-80s arrived to finish off the Yaks but discovered the revetments to be empty.

Over the next four days the MiG-15s made no further interceptions, but the KPAAF continued to launch four-ships of Yak-9Ps from Antung to engage UNC aircraft that approached the Sinuiju area. A flight of Yaks damaged two B-26s on 5 November, but engagements with F-51s on the previous day and again on 6 November had shown up the inexperience of the new KPAAF pilots and a number of Yaks were shot down. After suffering heavy losses, the 56th JHY was withdrawn from combat the next day. Meanwhile, most of the tasking for UNC aircraft during that week involved covering the withdrawal of the 8th Army back to a defensive line on the Chongchon River. In one intense action on 4 November, flights of B-26s held back CPVA forces as the US 21st Div retreated through Chongju (Jeongju) on its return from the farthest point of its advance at Chonggo (Chungho), just 18 miles from Sinuiju. At Pakchon the F-51s of 77 Sqn RAAF flew CAS missions for the British Commonwealth 27th Brigade as it fought to hold the bridge over the Taeryong River. This was the first time that the RAAF pilots had directly supported the troops of the 1st Royal Australian

Regiment (RAR). By 7 November the 8th Army was safely across the Chongchon. The night of 1 November had seen the first raids by the Tigercats of VMF(N)-542 over Sinuiju as they sought to interdict the stream of traffic from China passing through the city. These raids continued nightly until 9 November.

In the east of the country, X Corps had finally disembarked at Wonsan on 26 October. Air support was provided by VMF-312 and VMF(N)-513, which had deployed to Wonsan (K-25), as well as the units embarked on the carriers USS *Valley Forge*, USS *Leyte*, USS *Sicily* and USS *Badoeng Strait*; the USS *Philippine Sea* had already returned to Japan on 23 October and both USS *Leyte* and USS *Valley Forge* would soon follow. The immediate concern of 1st Marine Div was to secure the area against guerrilla action and minor actions were fought at Kojo, to the south of Wonsan, and Majon-ni, to the west of Wonsan. In both cases, CAS missions by 1st MAG aircraft were integral to the action on the ground. The 1st Marine Div also pushed northwards to relieve the ROKA 1st Corps and secure the hydro-electric power stations on the Changjin (Jangjin) Reservoir, which was also known as the Chosin Reservoir. In turn, the ROKA 1st Corps would be reinforced by the US 7th Infantry Div to push towards the Yalu River.

An F-51D Mustang of the 67th FBS/ 18th FBG in late 1950 or early 1951. This aircraft crashed near the Taedong River in North Korea on 9 June 1951; its pilot, Capt Jack H. Hederstrom was declared Missing in Action. (USAFM)

A B-26 firing a 5-inch rocket during a daylight mission over snow covered terrain in North Korea. Above it two more missiles that have been fired by another B-26 can also be seen. (USAFM)

After marching southwards through the central highlands, the CPVA 42nd Corps had swung eastwards to move against the Changjin and Fusen Reservoirs. At the same time, the US Marines began to advance along the Sudong Valley, which ran northwards from the port of Hamhŭng up to the reservoir. This valley would be their Main Supply Route (MSR) since it carried the narrow-gauge railway line from Hamhŭng to the village of Yudam-ni on the western arm of the Changjin Reservoir. The opposing forces collided at Sudong (Hagichon), almost halfway between Hamhŭng and Changjin, on 2 November. The ensuing battle lasted four days during which numerous CAS sorties were flown by the Corsairs of VMF-312 and VMF(N)-513.

While the troops of the CPVA fought the US Marines near Changjin and also forced the 8th Army to retreat back across the Chongchon River, the B-29s of the FEAF started an incendiary campaign against the northernmost cities of North Korea. These were seen as both arsenals and shelters for the KPA. In addition, the Korean ends of all bridges connecting the country to Manchuria were to be destroyed. Of particular interest were the 'Sinuiju bridges', two substantial structures, one carrying the road and the other carrying the railway, which connected Sinuiju to Antung. These three-quarter-mile-long bridges were solidly built and bombing them presented a series of problems to the B-29 crews: firstly, they were not allowed to fly north of the Yalu River, which constrained their attack directions; secondly, they had to bomb from above 18,000ft in order to remain clear of anti-aircraft fire, which made weapon aiming against such a small target very difficult; thirdly, this challenge was exacerbated by crosswinds at altitude of up to 120kts. The new bombing offensive started on 4 November with an incendiary raid directed against Kanggye, but the B-29 crews found their target covered by cloud and dropped their bombs on Chongjin instead. Kanggye was attacked in fine weather the next day by 21 B-29s of the 19th BG.

ABOVE:
A line-up of North American RB-45C Tornado reconnaissance aircraft of the 91st Strategic Reconnaissance Group at Kimpo (K-14). The 91st SRG used the RB-45C for missions over 'MiG Alley,' but one aircraft was shot down by St Lt A.F. Andrianov of the 29th GvIAP in a MiG-15 on 4 December 1950. (USAFM)

LEFT:
Two F-80C Shooting Stars of the 36th FBS/ 8th FBG at Suwon (K-13). (USAFM)

The 64th IAK MiG-15 units joined combat again on 6 November and on each of the following four days. On the first day, a patrol from the 72nd GvIAP intercepted a flight of F-51s and on the second both the 28th GvIAP and 72nd GvIAP were in action. Kill claims were made on both sides, but no losses were acknowledged. In any case, the claims by MiG pilots were made for head-on firing passes, which are unlikely to have been successful. A bombing raid by B-29s against the two bridges at Sinuiju was planned for 7 November but was delayed by 24 hours because of the weather.

The following day, a force of 79 bombers set out for the bridges. Before they arrived over the target, flights of F-51s and F-80s were tasked with suppressing anti-aircraft artillery in the area. Eight MiG-15s of the 72nd GvIAP launched to intervene and during the ensuing mêlée at 18,000ft, 1st Lt R. J. Brown, flying an F-80 from the 16th FIS, scored hits on the MiG-15 of St Lt A. E. Sanin. The latter aircraft disengaged by diving steeply and jettisoning his external fuel tanks, leading Brown to believe that he had shot down the MiG; however, Sanin landed his, although damaged, aircraft safely at Mukden. Other combats occurred during the course of the day, but there were no verified kills.

After replenishment, the aircraft carriers of TF77 departed Sasebo harbour in Japan on 5 November. On the same day HMS *Theseus* left Korean waters. With an unserviceable catapult, she could only launch aircraft without external stores, so her aircraft had been limited to mounting defensive CAPs over TF95. While HMS *Theseus* headed for Hong Kong for repairs, USS *Leyte*, USS *Valley Forge* and USS *Philippine Sea* braved heavy seas and winds of up to 50mph, caused by Typhoon Clara, as they sailed up the east coast. Because of the difficulties encountered by FEAF bombers in attacking the bridges across the Yalu, the aircraft of TF77 were also tasked against them. The naval efforts started on 9 November when USS *Valley Forge* and USS *Philippine Sea* both launched their air wings against the Sinuiju bridges. During the morning, ten MiG-15s from the 139th GvIAP took off from Liaoyang to intercept the strike wing from USS *Philippine Sea* as it approached Sinuiju. The fighter escort of Panthers from VF-111 engaged the MiGs and during the combat Lt Cdr W. T. Amen shot down a MiG-15 flown by Kpt M. F. Grachev. This was the first jet-versus-jet combat kill that was recognized by both sides. Later in the morning, six MiG-15s from the 72nd GvIAP were flying a CAP near Sinuiju when they saw a single RB-29 escorted

Just above the centre of the photo, a USN AD-3 Skyraider pulls out from a dive-bombing pass, after releasing a 2,000lb bomb during a raid on the bridges across the Yalu River at Sinuiju in mid-November 1950. Note the numerous bomb craters near the bridges. (US Navy)

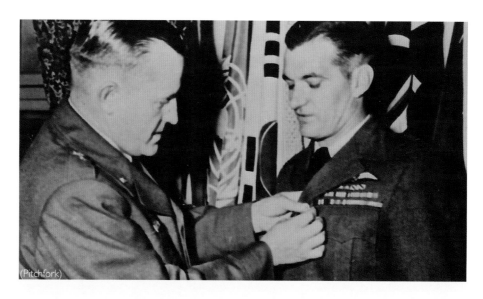

(Pitchfork)

Wg Cdr J.E. JOHNSON, RAF
RB-26, 162 TRS, 26 October 1950

On 26 October a RB-26 was dispatched on a daylight routine reconnaissance mission. Previous to this date, two F-51 fighter aircraft were always detailed as close escort but owing to the continued absence of enemy aircraft the fighter escort has been discontinued. When over enemy territory some 70 miles north of the bomb line and a few miles south of Kanggye, the pilot saw five enemy trains, consisting of engines and freight cars, moving slowly towards Kanggye. The pilot proceeded to take photographs from 5,000ft and attempted to contact the nearest TACP or Mosquito aircraft. However, although neither of these two control organisations could be contacted, the pilot was able to locate a section of two F-51 and a section of two F-80 aircraft. The pilot of the RB-26 passed the necessary map co-ordinates to the fighter-bomber aircraft and requested them to proceed to the target area as soon as possible. The fighter-bomber pilots called their TACP and received permission to leave their pre-arranged area. Meanwhile all five trains had stopped, and their crews were observed to make an undignified and hurried departure. The two F-80s were only armed with 50-calibre guns and they proceeded to attack the engines. Some steam was seen to come from the engines after this attack. The two F-51s then commenced shallow, low-level attacks with napalm and 5-inch HVAR. The engines and most of the freight cars were either damaged or destroyed. During all this attack, the RB-26 circled above and took colour film of the entire episode with a hand-held motion camera. Afterwards the reconnaissance aircraft climbed back up to 5,000ft and took another series of photographs for damage assessment purposes.

by 16 F-80s. While four MiGs engaged the escort fighters, the other two attacked the RB-29, riddling it with cannon fire. The aircraft managed to recover to Japan but crash-landed short of the runway at Johnson AFB; five crew members were killed.

The next day dawned cold but clear, with excellent visibility, and another 'maximum effort' naval airstrike was launched against the Sinuiju bridges by USS *Leyte* and USS *Philippine Sea*; the former mounted 83 sorties that day. Eight MiG-15s from the 28th GvIAP and another six from the 72nd GvIAP were launched to intercept these raids. The Soviet pilots were successfully held off by the Panther escorts and the Skyraiders and Corsairs were able to carry out their attacks unmolested by enemy aircraft. Fighter escorts, this time F-80s, also foiled an attack by the MiGs of the 72nd GvIAP that attempted to engage two B-29s near Sinuiju. However, an hour later B-29s from the 307th BG which were bombing the town on Uiju, ten miles upstream of Sinuiju, were less lucky. Eight more MiG-15s from the 139th GvIAP led by Mr G. I. Kharkovsky were scrambled and despite the efforts of the escorts, Kharvovsky and his wingman Lt Yu.I. Akimov shot down one bomber and possibly damaged another.

Naval airstrikes and FEAF bomber raids against the bridges over the Yalu continued over the next five days. Many of the raids were intercepted by MiG-15s, but despite kill claims from both sides most of the combats were inconclusive, although aircraft of both

The scene on the flight deck of USS *Philippine Sea* (CV-47) in the midst of a snowstorm off the Korean coast on 15 November 1950. Conditions at sea were often very challenging in the winter months. (US Navy)

sides were damaged. The only success against the bridges was achieved by a combined strike by USS *Leyte* and USS *Valley Forge* on 12 November, which dropped one span of the Sinuiju road bridge. The fighter escorts also proved successful in keeping the MiG-15s away from the B-29s, although two B-29s were seriously damaged by MiGs on 14 November. B-29s also continued the incendiary campaign, burning many of the towns and cities in North Korea that were thought to be sheltering KPA and CPVA troops, supplies or equipment. In the next week the weather turned, and heavy clouds brought snow and freezing conditions. Operations were also hampered by the fact that by now there were just ten-and-a-half hours of daylight each day. By 19 November the Yalu River was sufficiently frozen to carry road traffic.

On 7 November UN ground forces had been surprised to find that the CPVA forces had disappeared overnight. Having probed the UNC defences and gained an insight into their new enemy, the Chinese had withdrawn to re-supply and prepare for a larger offensive. However, the UNC commanders interpreted the withdrawal by the CPVA as a sign that it had been successfully beaten off. Based on the estimate that the UNC was facing a CPVA numbering some 70,000 troops in Korea, Gen MacArthur prepared for a final offensive to reach the Yalu River by Christmas 1950. UNC ground forces moved forward to consolidate their positions and by 23 November, the eve of the planned offensive, the 8th Army frontlines ran from the mouth of the Chongchon River, following an arc extending ten miles beyond the river for almost 35 miles, then crossing the river and running due eastwards for a further 30 miles. There was then a large gap between the easternmost point of the 8th Army and the westernmost positions of X Corps, which were manned by the 1st Marine Div at the Changjin Reservoir. The remainder of X Corps held unconnected positions spread across the northeast of the country: the US 7th Div was at Hyensanjin (Hysan) on the Yalu River, the ROKA 3rd Div held Hapsu, some 30 miles to the east, and the ROKA Capital Div was positioned at Chongjin on the east coast.

Day-to-day air operations both in support of the ground forces and against targets between the bomb line and the Yalu River continued as the weather allowed, but the opportunity was taken to redeploy some of the UN air units. The two F-80 groups, the 49th FBG and 51st FIG, remained at Taegu and Kimpo respectively but the 35th FBG, plus 77 Sqn RAAF, moved to Yonpo (K-27). Also supporting operations on the east coast were the USMC Corsair units VMF-212 and VFM-214, as well as VMF(N)-513 operating the Corsair and Tigercat, all based at Wonsan (K-25), and VMF-312 was embarked on the USS *Badoeng Strait*. They were joined at the end of November by VMF(N)-542. Two F-51 groups had also moved up to Pyongyang: 8th FBG were based at Pyongyang [K-23], while the 18th FBG plus the newly arrived 2 Sqn SAAF flew from Pyongyang East [K-24]. In TF77, USS *Valley Forge* sailed to Japan on 19 November, in preparation for returning to the US, leaving USS *Leyte* and USS *Philippine Sea* on station.

For the newly appointed Nationalist government of South Africa the Korean War had provided an ideal opportunity to curry favour with the US and at the same time send a bold signal that it wanted to distance itself from the UK. By offering, on 4 August,

An F-51D Mustang of 2 Sqn SAAF at Chinhae (K-10). South African crews flew their first operational mission in Korea on 19 November 1950. This aircraft, flown by 2Lt Christoffel Lombard, was lost to ground fire over North Korea on 1 November 1951. (SAKWVA)

USMC ordnance men fill the napalm cannister on an F4U Corsair during a turn-around in December 1950. The aircraft also carries 5-inch rockets under the wings and a bomb on the centreline weapon station. (NARA)

A pair of North American F-86 Sabres of the 4th FIG get airborne in early 1951. The Sabre was the only UN aircraft that was able to meet the MiG-15 on an equal footing. The black-and-white identification stripes were replaced by a yellow band in late 1951. (NARA)

a squadron of fighter aircraft directly to the UNC and thus, indirectly, to the US, the South Africans stepped away from the policy of the previous administration under Jan Smuts of putting their armed forces at the disposal of the British Commonwealth. The unit, 2 Sqn South African Air Force (SAAF), would be equipped with US-built aircraft and integrated into the FEAF command structure. Thus, it would not be part of any British Commonwealth air group. Personnel for the unit, including many pilots who had flown the F-51 in combat during World War II, departed Durban on 26 September. After arrival in Japan they were equipped by the USAF, which also supervised a swift refamiliarization with the F-51. The unit moved to Pusan East (K-9) on 16 November and later moved up to Pyongyang-East. The first operational sortie by 2 Sqn SAAF was a CAS mission flown by two aircraft on the morning of 19 November against enemy vehicles close to the Chongchon River.

There were changes, too, on the other side of the Yalu River. It was Soviet policy to rotate MiG-15 units through the 64th IAK in the combat theatre, and on 30 November the 151st GvIAD was withdrawn and tasked with training Chinese pilots. The 28th IAD was also withdrawn across the Yellow Sea to Shandong in order to train Chinese pilots. Its place in the 64th IAK was taken by the 50th IAD, comprising the 29th GvIAP and the 177th IAP. Both units were based at Anshan and were equipped with the improved MiG-15bis. The MiG-15bis had a more powerful VK-1 engine than the RD-45F of the earlier model and also incorporated improvements to the flying controls and armament.

The UNC offensive started on 24 November and in the first two days the 8th Army made good progress, advancing steadily almost ten miles northwards against only light opposition. At the same time the B-29s renewed their attacks on the bridges over the Yalu River. The B-29 raids succeeded in dropping one span of the railway bridge at Manpojin (Manpo) on 25 November and two spans of the road bridge at Chongsonjin (Chongson) the next day.

THE SECOND CHINESE OFFENSIVE

The Chinese, however, had also planned an offensive with the 300,000 troops they had already deployed to Korea. The CPVA offensive started in the darkness of the night of 26 November and over the next few days UNC forces were pushed relentlessly southwards. UNC air support was limited during 27 November because of snowstorms, but in the early hours of 29 November the US 2nd Div called for CAS from B-26s to enable it to disengage from CPVA before it was encircled. Night-time CAS was almost unheard of because of the hazards to friendly troops, but the US soldiers identified their positions by use of phosphorous shells, enabling the B-26s to fire accurately at CPVA positions.

An F9F-2B Panther of VMF-311 at Pusan East (K-9); unlike most other USMC units, VMF-311 operated entirely from land bases during the Korean War. This particular aircraft, flown by Lt Richard W. Bell was shot down by PPK Evgenii Pepeliaev in MiG-15 of the 196th IAP on 21 July 1951 (NARA)

The F-51s of 2 Sqn SAAF also flew 43 sorties in support of the 8th Army between 27 November and 2 December. Typically, three SAAF F-51s would be accompanied by USAF F-51s and the weapons load would comprise two napalm tanks and six HVARs. Frequently, the job of the CAS aircraft was to clear roadblocks that had been set up by infiltrating CPVA units or guerrillas behind the lines in the path of retreating UN forces. In the afternoon of 30 November, numerous airstrikes helped clear CPVA roadblocks on the pass through the hills between Kunu-ri (Kaechon) and Sunchon. Thanks to intensive air support, the 8th Army was able to extricate itself from the Chinese onslaught and retreat south of the Chongchon River, and by 1 December, the UN frontline ran between Sukchon and Sunchon. But the situation was fluid and the retreat continued: Pyongyang and Chinnampo were evacuated on 5 December. The latter operation was covered by aircraft from HMS *Theseus*, which had arrived back on station that day.

In the east, the brunt of the CPVA offensive had been borne by the UN troops at the Changjin Reservoir: 1st Marine Div on the western side and the 31st Regt from the US 7th Div (known as 'Task Force Faith') on the eastern side. The remainder of X Corps and the ROKA divisions withdrew to Hungnam, where they formed a defensive perimeter, awaiting rescue from the sea. Meanwhile, though completely

A B-26 Invader on its bombing run during a daylight strike against a KPA/ CPLA barracks and storage area in February 1951. (USAFM)

An F-51D Mustang of 2 Sqn SAAF preparing for take-off from Chinhae (K-10), armed with rockets and bombs. This aircraft, flown by 2Lt C.J. Pappas who was declared was missing after a strafing attack on 4 November 1951. (SAKWVA)

surrounded, the 1st Marine Div, which now included the British 41 Commando Royal Marines, began a fighting withdrawal from the reservoir. With enemy forces blocking their way, Maj Gen O. P. Smith, commanding the 1st Marine Div, characterized the action not so much as a retreat, but 'an attack in another direction'. Conditions were harsh, with temperatures of -26° C and snow on the ground. The only consolation was that the frozen reservoir provided an escape route for the survivors of Task Force Faith after it was decimated on 1 December.

During the next fortnight, the full might of naval air power was concentrated on the needs of the 1st Marine Div as it fought its way southwards down the Sudong Valley. When poor weather prevented the launching of aircraft from the carriers on 1 December, the entire B-26 force of the 5th AF was put at the disposal of X Corps. The Corsairs of VMF-212 and VMF-214 flying from Yonpo, plus those of VMF-312 operating from USS *Badoeng Strait*, worked at maximum effort to support their ground-based comrades. Each day, 1st MAW aircraft flew around CAS 130 sorties, while the carriers USS *Leyte* and USS *Philippine Sea* each contributed a further 70 sorties per day. The Marines were also supplied by air drops and in the first few days C-47s of the Tactical Air Lift were able to use the airstrip at Hagaru, at the head of the Sudong Valley. At 3,000ft above sea level and measuring just under 1,380m

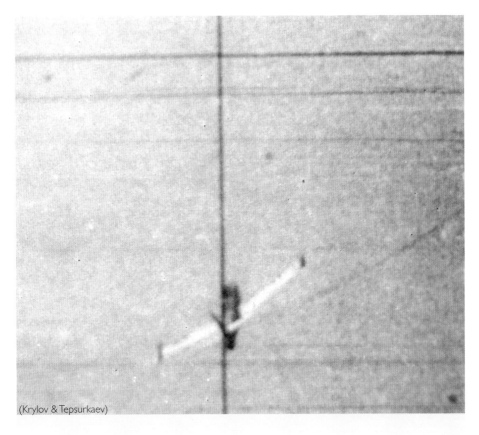

(Krylov & Tepsurkaev)

St Lt A. V. SIMATOV, VVS

MiG-15, 177 IAP, 20 January 1951

On instructions from the auxiliary command post, in a formation of six MiGs, we headed to the area where a group of enemy ground attack aircraft had been detected. Climbing to 1,000 metres, we soon spotted four F-84s, an element of which was attacking a target, while the other element provided cover. Sychev and Andriushkin went after the covering element, while Kormilkin and I attacked the other pair of F-84s. However, just then I saw an F-84 diving towards us and reported this to my leader. When the bogey closed to within firing range, my leader made a hard, left-hand climbing turn and I followed him. The enemy flashed past beneath us and then commenced a gentle turn back in our direction. Warning the leader, I turned into the opponent's attack and we passed head-on, after which I banked sharply to the left. The bogey banked around to the right and again we passed head-to-head. As we closed, I spotted a MiG-15 that was coming at right-angles to our plane of manoeuvre. I quickly alerted him (he turned out to be Kpt Fomin) and with a left-hand turn he turned he dropped in behind the enemy, attacked him from close range and shot him down.

Ensign Jesse L. Brown, the first African American naval fighter pilot, in the cockpit of an F4U-4 Corsair of VF-32 embarked on USS *Leyte* (CV-32) in 1950. Brown was killed while leading a section of Corsairs in support of the 1st Marine Division near the Changjin reservoir on 4 December 1950. (US Navy)

long, the strip was only half completed, but it was just sufficient for the C-47s to evacuate the wounded and also to fly in replacement troops to keep the division at fighting strength. On 6 December, aircraft from USS *Leyte* flew night CAS missions under the illumination of flares dropped by night-intruder aircraft. The following day C-119s dropped sections of bridging to enable the Marines to cross a chasm where the permanent roadway had been destroyed. After two weeks of bitter fighting, the 1st Marine Div reached the sanctuary of the Hungnam Perimeter on 11 December. Air power had played an important part of the battle, but it was at a cost of 11 Corsairs and nine Skyraiders lost on operations. One loss, on 4 December, was that of Ens J. L. Brown, the first African-American to qualify as a naval fighter pilot. While leading a section of Corsairs from VF-32, he was hit by ground fire and when he forced-landed five miles behind CPVA lines he was trapped in his aircraft, which began to smoke. Seeing that drastic action was needed to save his comrade, Lt T. J. Hudner crash-landed his own Corsair next to Brown and attempted to free him. Unfortunately, despite the valiant efforts of Hudner and the crewman from a USMC rescue helicopter, Brown died of his injuries.

Front-line troops were not the only UNC personnel under attack: on 28 November a KPAAF Po-2 'night heckler' bombed the 8th FBG base at Pyongyang (K-23), killing one serviceman and damaging 11 F-51s. Two more similar raids followed over the next few nights. As the CPVA advance began to threaten the northerly airfields, the 5th AF flying units that had moved up to North Korea less than a month previously began to withdraw back south: the F-51 groups at the two Pyongyang airfields moved to Seoul (K-16) and Suwon (K-13), while the units at Yonpo (K-27) moved to Pusan (K-1). However, armed reconnaissance sorties continued north of the bomb line, as did B-29 raids.

The MiG-15s of the 29th GvIAP started flying operational sorties on 1 December. For the first few days in their new theatre they were very cautious, and they avoided battle until they were thoroughly familiar with the tactical situation. Their first blood came on 4 December, when four MiG-15s led by Kpt L. P. Vvedensky were scrambled to intercept a high-flying reconnaissance aircraft flying at altitude over Antung and heading for Mukden. It was a North American RB-45 Tornado, which had replaced the vulnerable RB-29 for missions close to the Yalu River. Flying at 35,000ft, the RB-45 crew members probably thought that they were invulnerable to Chinese fighters, but as they approached Antung for the second time, they were intercepted by MiG-15s. The RB-45 was shot down and St Lt A. F. Andrianov was given credit for the kill.

The Soviet unit incurred its first casualty later that day, when St Lt K. V. Rumiantsev flew into the ground while engaging a formation of F-80s. Over the next few days, the MiGs began to venture as far south as Songchon and there were many engagements with F-80s. Although the Soviet pilots made some kill claims, no corresponding losses were recorded amongst UN aircraft. However, two more MiG-15s and their pilots were lost on 6 and 7 December.

Meanwhile, on 4 December B-29s had bombed the towns of Anju and Pakchon, which had so recently been behind the UNC lines. On the next day, Sunchon and

KPAAF pilots are briefed in front of a Lavochkin La-9 fighter in late 1950 or early 1951. After the 56th JHY had been decimated, the KPAAF started to rebuild itself in China. (Cooper/ Grandolini)

ABOVE:
A Lockheed RF-80A Shooting Star reconnaissance aircraft of the 15th TRS. In this variant, the nose armament of the fighter variant was replaced by a camera pack. Two US Navy Consolidated PB4Y-2 Privateers can be seen in the background. (NARA)

RIGHT:
An F4U Corsair of VF-113 traps aboard USS *Philippine Sea* (CV-47) after a mission over Korea, in early December 1950. Most of the missions flown at this time were in support of the US 1st Marine Division as it fought its way south from the Changjin reservoir. (US Navy)

A Douglas C-47 Dakota dropping supplies to the 1st Marine Div during the fighting withdrawal from the Changjin Reservoir. Once the division moved southwards, the transport aircraft could no longer use the short airstrip that had been cleared near the reservoir itself. (NARA)

A flight of three Republic F-84E Thunderjets of the 27th FEG, which deployed to Korea in late November 1950 to act as fighter escort to bomber aircraft. Unfortunately, the straight-wing F-84 was no match for the swept-wing MiG-15 in air-to-air combat and it was soon switched to the ground-attack role. The aircraft nearest the camera was shot down by anti-aircraft fire near Sinanju on 13 October 1951. (USAFM)

Sukchon were bombed and 2 Sqn SAAF lost its first aircraft. While rocketing a supply dump, Capt J. F. O. Davis flew into secondary explosions caused by his own weapons and forced-landed nearby. Fortuitously, he was rescued soon afterwards by a US Army L-5 observation aircraft crewed by Capt J. Lawrence and Capt L. Miller.

THE SABRE AND THUNDERJET ENTER COMBAT

The arrival of the MiG-15 over North Korea and its obvious superiority over the F-80 and the Panther had caused Gen Stratemeyer to request more modern equipment for the 5th AF. On 8 November, the 27th Fighter Escort Group (FEG), based at Bergstrom AFB, Texas, and equipped with the Republic F-84E Thunderjet, had been given notice to deploy to Korea. So had the 4th FIG, from Wilmington, Delaware, which flew the North American F-86A Sabre. The aircraft of both units were transported across the Pacific by ship and after arrival in Japan the units were sent to Korea. The 4th FIG deployed to Kimpo (K-14), while the 27th FEG went to Taegu (K-2). The 27th FEG flew its first mission on 7 December and, despite being equipped and

Maintenance crews working on an F-86A Sabre of the 4th FIG, Kimpo (K-14), January 1951. (Joe Scherschel/ The TIME LIFE Picture Collection via Getty Images)

trained to escort heavy bombers, it was pressed into the ground-attack role. Led by Col D. J. M. Blakeslee, four rocket-armed F-84s carried out an armed reconnaissance in the Chinnampo area, knocking out several locomotives and strafing enemy positions.

During the course of the next week, the area between the Yalu and Chongchon Rivers became a dangerous place for F-80s. MiG-15s patrolled the area and there were almost daily clashes. Soviet pilots claimed to have shot down some 16 F-80s during the course of December, but only one or two losses were recorded by the USAF, indicating that despite having been seriously damaged, most of the aircraft attacked by the MiGs had managed to return to their base. Indeed, over the months of combat the F-80 had consistently shown its ability to absorb a substantial amount of damage, including hits from 40mm shells, to both airframe and engine.

The 4th FIG started operational flying on 17 December. That afternoon, Lt Col B. H. Hinton led four F-86s on a fighter sweep along the Yalu River. His flight included Flt Lt J. A. O. Levesque RCAF, a Canadian exchange officer with the 4th FIG who thus became the first Canadian to fly a jet combat sortie over Korea. Since there was a 199-mile transit to and from the operating area, the flight flew at a leisurely 0.62 Mach in order to conserve fuel. It was a tactical error that might have cost them dearly, but for the fact that the Soviet pilots that day had not yet expected to see F-86s in Korea. They assumed that the swept-wing aircraft were friendly MiGs and ignored them. As a flight of MiGs passed under them, Hinton led the F-86s into the attack. He dived unseen behind the MiG element leader, Podpolkovnik (Lt Col – Pplk) Ya.N. Efromeenko, and shot him down. Two days later, F-86 pilots claimed to have shot down two more MiG-15s, but Soviet records indicate that these aircraft landed safely, although in one case the aircraft was peppered with 18 bullet holes.

The first large-scale jet fighter engagements occurred on 22 December. During a morning dogfight between eight F-86s and eight MiG-15s, Capt L. V. Bach was shot down by Kpt N. E. Vorobev, becoming the first F-86 loss of the conflict. However, that afternoon, another battle involving eight MiG-15s and 12 F-86s resulted in two MiG-15s, flown by St Lt S. A. Barsegian and Lt A. A. Zub, being shot down.

The evacuation of the X Corps rear guard from Hungnam was completed on 24 December. At the same time in the west of the country, the 8th Army was attempting to hold a line along the Imjin River, just north of Seoul. Whenever the weather

An F-84E Thunderjet of the 8th FBS/ 49th FBG in the snow (probably in December 1951), illustrating the challenges of operating in the winter conditions in Korea. (USAFM)

Two F-82G Twin Mustangs of the 339th F(AW)S preparing for a patrol from Misawa in early 1951. The mounting for the SCR-720C radar in a pod protruding between the cockpits is clearly visible in this view. (USAFM)

allowed, the B-29s continued to strike towns and bridges in North Korea. The targets for these bombers, as well as for the B-26s and fighter-bombers, were now framed in Interdiction Campaign Number 4. This plan divided Korea north of the 37th Parallel into 11 zones, each based on one of the main communications routes. The three zones in the far northeast, between Wonsan and the Tumen River, were delegated to TF77, while 5th AF was responsible for the remaining eight zones. Having been used to operating in conditions of air superiority where multiple attacks could be made against each target by single aircraft, the bombers now had to contend with the threat of the MiGs. Bombers now flew in formation and were usually escorted by fighters. After a directive from Gen MacArthur, on 23 December, that two-thirds of the FEAF bomber effort should be concentrated against towns and villages sheltering enemy troops, most of the bombers were diverted from Interdiction Campaign Number 4, which consequently met with little success. Another major factor limiting the success of the interdiction campaign was a complete underestimation of the ingenuity of the Chinese and North Koreans in repairing or replacing damaged bridges. During December, 5th AF aircraft flew 7,654 armed-reconnaissance sorties; initially these were highly successful, as CPVA troops massed southwards in pursuit of UNC forces, presenting lucrative targets, but from the middle of the month the Chinese reverted to strict camouflage discipline and movement by night, which greatly reduced the success rates of UNC aircraft.

The Soviet deception about their involvement in the air war had been largely successful, and the UNC pilots believed that most of the MiG-15s were flown by Chinese pilots. However, they also believed that a handful of Soviet instructors, who they nicknamed 'honchos', were helping the Chinese. In any case, from mid-December, the Chinese participation in the Korean War was no longer restricted to ground forces. During the second half of 1950, the CPLAAF had undergone a massive training programme and by the autumn some units were nearing combat readiness. One such unit was the 4th *Hángkōng Shī* (HS – Aviation Division), which was equipped with the MiG-15. The division, which comprised the 10th and 12th *Fēixíng Tuán* (FT – Flight Regiments) moved from Shanghai to Liaoyang in late October, in anticipation of a combat role. This move reflected the CPLAAF leadership plan to rotate units through the Korean theatre under Soviet supervision in order to give them some combat experience. After an intensive work-up, the first squadron-sized sub-unit, the 28th *Fēixíng Dàduì* (FD – Flight Brigade), which was part of the 10th FT and commanded by Li Han, deployed to Antung on 21 December. The unit flew its first combat mission on 28 December. On this first sortie, Li Han led four MiGs from the 28th FD to follow eight Soviet MiGs from the 29th GvIAP. During the patrol, the Soviet pilots sighted a formation of F-80s and dived to engage them, but the Chinese pilots, being inexperienced and unable to communicate, were left behind and returned to their base. This pattern would continue until the Chinese pilots had gained enough experience to understand what was happening around them and until communications difficulties were resolved.

Engagements between MiG-15s and UN fighters near the Yalu River continued through 30 December, but as UNC ground forces continued to fall back ahead of the CPVA, so UN airpower became focussed on events further south. The Chinese Third Phase Offensive opened on 1 January and 5th AF aircraft flew over 500 sorties each day to support UNC troops over the next four days. The efforts of USS *Valley Forge* were also dedicated to CAS missions in the centre of the country. But the CPVA pressure was relentless and Seoul was retaken by the CPVA and KPA on 4 January. Kimpo and Suwon had already been evacuated the previous day and both the 4th FIG and the 51st FIG were withdrawn to Japan, moving to Johnson AFB and Tsuiki AFB, near Kitakyushu, respectively. The F-86s no longer had the range to reach the Chongchon-Yalu area, so for the time being, combat between the MiG-15 and F-86 ceased. B-29s attacked Pyongyang with incendiary bombs on 3 and 5 January. During daylight hours, B-26s of the 452nd BG attacked targets in the enemy rear areas and by night the job was continued by the 3rd BG, which had become the night specialists. The night intruders had become more effective when they started using US Navy Mk VIII flares, which were more reliable than the USAF parachute flares. Detonating at 5,500ft, the Mk VIII flares provided good illumination for four to five minutes, giving plenty of time for B-26s to find and attack targets. In a combat assessment on 2 January, a C-47 'Lightning Bug' dropped 129 flares over the course of five hours.

After its evacuation from Hungnam, the 1st Marine Div (USMC) had deployed to Masan before moving up to hunt down guerrilla groups operating in the area west of Pohang. However, most of its air support remained at sea: USS *Sicily* and USS *Badoeng Strait* were patrolling off the west coast with, respectively, VMF-214 and VMF-323 embarked, while on the east coast VMF-212 aboard the USS *Bataan* (CVL-29) was carrying out armed reconnaissance sorties along the coast up to the

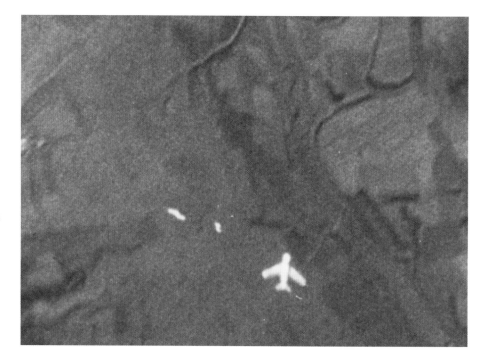

39th Parallel. In addition, VMF-311 had arrived in theatre in the previous month and was flying ground-attack missions with its Panthers from Pusan East (K-9). Since they were not required by 1st Marine Div, the 1st MAW aircraft were tasked directly to support the 8th Army, X Corps and the ROKA Corps as the retreat continued. The USMC aircraft alternated with USAF formations working with the army, but once again the doctrinal differences between the USN/USMC on one hand and the USAF on the other, began to cause problems.

The US Navy and US Marine Corps understanding of the CAS mission was the support of troops in actual contact with enemy forces; it was controlled directly by a FAC who was embedded within ground forces at battalion level. Higher command levels were kept informed, but they indicated their approval by remaining silent and if an airborne spotter was needed because the ground-based FAC needed a better view, the man on the ground nevertheless retained overall control. In the USAF concept, the term CAS applied to operations against enemy forces which were close to, but not in contact with, friendly troops, a role which in later years would be defined as Battlefield Air Interdiction (BAI). Requests for CAS were sent through a formalized air force command chain and based at division level. Since most FACs were airborne as 'Mosquitoes', there was also a physical disconnection between the ground troops and their FAC. The advantage of the air force system was that it was extremely flexible: the Mosquito and the support aircraft had great freedom of movement and air power could be projected beyond the immediate battle line. Its weaknesses lay in the separation between ground and air and also in that radio channels became blocked by the sheer volume of traffic. A solution to this latter problem was found in late January

in 'Mosquito Mellow', a C-47 equipped with a 20-channel VHF radio which could communicate with HQ units, airborne FAC and support aircraft and also act as a filter to keep a manageable traffic load on each frequency.

With the help of air support, the 8th Army disengaged from CPVA forces in order to withdraw to a new Defensive Line D, also known as the 'Dog Line', which ran from Pyongtaek in the west, through Wonju to Samchok on the east coast. It was here that the Chinese offensive was finally halted on 7 January. A band of low cloud and snow brought flying to a halt over the next few days and it was not until 11 January that the weather conditions improved sufficiently for air operations to resume. In the afternoon, at the request of the 8th Army, ten B-29s from the 98th BG bombed Wonju, which was occupied by the KPA 5th Div. By now the need for CAS sorties had dissipated, and from mid-January the 5th AF fighter-bombers concentrated on armed reconnaissance missions. Operating now from Chinhae (K-10) 2 Sqn SAAF, along with other units of the 18th FBG, mounted 16 sorties per day, searching for

targets on the roads between Seoul and Sarawon, and between Seoul and Chorwon. Naval aircraft were also busy on similar missions on the coastal strips: the three carriers of TF77, the USS *Leyte*, USS *Valley Forge* and USS *Philippine Sea* were on station off the east coast, while HMS *Theseus* and USS *Bataan* alternated their duty in the Yellow Sea.

Throughout the winter months the UNC maritime patrol aircraft, Lockheed P-2 Neptunes of US Navy VP-6 operating from Tachikawa near Tokyo, the Martin PBM-5 Mariners of VP-892 and the Sunderlands of the RAF FEFBW, continued the unglamorous task of anti-mine and anti-submarine patrols around the Korean coast. The flying boat crews had to face particularly arduous conditions, in draughty, unheated aircraft flying in temperatures as low as -20°C; the RAF crews were extremely grateful to be supplied with Irvine flying suits by the US Navy. On 15 January, a Sunderland captained by Flt Lt H. J. Houtheusen was flying a routine anti-submarine patrol around the refuelling task force in the Tsushima Straits when the crew picked up a Mayday call from the Wonsan area. On the resumption of carrier air operations that

A winter scene on HMS *Theseus* (R-64): Hawker Sea Fury FB11s and Fairy Firefly FR5s on a snow-covered deck in the winter of 1950–51. (Thomas)

day, USS *Valley Forge* had launched a strike force to carry out armed reconnaissance sorties near Wonsan and during the course of the mission, one of the Corsairs from VF-64 had been so badly damaged by anti-aircraft fire that the pilot, Lt E. J. Hofstra, was forced to ditch in choppy water just off the coast. In falling darkness, Houtheusen and his crew located Hofstra and landed in the open sea to rescue him. Conditions were so rough that Houtheusen had to shut down all four engines, but after Hofstra was hauled aboard suffering from hypothermia, he was able to start again and take off from the rough water.

The rescue of downed airmen had become a priority for UNC forces and helicopters proved to be the most versatile aircraft for the role. Six Sikorsky H-5 rescue helicopters of Detachment F from the USAF 3rd Air Rescue Squadron had been based in Korea since the previous August and both the USN and USMC flew the HOS3 helicopter (which was identical to the H-5) from their ships for the same purpose. However, the different outcomes of two rescue attempts, experienced by USMC Corsairs operating from USS *Bataan*, illustrated how outside conditions such as the presence or absence of enemy forces and the prevailing weather were major factors in the outcome of such missions. On 18 January, Capt R. G. Patterson from VMF-212 was shot down near Suwon and was successfully rescued by a USAF Sikorsky H-5 helicopter from Pyongtaek just 29 minutes later. Two days later, Capt A. H. Agan ditched near Inchon, but by the time the rescue helicopter from USS *Bataan* reached him 70 minutes later, he had died of exposure.

After successfully driving the UNC troops from North Korea and out of Seoul, the CPVA took the opportunity to regroup. Conscious of stretching supply lines and their lack of supporting air cover, CPVA and KPA forces withdrew from the UNC frontlines. For the CPLAAF, the removal of the F-86 from the Chongchon-Yalu area gave the pilots of the 10th FT time to consolidate their skills. The unit was brought up

Flt Lt H.J. 'Bert' Houtheusen (kneeling on left) and his 88 Sqn RAF Sunderland crew with Ensign Edward J. Hofstra (kneeling centre), a Corsair pilot from VF-64, after rescuing him from the sea off Wonsan on 15 January 1951. (Pitchfork)

Ground crews spraying an F-51D Mustang of 2 Sqn SAAF in an attempt to de-ice it on a cold winter day. The aircraft has already been loaded with napalm cannisters under the wings. (SAKWVA)

to full strength when the 29th FD and 30th FD joined the 28th FD at Antung. Rather than remaining in Manchurian airspace, the combined Soviet/Chinese MiG-15 force now operated in the area between the Yalu and Chongchon Rivers, which had become known to UNC aviators as 'MiG Alley'. The KPAAF also rejoined the fray, basing the 56th JHY (now equipped with both the Yak-9P and the Lavochkin La-9) and 57th PHY at Sinuiju, with a forward detachment of Yak-9s operating from Pyongyang (K-23). Two KPAAF fighters intercepted a formation of B-26s attacking Pyongyang on 15 January, but no losses were reported by either side.

USS *Princeton* (CV-37) joined USS *Philippine Sea* in TF77 on 19 January, releasing USS *Valley Forge* and USS *Leyte*, which returned to Japan for replenishment. The carrier aircraft were providing CAS to ROKA ground forces in the east of the country, as well as carrying out armed reconnaissance sorties to the north of the bomb line. Armed reconnaissance behind CPVA/KPA lines continued to be the main role, too, of the F-51, F-80 and B-26 units in mid-January. The main focus was the double-track railway line and roadway running from Seoul northward through Pyongyang to Sinuiju; but the many small roads and railway spurs in the centre of the country which were also used by the CPVA/KPA to bypass blockages in the main routes were covered as well.

Late 1950: A rocket-armed F9F-2B Panther of VMF-311 is refuelled at Pusan (K-9) ready for another mission. This aircraft did not recover from a strafing pass near Kaesong on 2 January 1951; the pilot Lt Marshal E. Simonson was killed. (NARA)

KPA-sponsored guerrillas were active, too, behind UNC lines. An area in the southwest of the country, near Kwanju (Gwangju), was particularly affected, but by 20 January the ROKA IX Div had contained the guerrillas there. On that day, each of the squadrons of the 18th FBW, including 2 Sqn SAAF, dispatched four aircraft to attack rebel villages, killing over 500 guerrillas in the process.

In the morning of 21 January, some 30 Soviet MiG-15s took off to intercept formations of UNC aircraft approaching Anju. Between six and 12 MiG-15s from the 29th GvIAP duelled with four F-80s of the 49th FBG escorting an RF-80 and Lt A. I. Bondarenko shot down one F-80. A little later, six more MiG-15s from the 29th GvIAP were accompanied by Chinese pilots from the 10th FT when they bounced two flights of F-84s from the 27th FEG as they dive-bombed a bridge over the Chongchon near Anju. During this engagement, Li Han scored the first kill for the CPLAAF when he shot down the F-84 flown by Lt G. W. Simpson.

Two days later, the 5th Air Force attempted to neutralize the KPAAF operations with two major airstrikes against Sinuiju (K-30) and Pyongyang (K-23) airfields. In the first raid, 33 F-84s carried out a dawn attack on Sinuiju airfield. The Soviet and Chinese airmen were taken by surprise and two flights of F-84s had completed their strafing runs by the time the first MiG-15s took off from Antung. In the ensuing mêlée between the F-84s and 20 Soviet MiG-15s, with another eight Chinese MiG-15s, two Soviet MiGs were severely damaged and another was shot down, and two Chinese MiG-15s were also lost. The Soviet pilots claimed six kills against F-84s, but no losses were recorded by the USAF that day, although it seems likely that a number of aircraft were badly damaged. During the combat, Lt J. Kratt of the 523rd FES was credited with two MiG-15 kills. Later in the morning a force of 46 F-80s strafed the anti-aircraft batteries around Pyongyang before 21 B-29s of the 19th BG and 309th BG from Okinawa bombed the airfield.

ABOVE:
The tactical
reconnaissance version
of the Mustang was the
RF-51D, seen here in
the markings of the 45th
TRS/ 67th TRG. The
camera lenses, on the
port side of the fuselage
are visible on the right
bar of the national
insignia. (USAFM)

LEFT:
A Sea Fury FB11 of
No.807 NAS about to
be catapulted off HMS
Theseus (R-64) for a
mission over Korea in
early 1951. (Thomas)

After two weeks of cautious probing to try to locate the CPVA formations, UNC ground forces launched Operation *Thunderbolt*, an advance into contact with the CPVA, on 25 January. Over the next six days, UN troops moved slowly northwards, recapturing Suwon in the process. Although the airfield at Suwon was not usable for jet operations, it could nevertheless be used for resupplies. But the ground situation was still uncertain, and the F-80s of the 49th FBG and F-84s of the 27th FEG were pulled back from Korea to Japan, moving to Tsuiki and Itazuke respectively. With the F-86s no longer able to reach past Pyongyang and being used instead for ground-attack

An F-84E Thunderjet of F-84 the 154th FBS (Arkansas ANG)/ 136th FBW takes off from Taegu (K-2) armed with 5-inch rockets. This particular aircraft was shot down while attacking marshalling yards to the south of Sukchŏn on 10 March 1952, killing the pilot, Lt Robert D. Canfield. (USAFM)

mission, the 5th AF had effectively withdrawn from operating in MiG Alley, leaving the Soviets and Chinese claiming air superiority over northern Korea. Reconnaissance flights into the northwest corner of Korea by RF-80s continued, often escorted by F-80s. These were intercepted regularly by Soviet and Chinese aircraft and although there were no losses on either side, many aircraft were damaged in combat.

The beginning of February 1951 brought changes to the Soviet and Chinese order of battle. Keen to give more CPLAAF pilots combat experience, the Chinese replaced the 10th FT at Antung with the 12th FT. It was an ill-considered move, however, since the pilots within this regiment each had only 15 hours of experience flying the MiG-15. Their inexperience became evident on 10 February when two aircraft collided during a scramble take-off and another ran out of fuel and crashed. The unit remained at Antung for the rest of the month but redeployed to Liaoyang in early March. Meanwhile, the Soviet 50th IAD had been withdrawn from combat and the 28th GvIAP from the 151st GvIAD was recalled to the frontline.

The USAF also had to rest their aircrew and share the experience of combat, but rather than rotating entire units through the operational theatre as the Soviets and Chinese did, they chose instead to rotate individuals through the operational units. Every crew member in the continental USA could expect a posting to Korea for an operational tour of 100 missions. In mid-January 1951, this included Flt Lt S. W. Daniel of the RAF, who had joined the 1st FIG at Victorville AFB, California, as an exchange pilot flying the F-86 the previous summer. Daniel was the first of a number of RAF pilots who flew combat operations in the F-86 and F-84 under the auspices of the USAF. The system of individual rotations worked well because it allowed the flying units in Korea to retain a constant level of experience and not to have to start from scratch and re-learn the same lessons. By 10 February, UNC forces had recaptured Suwon (K-13) and Kimpo (K-14) airfields but both airstrips had been too badly damaged to be used immediately by jet aircraft. With UNC troops steadily advancing and the prospect of jets being brought back to Korea, the fortunes of war seemed once again to have swung in favour of the UNC.

Loading the ammunition for the six 0.5inch Browning M-3 machine guns in the nose of an F-80C Shooting Star of the 80th FBS/ 8th FBG at Kimpo (K-14). (USAFM)

B-29 Superfortress of
the 98th BG bombing
industrial targets in
North Korea in January
1951. (USAFM)

CHAPTER 5

OFFENSIVE, COUNTER-OFFENSIVE AND STALEMATE

11 FEBRUARY–31 DECEMBER 1951

In the first weeks of February 1951, six CPVA Armies (each of three divisions) faced UNC forces in the western half of the country, with three KPA Corps facing ROK forces in the eastern half. By 10 February, most of the CPVA was holding positions to the north of the Han River, with the exception of the 38th Army, which remained on the southwestern side of the river bend opposite Yangpyong (Yangpeong). Despite the efforts of UNC aircraft to interdict their supply lines, the CPVA and KPA continued to re-supply their front-line forces successfully. UNC jet fighters operating from Japan, as they had at the very beginning of the conflict, could no longer contest the airspace north of Pyongyang: thus, the MiG-15s of the Soviet 29th GvIAP and the Chinese 12th FT at Antung enjoyed air superiority in the area nicknamed 'MiG Alley'. Across the Yalu River, the KPAAF 56th JHY and 57th PHY remained at Sinuiju, from where they periodically intercepted UNC aircraft operating north of Pyongyang.

CHINESE COUNTERATTACK

During Operation *Thunderbolt*, UNC forces had advanced steadily northwards and as they reached the Han River it seemed that Seoul could be retaken imminently. Meanwhile, night interdiction and reconnaissance sorties by UNC aircraft regularly brought back reports of mass movements of vehicles in North Korea during the hours of darkness, but subsequent daylight armed reconnaissance sorties could find little evidence of supplies or of transportation. The CPVA/KPA had become experts at re-routing transport around obstructions or damage caused by UNC bombers and at sheltering and camouflaging their logistic support. A new plan was therefore devised at HQ 5th AF in order to make the daylight armed reconnaissance missions more

Three McDonell F2H-2 Banshees in service with VF-172 being prepared for an operation on the flight deck of USS *Essex* (CV-8) in 1951. (US Navy)

RIGHT:
A casualty is transferred from a US Army Hiller H-23 Raven helicopter. (CORBIS via Getty Images)

TOP LEFT:
Helicopters were used very successfully for casualty evacuation during the Korean War. Here, wounded personnel are being loaded into a US Marine Corps Sikorsky HOS3 (Dragonfly) on Kari San Mountain, 23 May 1951. In USAF and US Army service, the machine was designated the H-3. (CORBIS via Getty Images)

LEFT:
Personnel of the US Army 8225th Mobile Army Surgical Hospital (MASH) in front of a US Army Bell H-13 Sioux in October 1951. (NARA)

A heavily laden bomb-armed F-80C Shooting Star of the 51st FIG takes off using JATO over an F-86 Sabre of the 4th FIG at Suwon (K-13) in 1951. (USAFM)

effective. Firstly, all reports of night movements were to be collated to provide clues as to where transport might be hiding and where supply dumps might be located. Secondly, the area between the bomb line and 50 miles north of it was divided into three areas, each of which was allocated to an individual fighter-bomber group. The 18th FBG, 35th FBG and 1st MAW were tasked with continuously patrolling their own the area of responsibility. In this way, the pilots would become so familiar with their assigned area that they would learn to recognize potential hiding places or camouflaged equipment. The new tactic paid dividends: in February the 5th AF estimated that it destroyed 1,366 enemy vehicles, more than double the number of the previous month.

The northward advance of UNC forces, Operation *Thunderbolt* on the western UN flank and Operation *Roundup* in the centre of the country, continued through the first ten days of February. By using the forward airstrips at Taegu West (K-37) and Taejŏn (K-5), Mosquito T-6 aircraft could stay airborne virtually continuously over the frontlines. They were supported by the 'Mosquito Mellow' C-47 radio relay aircraft that remained on station 20 miles behind the lines. The controllers also ventured ahead of UN columns, calling in airstrikes to clear the way ahead. For example, on 6 February, Capt D. E. Wilkinson, 'Mosquito Cobalt', located a body of CPVA troops near Yangpyong and called in strikes by four F-84s, six Corsairs and six B-26s. However, the UN advance was brought to a sudden halt on 12 February by heavy counterattacks by the CPVA/KPA between Yangpyong and Hoengsong (Hoengseong). During the battle of Hoengsong, two T-6s consecutively took the callsign 'Mosquito

Liberator' to operate over the town and direct airstrikes by Corsairs, F-80s, F-84s and F-51s against the attacking CPVA troops. Despite the efforts of supporting aircraft, US and Netherlands troops were ejected from Hoengsong on 13 February in the face of overwhelming force. The CPVA then moved southwards to invest US and French troops in the village of Chipyong-ni, while another push by CPVA and KPA struck towards Wonju. For the next three days, despite strong winds, Chipyong-ni was given the highest priority for air support. Three flights of fighter-bombers attacked CPVA troops with napalm in the afternoon of 14 February and they were followed by an aerial re-supply by 24 C-119s. The next day, airstrikes again helped the defenders to fight off Chinese attacks. During the day, H-5 helicopters braved the weather conditions to evacuate casualties.

The techniques for night CAS by UN B-26s were perfected during February by employing ground controllers with AN/MPQ-2 narrow beam radars to direct the bombers to their target. When the controller received the co-ordinates of the target, he could plot them accurately on the radar scope and direct the aircraft towards it. The controller gave the bomber a countdown to weapon release, with surprisingly accurate results. In daylight, the B-29s were in action over northwest Korea on 14 February. Just before midday, ten MiG-15s led by Mr P. B. Ovsyannikov scrambled to intercept a formation of eight B-29s escorted by eight F-80s. Two of the MiGs, led by Pplk V I. Kolyadin, engaged the bombers and although the fighter escorts interrupted his first firing pass, Kolyadin attacked again and was credited with shooting down a B-29. However, once again, the Soviet pilot had fired out of range and no losses were reported by the USAF crews.

The last F-51D Mustang off the production line, serving in Korea with the 39th FIS/ 18th FBG in 1951. It crashed on 18 October 1951 after its coolant system was damaged by ground fire. (USAFM)

(RAAF Museum)

77 SQUADRON RAAF, COMBAT REPORT
Meteor Close Escort, 5 September 1951

Pilots were briefed to provide close escort to two RF-80s from rendezvous over Tan-Do to a target in the Sinuiju area. Each aircraft was armed with full loads of 20mm ammunition. They were airborne under the callsigns of Anzac Able and Baker, in two flights of four aircraft. After being cleared by Shirley, two aircraft aborted, one with inoperative guns and one escorted him back to base. Rendezvous was established with the RF-80s but after one RF-80 had made two passes he returned to base. The other RF-80 was in the target area for about 17–18 minutes and covered the railway line from Sonchon to Chongju. At 1735K twelve MiG-15s were sighted at 26,000ft – 2,000ft above the Meteors - heading 310° on a reciprocal course to the Meteors. The MiGs flew past the Meteors, turned 180° and attacked from six o'clock high. Combat discipline was very good. Six MiGs came down first and friendly flights broke left. The MiGs followed round in pairs, two would fire then pull up; second two would fire then pull up; third two would fire then pull up, all in formation. While the first six drew off and re-grouped, second six would come in and repeat the tactics of the first. The encounter lasted about 5-6 minutes, during the course of which Able One and Three fired two bursts each with no observed results. Baker Four fired one burst then received a hit which threw him on his back and the aircraft went into a long dive out of control. The pilot could see that his tail assembly was damaged and made no attempt to pull out too quickly, or to use speed brakes for fear of applying strain to the damaged part. The aircraft gradually flattened out and pilot was able to regain control at 10,000ft. Baker Four received major damage to his port tailplane. When the first six MiGs drew off to re-group, Able Three observed one to be emitting white smoke.

Chipyong-ni was relieved on 15 February, but the CPVA/KPA drive towards Wonju continued for another four days before it was halted. UNC ground forces were supported by airstrikes, including aircraft from the carriers of TF77 sailing off the east coast, which carried out both CAS and armed reconnaissance missions. On the west coast, the Sea Furies and Fireflies of HMS *Theseus* hunted for targets of opportunity in the area of Chinnampo and, like the Corsairs and Skyraiders of TF77, their main concentration was against bridges. The weather provided a challenge to pilots, with low cloud often covering the hilltops and forcing them to stay low in narrow valleys. On the day that Chipyong-ni was relieved, Lt D. W. McKellar of 2 Sqn SAAF was killed when his F-51 hit a hillside while manoeuvring for a strafing pass and the previous day two F-51s from 77 Sqn RAAF had been lost when they collided in cloud. On 21 February a flight of four F-80s from the 49th FBG were caught out when the weather closed in on Taegu and they had to force-land on the banks of the Naktong River.

With the Chinese and North Korean forces halted, it was the turn of the UNC to take the initiative and Operation *Killer* was designed to retake the territory seized by the CPVA/KPA. A re-arming and refuelling detachment for F-86s was established at Suwon (K-13) on 22 February and on the same date, the 334th FIS was deployed to Taegu (K-2); however, even with these arrangements in place, the F-86 could not reach beyond Pyongyang. Nevertheless, some small-scale B-29 formations escorted by F-80s raided into the north. On 25 February, 12 MiG-15s from the 28th GvIAP intercepted a box of four B-29s at Kaechon, ten miles east of Anju. The MiG pilots carried out a sustained attack against the bombers, which maintained tight formation and kept up heavy defensive fire. Having seen their shells registering on the B-29s and smoke issuing from some of the aircraft, the Soviet pilots had to disengage as they ran short of fuel. They confidently reported that they had damaged at least three bombers, but they were credited by their command centre with having shot down all four aircraft. In fact, no losses were reported by the FEAF.

Despite solid cloud cover in the last week of February the UNC ground forces were strongly supported by fighter-bombers as they pushed northwards. Once again Mosquito

Fully armed with two 500lb bombs and eight 5-inch HVARs, this F-84E Thunderjet of the 8th FBS/ 49th FBG is at readiness - complete with ground power unit and cockpit ladder attached. It is parked on the ubiquitous PSP. (USAFM)

The RATOG rocket pods are easily visible on this bomb-armed Firefly FR5 of N0.810 NAS as it launches from HMS *Theseus* (R-64) for a mission over Korea in March 1951. (Thomas)

controllers called in aircraft to attack enemy troops near Seoul and Hoensong using napalm and gunfire. Air support was not limited to bombing and strafing, for during the advance through the hilly country around Wonju some 1,350 tons of supplies were air dropped to UNC troops by C-119s of the 314th Troop Carrying Group (TCG). Beyond the frontline, the 'truck hunting' method of armed reconnaissance was further improved by the 'Circle Ten' technique. In this development, the RF-51s of the 45th TRS were dispatched for a pre-dawn reconnaissance in a ten-mile circle around the most likely positions of enemy vehicles, based on the reports of the previous night. The RF-51 pilots then reported any sightings, leading F-80s and F-84s directly to their targets.

Another B-29 raid was mounted on 1 March, when 18 B-29s from the 98th BG were tasked against the bridge at Kogunyong (Cheonggang) between Chongju and Sinuiju. After taking off from Yokota, the bombers were delayed by winds that had not been forecast, so they arrived late at the rendezvous point with the escort of 22 F-80s. As a result, the F-80s ran short of fuel and had to turn back early, leaving the B-29s to continue unescorted to their target. Eight MiG-15s led by Mr P. B. Ovsyannikov were scrambled to intercept the bombers, followed a few minutes later by another six MiGs led by Pplk V. I. Kolyadin. Three of the MiGs returned to Antung after suffering technical problems, leaving 11 fighters to engage the bombers. The MiGs caught the B-29s just as they turned for home and subjected them to a heavy attack, leaving ten of the B-29s severely damaged. Three of the bombers had been hit so badly that they had to make emergency landings at Taegu. It was this encounter that made 5th AF commanders realize that they had lost air superiority over northwest Korea.

The stakes were raised in the following days as both sides reinforced their fighter forces. On 2 March the Soviet 151st GvIAD was strengthened by moving the 72nd GvIAP from its training role at Anshan to join the 29th GvIAP at Antung. Four days later, the US 4th FIG was also reinforced. The 334th FIS moved forward to Suwon and its place at Taegu was taken by the 336th FIS, which in turn started to rotate its F-86s through Suwon for sorties into MiG Alley. On the same day the F-86 squadrons began to launch sequential flights of four aircraft into MiG Alley separated by short intervals to ensure a continuous presence there. Their role was simply to keep the MiGs tied up so that they could not interfere with ground-attack aircraft operating in the area. The first week of F-86 patrols resulted in wary sparring, but no engagements with the MiG-15s. The first major combats occurred on 12 March, a day in which the 151st GvIAP flew 56 sorties.

That morning, 12 MiG-15s launched in response to an air raid warning and fought a lengthy battle with 12 F-86s. Both sides made kill claims, but in fact neither side suffered any losses. By the afternoon the cloud structure had built up and while one formation of MiG-15s distracted the F-86 screen, 12 more MiG-15s bounced four F-80s from the 8th FBG which were attacking a target near Sinuiju. During the dogfight, two MiG-15s flown by St Lts V. F. Bushsmelev and V. P. Sokov collided when they both tried to shoot the same F-80. After a short break caused by poor weather, the air-to-air engagements started again and there was another fatal mid-air collision on 17 March. This time a MiG-15 flown by Kpt V. M. Dubrovin and an F-80 flown by Lt H. J. Landry collided head-on, as four MiGs and four F-80s fought in and out of cloud a few miles southeast of Sinuiju. Both pilots were killed.

Flooding due to heavy rain was a major problem in the summer months, as illustrated here at Pyongtaek airfield (K-6) in the summer of 1951. The AT-6 Texans used by the 'Mosquito' airborne FACs are dispersed on the airfield. (USAFM)

Two four-ship flights of bomb-carrying F-84E Thunderjets of the 8th FBS/ 49th FBG set out for a mission over North Korea in late 1951. (USAFM)

The UNC Operation *Killer* had successfully regained the ground lost earlier to the CPVA and KPA by 6 March and had been superseded by Operation *Ripper*, which sought to recapture Seoul and advance to the Imjin River. The US 25th Division started to cross the Han River on 7 March, supported by over 570 sorties by 5th AF and 1st MAW aircraft. The effort was repeated the following day and 22 B-29s also struck a CPVA supply depot at Chunchon. Seoul was recaptured for the second time on 14 March, and nine days later, to cut off retreating CPVA forces, the US 187 Airborne Regiment carried out a parachute assault to capture the town of Munsan, a chokepoint where the road between Seoul and Kaesong crossed the Imjin River. The area around the drop zone was worked over by 56 B-26s from the 3rd BG and 452nd BG before nearly 3,500 paratroopers were delivered by a fleet of 72 C-119 Flying Boxcar and 48 Curtiss C-46 Commando transport aircraft. Once the troops were on the ground, CAS was provided by a force of 31 F-51s, 50 F-80s and 31 F-84s.

On the same day, the FEAF B-29s revisited Kogunyong, but this time they were escorted by a sizeable force of Sabres and the 12 MiG-15s which were scrambled to intercept the bombers were unable to penetrate the escort screen. Perhaps emboldened by this success, the FEAF sent its B-29s to the Yalu bridges on 29 and 30 March. On each day some 30 bombers were supported by a high cover screen of F-86s and close escort of F-80s from the 8th FBG and 49th FBG. Once again, the escorts managed to fend off most of the MiG-15 attacks, but even so one B-29 was lost on 29 March and another seriously damaged the following day.

By the end of March, the battle lines ran from the Imjin River in the west to the Hwachon Reservoir in the centre of the country, and then to Yangyang on the east coast. Naval aircraft had flown armed reconnaissance and CAS sorties throughout the month. On the east coast, the Panthers of TF77 were employed in the armed reconnaissance role, combing the highways and railway lines between Wonsan and Songjin (Gimchaek), hunting railway trains, vehicles and supply dumps and also bombing the bridges. On the west coast, the same tasks were performed over Chinnampo and the Ongjin Peninsula by Sea Furies and Fireflies from HMS *Theseus* until they were relieved in TF95 by the Corsairs of USS *Bataan* on 1 April. Meanwhile, the Corsairs and Skyraiders from USS *Princeton* and USS *Boxer* were dedicated to CAS sorties. The F-51, F-80 and F-84 units were busy, too, with armed reconnaissance and CAS missions every day. The weapon of choice for these roles was still napalm because it was very effective against area targets without needing to be dropped accurately.

Bombs explode on the newly constructed airfield at Saamchan on the banks of the Chongchon River, during a raid by B-29 Superfortress on 18 October 1951. (USAFM)

But it was a particularly horrible method of killing and the use of napalm troubled the conscience of many pilots: one F-84 pilot, Sqn Ldr M. C. Adderley, an RAF officer who flew 100 combat missions with the 27th FEG during the first half of 1951, thought it an evil and abhorrent weapon. Another antipersonnel weapon, the proximity-fused fragmentation bomb, was beginning to prove its usefulness and, in some cases, replace napalm. After some initial problems with aircraft self-damage by these weapons, local modifications were made to the bomb racks on F-51s, F-80s and F-84s to stop the weapons from arming until they had fallen a safe distance from the dropping aircraft.

The Soviet 151st GvIAD was withdrawn from Antung on 2 April and its place in the 64th IAK was taken by the 324th GIAD, comprising the 176th GvIAP and the 196th IAP. The newcomers had their first taste of combat on 3 and 4 April when they tangled with F-86s. The F-86 pilots, unaware of the changeover in MiG-15 units, noticed a new, aggressive attitude in their opponents. Despite this, the lack of operational experience in the MiG pilots showed as they fought the F-86s in cloud-filled skies. On 3 April Capt J. Jabara of the 334th FIS shot down a 176th GvIAP MiG-15 flown by St Lt P. D. Nikitchenko, and two more MiG-15s were heavily damaged that day. Over the next few days there was too much low cloud for the B-29s to operate near the Yalu River, but daily clashes between F-86s and Sabres continued. There was an improvement in the weather on 7 April and 16 B-29s of the 98th and 307th BGs were tasked to bomb the bridges over the Yalu at Sinuiju and Uiju on that morning. It had also been decided that the 27th FEG should be employed in their primary role, as escort fighters, so 48 F-84s accompanied the bomber force. A high cover screen of

An F-80C Shooting Star of the 36th FBS/ 8th FBG in mid-1951. The aircraft was lost on 31 August 1951 after being set on fire by anti-aircraft fire; the pilot, Lt Jack E. Henderson, was posted as Missing in Action. (USAFM)

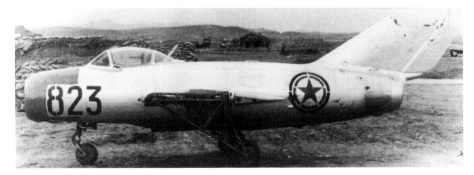

F-86s were also on station in MiG Alley. As the bombers approached, 22 MiG-15s from 176th GvIAP were scrambled from Antung, in four sections. Six MiGs tackled the F-86s, while the rest tried to force their way through the close escort. The F-84s did well and shot down one MiG-15, but two pairs of MiGs managed to slip through and attack the bombers. Kpt I. A. Suchkov shot down one B-29 and another was badly damaged by Kpt S. P. Subbotin. The bridge at Sinuiju remained standing.

Five days later, the FEAF made a final attempt to destroy the bridge at Sinuiju. This time the bomber force was to consist of 48 B-29s, drawn from all three bombardment groups, escorted by 54 F-84s from the 27th FEG with high cover provided by the 4th FIG. Unfortunately, a number of bombers experienced technical issues, so by the time the bomber formation set out for the target, there were only 39 B-29s and the formation had become stretched out. The 196th IAP launched 14 MiG-15s from Antung in two sections, followed a few minutes later by another two sections of eight and six MiG-15s from the 176th GvIAP to meet the bomber raid. It seems that all four sections intercepted the first formation of eight B-29s from the 19th BG. Despite the efforts of the escort fighters, the 28 MiG-15s were able to get through to the bombers, carrying out high-speed firing passes on their quarry. In the chaos of close combat, the F-84 pilots became confused and started shooting at F-86s as well as MiG-15s. Two B-29s were shot down by the MiGs and a third was so badly damaged that it had to make an emergency landing at Suwon on just two engines. Some 15 minutes after the first scramble, a further four MiG-15s from the 176th GvIAP took off, but they became

RIGHT:
Gun camera film from
the MiG-15 of Kpt Ivan
A. Suchkov of the 176th
GvIAP/ 324th IAD during
the engagement with
B-29s over Sinuiju on
7 April 1951. Suchkov
was credited with a
confirmed kill and one
B-29 of the 371st BS/
307th BG was shot
down.
(Krylov & Tepsurkaev)

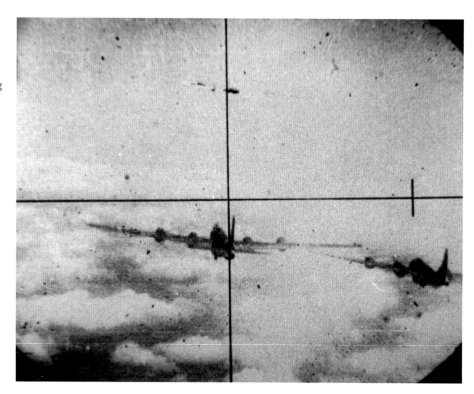

BELOW:
Lt T.G. Nielson, USNR
flying an F9F-2 Panther
of VF-721 aboard USS
Boxer (CV-21) as escort
for a reconnaissance
aircraft, near Sinpo,
North Korea on 9 June
1951. (US Navy)

entangled with the escort fighters. Finally, ten minutes later, eight more MiG-15s from the 196th IAP led by Kpt B. V. Bokach launched to join the fray. This formation intercepted the second bomber formation, comprising 12 B-29s from the 307th BG, and Kpt B. S. Abakumov succeeded in shooting down one of the bombers, although his aircraft was badly damaged afterwards by an F-86. The final force of 19 B-29s from the 98th BG was fortunate in that most of the MiG-15s were on the ground re-arming and refuelling when they reached the target area, so they were unmolested. There were no MiG-15 losses that day, and in addition to the three B-29s shot down and the damaged aircraft at Suwon, another four B-29s had been severely damaged, including one that also had to land in Korea. It was a rate of attrition that the FEAF could not afford and as a result of 'Black Thursday', daylight deep penetration raids by B-29s were discontinued for the time being.

On 17 April, FEAF bombers were in action again, though safely out of range of the MiGs, when they commenced a campaign against KPAAF airfields; over the next five days, the established airfields at Pyongyang, Yonpo and Wonsan were bombed, along with four new airfields which were being built to the southeast of Pyongyang. Air-to-air engagements between MiG-15s and UNC jet aircraft continued in MiG Alley through the rest of April. By 22 April the facilities at Suwon (K-13) had been improved sufficiently for the 336th FIS to join its sister squadron there, which enabled the two squadrons to co-ordinate their operations and fly larger formations. On that day 20 MiG-15s from the 196th IAP and another 16 MiGs from the 176th GvIAP

This B-29 Superfortress was badly damaged during a bombing raid on the bridges over the Yalu River on 1 March 1951 and was forced to divert to Seoul (K-16). It eventually completed 45 missions over North Korea. (NARA)

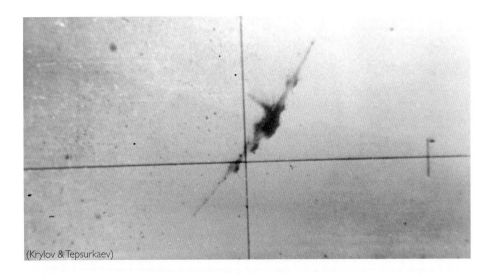

(Krylov & Tepsurkaev)

St Lt A.N. NIKOLAEV, VVS
MiG-15bis, 17th IAP, 27 October 1951

We had just emerged from the clouds when we ran into enemy fighters. I and my leader Volkov somehow wound up off to one side of the dogfight. Soon I saw a group of British Gloster Meteors below and to the right and notified my leader about this. They presented an enticing target because the Meteors were slower and less manoeuvrable than our MiGs. However, the leader answered me: 'We're going after the big ones!' That's when I spotted the 'big ones' - the famous B-29 Superfortresses that had dropped the atomic bomb on Japan in 1945. They were flying in two groups of four, in a diamond formation. I was very upset when my leader opened fire on the bombers at a very long range, and his fire inflicted no damage on them. Even before reaching the B-29 formation, he pulled out of the attack in a chandelle to the left. I decided to press the attack, since I didn't see any enemy fighters around. From a range of 400 metres I opened fire, targeting the left engine on one of the B-29s. The cannon fire shook my aircraft and at maximum speed I flashed past above the bombers. I pulled out of the attack into a chandelle to the left, gained altitude and took a careful look around. I didn't see anything other than the B-29 formation. The B-29 I had attacked had dropped out of the formation and was engulfed in flames. I decided to attack another B-29 and went after it just as I had the first one. As I was passing over the Superfortress formation I heard a powerful thump against my aircraft. The thought flashed through my head 'They've hit me, the swine!' However, my aircraft continued to climb steadily, there were no flames and I pointed my MiG towards home. Several enemy fighters were rushing to intercept me, but I avoided their attacks.

ABOVE: Gloster Meteor F8s of 77 Sqn breaking away, after the unit converted from the Mustang in mid-1951. The nearest aircraft was shot down by anti-aircraft fire on 15 June 1953, but the pilot Sgt Donald W. Pinkstone ejected successfully. (State Library of Victoria)

LEFT: F-84 Thunderjet pilots Lt. Arthur Oligher (left) and Capt Harry Underwood of the 182nd FBS (Texas Air National Guard)/ 136th FBG, discuss the air combat on 26 June 1951, when they scored the first jet combat victory for Air Guard pilots by shooting down the MiG-15 flown by St Lt Evgenii N. Arganovich of the 17th IAP. (USAFM)

bounced 12 F-86s from the 336th FIS just as they were about to leave the area on minimum fuel. However, the MiG pilots were in turn surprised by another 12 F-86s from the 334th FIS. A furious dogfight ensued and when two MiG-15s running low on fuel attempted to disengage and recover to Antung, Capt J. Jabara chased them to low level, shooting down the MiG-15 of Kpt E. N. Samusin. This was the fourth kill credited to Jabara in the conflict. The KPAAF also continued its sporadic operations through April. On 21 April, a pair of Corsairs from USS *Bataan* were jumped by four Yak-9Ps five miles west of Chinnampo. The Yak flying was, in the word of the USMC pilots 'aggressive but poorly executed' and three Yaks were shot down by the Corsairs.

THE CHINESE SPRING OFFENSIVE

Although the CPVA had given ground to the UNC, it was, at the same time, gathering its troops in preparation for another offensive. A confident *Yuan Shuai* Peng Dehuai had allegedly promised Mao Zedong that he would recapture Seoul as a May Day gift. The CPVA Fifth Phase Offensive opened in bright moonlight at midnight on 22 April. Using massive numerical superiority, night infiltration tactics and great courage, nearly 400,000 troops of the CPVA 3rd, 9th, 13th and 19th Army Groups surged towards UNC positions between the Hwachon Reservoir and the west coast. Meanwhile, the KPA 3rd Corps and 5th Corps attacked the ROKA forces holding the line between the Hwachon Reservoir and the east coast. A number of Douglas B-26 night-intruder bombers were immediately called in to attack under direction of the AN/MPQ-2 controllers, but their effectiveness was limited by the proximity of friendly

An F-82G Twin Mustang taking off from an airstrip in Korea in early 1951. This image illustrates the roughness of the operating surfaces on the airfields in Korea. (USAFM)

LEFT:
Two views of the nose of
MiG-15bis No. 1315325,
flown by Plk Yevgeny G.
Pepelyayev, commander
of the 196th IAP, showing
before and after repairs
to battle damage inflicted
during air combat on 6
October 1951.
(Krylov & Tepsurkaev)

troops. When daylight came, all tactical aircraft, including those from the carriers *Boxer*, *Princeton* and *Philippine Sea*, were tasked with CAS missions, or interdiction of the CPVA/KPA form-up areas. The 1st MAW, flying from Seoul (K-16) and Pusan West (K-1) also expended its maximum effort, flying 150 missions in direct support to UNC ground troops. The F-51s of the 35th FBG also moved forward to Seoul (K-16) so that they could be on task over the battle area as quickly as possible. With no air support of their own to keep UNC aircraft away from the battle area, the Chinese strength in numbers also became their undoing because the large masses of troops presented easy targets for UNC aircraft. In one instance, typical of many, a pair of F-80s of the 8th FBG led by Capt W. A. Alden attacked a body of 200 CPVA troops near the Imjin River, using 260lb fragmentation bombs, rockets and guns, killing most of them. On 23 April, FEAF aircraft flew 340 CAS sorties and claimed to have killed around 2,000 Chinese soldiers. That night, MPQ-2-directed B-26 and also B-29 strikes continued to take their toll on CPVA troops. Each B-29 could drop 40 500lb fragmentation bombs, with a kill zone covering a relatively wide area.

One ground action of particular note was the stand by the 1st Bn of the British Gloucestershire Regiment (The Glosters), on Hill 235, which held back the CPVA attack long enough for the US 3rd Div and ROKA 1st Div to make an orderly withdrawal. On the morning of 24 April, the Glosters were supported by an airstrike by napalm-dropping F-51s and after holding their position despite multiple CPVA assaults, another airstrike by a flight of F-80s destroyed a Chinese attacking force the next day. Although the Glosters were eventually overrun, the CPVA offensive in the west was largely spent by 29 April and the UNC forces were holding a line five miles north of Seoul. In the central area the fighting flared again on 26 May with a mass attack by combined CPVA/KPA troops in the Chunchon-Inje sector. The attack was defended robustly by the US X Corps, bolstered by fighter-bombers that killed an estimated 5,000 enemy soldiers on 17 May.

In the humid conditions, the propeller blades of this F4U-4 of VF-791 trace a helical vapour trail as the aircraft passes the 500-ft to go marker during take-off from the deck of USS *Boxer* (CV-21) on 6 July 1951. (US Navy)

Ground crew work on an F-84E Thunderjet of the 8th FBS/49th FBG in late 1951. (NARA)

At nighttime, MPQ-2-controlled B-29s also wrought havoc when they were directed against CPVA/KPA troops forming up for assaults. On the nights of 19, 20 and 21 May, the B-29s were tasked to bomb areas where large numbers of troops were reported to be preparing to make an attack. In each case the CPVA/KPA attack was completely foiled and reconnaissance the following day reported large numbers of enemy dead in the bombed areas. The offensive had run its course by 22 May and a massive MPQ-2-directed attack by 22 B-29s and 11 B-26s across the entire front on the night of 23 May smashed any remaining offensive spirit. With the CPVA on the defensive, UNC seized the opportunity to counterattack and by the end of May, most of the territory lost to the Chinese offensive had been regained.

During follow-up attacks by UNC forces against CPVA positions in the west of the country at the end of April, it became evident that the Chinese control of the Hwachon (Hwacheon) Reservoir represented a threat to operations in the Pukhan River valley below the dam. An attempt to take the dam by ground troops failed, so the help of TF77 was sought to disable the dam floodgates. An initial attempt by Skyraiders of VA-195 from USS *Princeton* on 30 April was unsuccessful: rockets and 2,000lb bombs had no effect on the structure. The following day, USS *Princeton* launched eight Skyraiders, and this time each carried a Mk 13 torpedo. They were supported by 12 flak-suppression Corsairs, and in an impressive feat of airmanship the Skyraiders led by Cdr R. C. Merrick dropped their weapons accurately, destroying two sluice gates and putting the dam beyond use by the CPVA.

Two McDonnell F2H-2 Banshees of VF-172 fly past USS *Essex* (CV-9) with hooks down prior to joining the landing pattern for the carrier, in late 1951. Like the Panther, the Banshee was mainly used for ground-attack missions. (US Navy)

The 64th IAK and KPAAF had been unable or unwilling to support the CPVA ground offensive, but the Soviet MiG-15 force on the Korean border was strengthened in early May. The 303rd IAD was ordered to join the 324th IAD and on 8 May the 18th GvIAP moved to Antung; the 523rd IAP would move to a new airfield at Tatungkao (also known as Miàoergōu), eight miles southwest of Antung, on 28 May. The airfields at Antung and Tatungkao became known collectively as the 'Antung Complex'.

Taking advantage of fine weather on 9 May, the 5th AF and 1st MAW launched a mass fighter-bomber raid against Suniiju airfield, which was being used by KPAAF Yak-9Ps, Lavochkin La-9s (of the recently formed 58th JHY) and Il-10s. Over 300 UNC aircraft were involved in the operation, including a fighter escort of F-86s, F-84s and USMC Panthers. The main strike force, which comprised the F-51s of the 18th FBG with 55 USMC Corsairs, was preceded by a defence suppression wave of F-80s. Several flights of MiG-15s were launched to counter the raid, but the only success was by St Lt A. M. Dostoevsky, who damaged an F-84. Two days later, USS *Princeton* and USS *Boxer* between them launched a force of 32 Skyraiders and 32 Corsairs with a top cover of 16 Panthers to attack four rail bridges to the east and northeast of Pyongyang. The attacks were successful in taking down spans on three of the bridges. Poor weather for much of the rest of the month curtailed aerial encounters in northwest Korea, although UNC fighter-bombers continued to support the ground troops and to interdict the lines of communication on a daily (and nightly) basis. A CAS mission by a flight of four F-84s led by Sqn Ldr Adderley on 21 May illustrates

An F7F-3N Tigercat of VMF(N)-513 taxying out for a sortie from Pyongtaek (K-6). (USAFM)

the testing conditions that fighter-bomber pilots had to face: in order to attack the targets allocated to them north of Seoul, the aircraft had to fly amongst the hills under a low cloud base with rain bringing the visibility down to less than a mile.

MiG-15s and F-86s fought again on 20 May over Tetsuzan (Cholsan), with each side claiming to have shot down three of the opposition. In reality, the only combat loss was one MiG-15: Kpt V. A. Nazarkin ejected from his aircraft after being shot down by Capt J. Jabara. This was the fifth MiG-15 to have been credited to Jabara, making him the first 'jet ace'. Two days later, St Lt F. A. Shebanov of the 196th IAP became the second jet ace. However, without wishing to detract from the achievements of these distinguished fighter pilots, it must be remembered that 'confirmed kills' on both sides did not necessarily reflect the actual outcomes of aerial combat.

At the beginning of April, the Soviet VVS Scientific Research Institute had been tasked to capture an F-86 so that it could be examined. A team of test pilots and experienced officers was formed as 'Group Nord' and equipped with new MiG-15bis aircraft. The group arrived in China in late April and set about preparing for their mission. All of the members of Group Nord were experts in their field but, unfortunately, they proved unable to work together as a team. On 31 May, 12 MiG-15s from Group Nord led by Pplk Dzuybenko chanced across a pair of apparently

Armed with rockets and bombs, this F-51D Mustang of 2 Sqn SAAF is ready for an operational sortie. (NARA)

unescorted B-29s near Anju. They had not seen the ten F-86s of the high cover escort, which dived to attack. In their first pass, the F-86s shot down the MiG-15 flown by Mr P. A. Perevozchikov and seriously damaged one other. For their pains, the MiG-15 pilots did not hit the B-29s. A further fatal accident six days later resulted in the abandonment of the project and the disbandment of the team.

OPERATION *STRANGLE*

On the last day of May, USS *Bonne Homme Richard* (CV-31) relieved USS *Philippine Sea* in TF77. The same day also saw the start of Operation *Strangle*, an interdiction campaign by UNC aircraft designed to stop the ability of the CPVA to resupply itself by road. North Korea was divided into three areas, one of which was allocated to each of 5th AF, 1st MAW and TF77. Aircraft were tasked with destroying bridges and damaging or blocking roads where they would be difficult to repair or bypass. For example, on 4 June, four F-51s from 2 Sqn SAAF led by Lt P. J. Strydom bombed a section of roadway just north of Chorwon, where it was cut into the hillside. The F-51s bombed the hillside, starting an avalanche that blocked the roadway.

The B-29 force was tasked against airfields, bridges, railway marshalling yards and supply centres. On 1 June four B-29s, escorted by F-86s, set out to bomb the railway bridge at Kwaksan (Gwaksan). The bomber formation was detected on radar and 37 MiG-15s, in five sections from both the 176th GvIAP and 18th GvIAP were launched to meet them. Unfortunately, the bombers were ten minutes late at the rendezvous point with their F-86 escort, so when the leader decided to carry out a second run on the target, the fighters were too short of fuel to stay with them. The first MiG formations were engaged briefly by the F-86s, but when the US fighters left because they were short of fuel, there followed a mix-up between MiG-15 formations, each of which thought that the other might be F-86s. However, one MiG-15 pilot from the 18th GvIAP, St Lt E. M. Stelmakh, saw the opportunity to engage the bombers and did so, shooting down one of the B-29s on his first pass and severely damaging another on his second. At that point another formation of F-86s arrived and Stelmakh was shot down by Capt R. Ramsbottom of the 336th FIS. A further 11 firing passes by the MiG-15s badly damaged a third B-29. Later in the day, eight MiG-15s from the 18th GvIAP encountered a flight of F-51s that was covering a rescue attempt on the B-29 crew lost earlier. The MiGs engaged the F-51s and shot down one of their number.

Interdiction missions by UNC aircraft continued into the hours of darkness; B-26s flew a total of 177 nighttime sorties between 27 May and 2 June, many of them against targets illuminated by flare-dropping C-47 aircraft. These latter aircraft could illuminate an area for up to four hours. The USMC squadron VMF(N)-513 also carried on the nocturnal interdiction campaign, using their Corsairs and Tigercats, which, being more manoeuvrable that the B-26, were better suited to the role than the USAF aircraft. The US Marines also used the Convair PB4Y-2 Privateer maritime patrol aircraft, known locally as 'Lamplighters', in the target illumination role, with great success.

US Marine ground crew servicing a Sea Fury FB11. This Royal Navy aircraft was loaned to the No.808 NAS of the Royal Australian Navy (RAN), operating from HMAS *Sydney* (R-17), for operations over Korea in late 1951. (NARA)

The fireball from an exploding napalm canister dropped on a CPLA/ KPA storage facility during an airstrike in March 1951. (USAFM)

A mixed formation of F4U Corsairs from VF-791 and AD Skyraiders of VA-702, from the Air Wing of USS *Boxer* (CV-21), photographed off the North Korean coast on 15 August 1951. (US Navy)

The USMC and USAF were not the only force to use the darkness: the KPAAF continued to use its Po-2 'night hecklers' and on 17 June two Po-2LSh aircraft led by La Woon-Yung bombed the flight line of the 4th FIG at Suwon (K-13), destroying one F-86, seriously damaging four more and slightly damaging another four aircraft. The Po-2 raids continued so regularly and punctually in the early hours that they became known by UNC personnel as 'Bedcheck Charlies'. UNC night fighters attempted to intercept the Po-2s, but they proved an elusive foe, although one Po-2 was shot down by B-26 pilot Capt R. M. Heyman of the 8th BS while he was returning from an interdiction mission on 23 June. Another Po-2 was shot down by a Tigercat flown by Capt E. B. Long from VMF(N)-513 on 30 June.

In the second half of June, the 'fighter screen' tactics used by the 4th FIG were effective in keeping the MiG-15s away from interdictor aircraft. There were regular battles in MiG Alley and both sides claimed victories and lost aircraft. On 18, 19 and 22 June the UNC pilots claimed seven kills against a loss of two F-86s, while in the same engagements the Soviets claimed to have shot down ten F-86s for the loss of two MiG-15s.

On 20 June, the KPA attempted to retake Sinmi-do Island, 15 miles south of Sonchon, with air support provided by eight Il-10s from the 57th PHY. The Il-10s were escorted by six Yak-9Ps from the 56th JHY, which were in turn covered by a high escort of 18 MiG-15s from the 176th GvIAP. By chance, a flight of four F-51s from the 18th FBG on their way to their interdiction target spotted the formation and attacked them. They were followed by two more flights of F-51s. In the ensuing combat, one Yak-9P was shot down and at least two Il-10s were severely damaged,

A bomb-carrying F-51D Mustang of the 67th FBS/18thFBG taxis past a ROKAF F-51 at an airfield in Korea. This aircraft was later transferred to the ROKAF. (USAFM)

AT-6 Texans used by the 'Mosquito' FACs at K-6 (Pyongtaek) in the spring of 1951. The open-air gravel pad on the right is the maintenance area. Although PSP has been laid down for the runway, the taxiways are simply dirt tracks. (USAFM)

before the MiG-15s intervened and Kpt G. I. Ges shot down the F-51 flown by Capt J. J. Coleman, his fifth kill of the conflict. Having opened fire from close range, Ges flew through the debris as the F-51 disintegrated, badly damaging his own aircraft.

On the ground, the frontlines now ran from the Imjin River in the west up to the 'Iron Triangle' (between Pyonggang, Chorwon and Kimhwa) and then across to Kansong on the east coast. Both sides could see that the positions were unlikely to change and negotiations to arrange an armistice started on 22 June 1951. However, there was little progress in the negotiations, which would continue for another two years. Meanwhile, both sides had also reinforced their air arms once more. The 17th IAP had moved to Tatungkao in mid-June, completing the deployment of the 303rd IAD. On the UNC side, the 27th FEG started a two-month handover of F-84 operations to the 136th FBG and 49th FBG, overseeing the conversion of both groups to the F-84. Amongst the pilots in the 136th FBG was Flt Lt P. H. L. Scott, an RAF pilot who was part-way through an exchange tour with the 78th FBG at Hamilton AFB near San Francisco.

Carrying external fuel drop tanks once more, MiG-15s began to venture as far south as Pyongyang and frequently attacked F-51s and F-80s operating north of Pyongyang. On 28 and 30 June, MiG-15s attacked separate flights of F-51s near Sinanju and shot

Kpt Vasilii F. Shulev
(on the left) chats to a
colleague of the 17th IAP
at Antung, autumn 1951.
A MiG-15 can be seen in
the background. Shulev
was credited with seven
confirmed kills. (I. Seidov)

down at least one F-51D. In fact, even without the intervention of MiGs CPVA/KPA anti-aircraft guns caused a steady attrition of UNC ground-attack aircraft: on 28 June alone, the anti-aircraft defences accounted for three F-80s, one Skyraider, one Tigercat and one Corsair. A force of 20 MiG-15s attacked F-51s again near Kandong, to the northeast of Kanggye, on 8 July, but the MiGs were, in turn, bounced by 35 F-86s, which shot down two MiG-15s for no loss.

The next day, the CPLAAF took part in combat operations once more. Eight Chinese MiG-15s from the 4th *Hángkōng Shī* (HS – Aviation Division), which included the 10th FT and 12th FT, were scrambled to intercept six B-29s of the 19th BG bombing the airfield at Sinanju. They were escorted by six Soviet MiG-15s from the 17th IAP. While the Soviet MiGs engaged the fighter escort, regimental commander Zhao Dahai led the Chinese MiGs to attack the bombers, which were now egressing from the target area over the sea. The MiG leader damaged one B-29, but because of his lack of combat experience, Zhao Dahai then slowed down to match the speed of the bombers and in so doing made himself an easy target. He was shot down either by the B-29 gunners or by one of the escorting F-86s. His MiG-15 crashed in shallow water almost 30 miles off the Taedung estuary and was recovered for examination, by UN naval forces 12 days later. The recovery of the wreckage on 21 July was undertaken under cover of fog and low cloud, which also kept the MiG-15s on the ground, but eight Panthers from VMF-311 established a CAP above the naval vessels in case of KPAAF attempts to intervene. As the Panthers started to recover, they became disorientated and flew north of Antung, before they fixed their position by seeing Sinuiju in a gap in the clouds. In the meantime, ten MiG-15s of 196th IAP which scrambled into the fog to intercept this violation of Chinese airspace caught the rear section of three Panthers, shooting down one and damaging a second so severely that it had to land at Kimpo (K-14).

An F-51D Mustang of 2 Sqn SAAF in the summer of 1951. This aircraft was shot down by ground fire on 24 November 1951 with the loss of its pilot, Lt George H. Krohn. (SAKWVA)

Gun camera footage of a KPAF Il-10 being shot down by Lt Col Ralph H. Saltsman in an F-51D Mustang of the 18th FBG on 17 June 1951. (USAFM)

RIGHT: Soviet MiG-15 pilots of the 17th IAP at Tatungkao, autumn 1951. First row, left to right: S.S. Bychkov, V.F. Shulev, S.S. Artemchenko, N.V. Sutyagin and F.P. Malunov; second row, left to right: N.A. Savchenko, A.S. Shirokov, N.Ya. Perepelkin, N.N. Kramarenko, M.F. Osipov and N.F. Miroshnichenko. (Igor Seidov)

BELOW: A damaged Sea Fury FB11 flown by Lt Doug McNaughton from No.804 NAS, HMS *Glory* (R-62) seen at Kimpo (K-14) after being hit by anti-aircraft fire on 16 August 1951. (77 Sqn RAAF)

For most of the rest of July and August the summer monsoon brought thick clouds from around 2,000ft all the way up to 35,000ft, so encounters between MiG-15s and F-86s in MiG Alley became less frequent. However, the 'night heckling' activities of the KPAAF Po-2s continued through the first half of the month until, on the night of 12 July, a Corsair from VMF(N)-513, vectored by the Ground Controlled Intercept (GCI) radar controller 'Dentist' based near Seoul, successfully shot down a 'Bedcheck Charlie' Po-2LSh. As a result of the heavy losses amongst Po-2 crews and aircraft, the KPAAF withdrew from night bombing for two months.

After analysis of the results of interdiction sorties over the previous months, on 18 August the focus of the UNC Operation *Strangle* switched from the road network to the railway system in North Korea. The planners at HQ 5th AF had decided that the railway was more important and more vulnerable than the roads; for the rest of August daily attacks by formations of upwards of 60 fighter-bombers would concentrate their efforts on a specified 15-to-30-mile stretch of railway line in northwest Korea, attempting to destroy the track and roadbed using 1,000lb bombs. Meanwhile, the aircraft of TF77 concentrated on the tracks in the northeast of the country. By night, the B-26s of the 3rd BG, which was now operating from Kunsan (Gunsan – K-8), kept up the pressure on the western arm of the rail system, whilst those of the 452nd BG flying from Pusan East (K-9) concentrated on the eastern side. During September, the F-51 wing comprising the 18th FBG and 2 Sqn SAAF also began to deploy detachments forwards from Chinhae (K-10) to Seoul (K-16), allowing them to spend longer on task.

Bombs hanging from the underwing weapons stations of an F-80C Shooting Star of the 35th FBS/ 8th FBG on a PSP dispersal at Taegu (K-2). (USAFM)

Fully loaded F4U-4
Corsairs of VF-24
and AD Skyraiders of
VA-65 ready for a mass
deck launch from USS
Philippine Sea (CV 47)
during the summer
of 1951.
(US Navy)

THE GLOSTER METEOR

During April, 77 Sqn RAAF had been withdrawn from operations in order to re-equip with the Gloster Meteor F8. Four experienced RAF instructors, led by Flt Lt M. Scannell, had arrived in Japan during February to supervise the conversion and by the end of July the squadron was ready for operations once more. The change of aircraft type had brought with it a change of role: having flown the F-51 in the ground-attack role, 77 Sqn RAAF would fly the Meteor in the fighter role. This was largely a result of an evaluation on 18 May in which Flt Lt Scannell flew a Meteor against an F-86 flown by Flt Lt Daniel and concluded that the Meteor was the equal of the F-86 in air combat. Unfortunately, the evaluation did not take into account the speed differential between the straight-winged Meteor and the swept-wing F-86 (or MiG-15) and nor did it highlight the poor rearward view from the Meteor cockpit; both of these shortcomings would soon become apparent. The first operational sortie by 77 Sqn with the Meteor was a fighter sweep, flown on 29 July. Sqn Ldr R. C. Cresswell led two flights, each of eight Meteors, into MiG Alley; one flight flew at 35,000ft and the other at 30,000ft and both were acting as top cover for F-86s flying at 25,000ft. No MiG-15s were encountered but the difficulties became evident in co-ordinating Meteors flying at around Mach 0.72 and Sabres flying at Mach 0.86. The Meteors were also employed as escort fighters for RF-80s and B-29s. It was during an RF-80 escort sortie on 25 August that 77 Sqn Meteors first encountered MiG-15s, but the result of the engagement was inconclusive.

On the same day, the USAF and USN carried out a successful combined operation when carrier-borne fighters escorted 35 B-29s attacking Rashin (Raseon). Three days earlier USS *Essex* (CV-9) had relieved USS *Princeton* off the east coast of Korea. On board USS *Essex*, the air wing included VF-172, which was equipped with

A Tupolev Tu-2 light bomber of the CPLAAF with crews of the 24th FT, 8th Division. (Dildy)

A line up of Gloster
Meteor Mk 8s in service
with 77 Sqn RAAF at
Kimpo in late 1951.
(State Library of Victoria)

the McDonnell F2H Banshee, and on 25 August, 12 Banshees and 11 Panthers from
USS *Essex* accompanied the B-29s to Rashin, but there was no aerial opposition to the
raid, so the Banshee remained untested in combat. At the same time the air group from
USS *Bonne Homme Richard* carried out a strike on bridges to the north of Chongjin.

The first Meteor combat loss occurred on the morning of 29 August, when two
flights, each of four Meteors, accompanied by 16 F-86s, carried out a fighter sweep
in the area of Chongju. A force of 24 MiG-15s from the 18th GvIAP launched from
Tatungkao to intercept them. Patrolling at 35,000ft, the Meteor pilots saw two flights
of six MiG-15s above them and two MiG-15s below them at 30,000ft. As the Meteors
dived to attack the low MiGs, they were in turn bounced by the rest of the MiG
formation. In the ensuing mêlée, St Lt L. K. Shchukin scored hits on the Meteor of
Sqn Ldr D. L. Wilson, severely damaging the aircraft and wounding Wilson, while
St Lt N. V. Babonin attacked the rear section of Meteors, shooting down Warrant
Officer (WO) R. D. Guthrie.

Throughout the month of September, with the exception of a short period of bad
weather between 21 and 24 September, daily engagements took place in MiG Alley.
Typically, Soviet MiG-15s launched in regimental strength of 24–26 aircraft and often
two entire regiments would launch to intercept formations of UN aircraft. These
were often group-strength formations of F-86s covering similar-sized formations of
fighter bombers, so dogfights involving 50-plus MiG-15s, 24 F-86s, 24 F-84s and
24 F-80s were not unusual. In the first few days of September, Meteors might also have
been involved, but late on the afternoon of 5 September, two flights of four Meteors

FAR RIGHT:
The dammed end of
the Hwachon Reservoir
under attack by Douglas
AD-4 Skyraiders of
VA-195 from USS
Princeton (CV-37)
on 1 May 1951. This
attack, using torpedoes,
successfully destroyed
one flood gate and
severely damaged
another. Earlier attempts
to deny the CPLA/ KPA
tactical use of controlled
flooding on the Pukhan
and Han rivers by
bombing the flood gates
had failed. (US Navy)

BELOW:
An F9F Panther of VF-51
readied for launch from
USS *Essex* (CV-9), with
F2H-2 Banshees of VF-
172 in the background,
off the Korean coast in
late 1951 or early 1952.
(US Navy)

escorting two RF-80 reconnaissance aircraft, which were reconnoitring the railway line between Sonchon and Chongju, were set upon by 12 MiG-15s from the 523rd IAP. The MiG-15s were able to use their superior performance to carry out diving attacks in pairs, firing on the Meteors and then zooming back up to height after each pass. Using this tactic, they seriously damaged one Meteor. This was the final straw for Wg Cdr G. H. Steege, commanding 77 Sqn RAAF, who pointed out that the Meteor was not well-suited to the air-to-air role. As a result, the Meteors were withdrawn from operations north of the Chongchon River. Battles continued to rage in MiG Alley, including one on 19 September when MiG-15s of the 523rd IAP evaded the F-86 screen and caught a formation of F-84Es. However, Capt K. L. Skeen of the 48th FBG turned the tables when he jettisoned his bombs and shot down a MiG-15 flown by Kpt I. I. Tiuliaev.

Earlier in the month, the CPLAAF had deployed the 55 MiG-15s of the 4th HS to Antung once more and after local familiarisation flights, the 12th FT flew its first combat mission of this tour on 25 September. The Chinese pilots were still very inexperienced in air combat and their initial performance was disappointing. Sixteen MiG-15s led by deputy regimental commander Li Wenmo took off to intercept 12 F-80s, covered by a screen of F-86s, which were attacking the bridge at Sinianju. As they attempted to engage the F-80s, the MiG-15s were bounced by the F-86 escort, which shot down one MiG and seriously damaged another. The 4th HS lost several more aircraft to UN fighters over next two days.

The KPAAF had also entered the fray once more midway through the month. A restored 3rd *Yagan Poggyeoggi Yeondae* (YPY – Night Bomber Regiment) under the command of *Daelyeong* (Colonel) Pak Den-Sik reinstated its nightly 'Bedcheck Charlie' raids with Po-2LSh biplanes. The first combat loss in this renewed campaign

was on 23 September, when a Tigercat flown by Maj E. A. van Gundy and M Sgt T. J. Ullhorn shot down a Po-2 which had just bombed Kimpo and damaged two F-86s. Another loss to anti-aircraft guns on 2 October marked the end of night raids by Po-2 for that year.

Although UNC ground-attack assets were primarily focussed on interdiction missions under Operation *Strangle*, CAS sorties remained an important part of the daily task. The period from mid-August to mid-October was one of intense fighting for UN ground forces of X Corps in the area of the Punchbowl, the circular Haean Basin, approximately 15 miles northeast of the Hwachon Reservoir. On 5 September, Bloody Ridge, to the west of the Punchbowl, was taken. But an assault on the high ground to the north of the Punchbowl had already begun and would continue until CPVA were driven off by US, ROK, French and Dutch troops on 21 September. Meanwhile, the month-long battles of Heartbreak Ridge, immediately north of Bloody Ridge, had commenced on 13 September. All of this activity was supported by UNC fighter-bombers, including aircraft from TF77, under the direction of Mosquito FACs. Over 1,600 CAS sorties were flown in support of X Corps during September.

That month saw the introduction to the 4th FIG of the F-86E, which progressively replaced the F-86A in Korea. The main difference between the two versions was that the F-86A had a hydraulically boosted flight control system, whereas the F-86E incorporated fully powered hydraulic controls, including an all-moving horizontal stabilizer. This modification markedly improved the aircraft's controllability, especially in the transonic speed range. The F-86E was also equipped with an AN/APG-30 ranging radar coupled to the gunsight, which improved its accuracy. By the end of the month, UNC pilots claimed to have shot down 14 MiG-15s, although in fact the Soviets lost just five MiG-15s and the Chinese lost a similar number. For their part, the Soviet pilots claimed 90 UNC aircraft downed, although the true losses to the MiG-15 were four F-86s, one F-84, one F-80 and one F-51 – just seven aircraft.

Damage to the rear fuselage of a Soviet MiG-15bis incurred during air combat in 1951. The Korean markings used by Soviet units to disguise their presence are clearly visible in this photograph. (Krylov & Tepsurkaev)

ABOVE:
The open panel under the cockpit of this North American F-86 Sabre shows the ammunition belts of the nose-mounted Browning 0.50-inch machine guns. (USAFM)

LEFT:
B-26B Invader of the 729th BS/ 452nd BG based at Pusan East (K-9) photographed on a daytime mission in 1951. (USAFM)

However, by far the largest part of UNC air operations were performed by ground-attack aircraft and the greatest threat to them was anti-aircraft fire. In comparison to the losses of seven aircraft to MiG-15 fighters, the losses to ground-based anti-aircraft fire during the month of September were 16 F-51s, 14 Corsairs, six Skyraiders, five B-26s, three Panthers, three F-84s and three F-80s – a staggering 50 aircraft. Four Mosquito T-6s were also lost in action. Furthermore, at least 15 UNC aircraft were lost in aircraft carrier launch or recovery accidents. Also, three transport aircraft, six helicopters, three artillery spotters, four B-26s and two B-29s were destroyed in accidents during the month.

The first week of October followed the pattern of the previous month, with daily clashes in MiG Alley. On 1 October one MiG and one F-84E were shot down and the following day an RF-80 and an F-84 collided during a dogfight with MiGs, but two MiG-15s were shot down during the course of the day. One of those Mig-15s, flown by St Lt C. Z. Moskvichev, was the third kill in Korea by Col F. S. 'Gabby' Gabreski, the top-scoring USAAF ace in Europe during World War II, who was now the deputy commander of the 4th FIG. However, it should be noted that on the same day six UNC ground-attack aircraft were lost to anti-aircraft fire, so ground fire remained

the greatest threat to UNC aircraft. On 5 October the Chinese 10th FT was in action again and claimed to have shot down three F-84s for the loss of one MiG-15, although no UNC aircraft were lost in air-to-air combat that day. Five days later the Chinese pilot Hua Longyi was credited with shooting down two F-84s in one sortie, but again no corresponding losses were recorded by UN units.

The air wings from TF77 carriers were active in the eastern half of Korea and on 9 October aircraft from USS *Essex* succeeded in isolating two trains by cutting the tracks immediately in front of and behind them. Aircraft from USS *Bonne Homme Richard* were also called in to capitalize on this target. The next day, aircraft from both carriers worked together again, mounting a raid against a KPA ammunition depot north of Hungnam. The depot was destroyed, and the naval aircraft left the area ablaze with many large secondary explosions. The third carrier in the task force, USS *Boxer*, had already left Korean waters, but it was replaced halfway through the month by USS *Antietam* (CV-36). On the opposite coast, the two carriers which alternated on station as Task Element 95.11 were USS *Rendova* (CVE-114) with the Corsairs of VMF-212 on board, and HMAS *Sydney* (R-17), which carried the 21st CAG comprising the Sea Furies of 808 NAS and Fireflies of 817 Sqn RAN.

F-84E Thunderjets of the 8th FBS/ 49th FBG undergoing servicing at Taegu (K-2) in late 1951 or early 1952. (NARA)

BATTLE OF THE AIRFIELDS

In early October, the main concern of staff at HQ 5th AF was the discovery of three
large airfields being built in the vicinity of Sinanju. The airfield at Saamchan had
been constructed alongside the Chongchon River at Kaechon, 15 miles northeast of
Sinanju, while the airfield at Taechon was situated in a loop of the Taeryong River,
some 20 miles north of Sinanju. The third airfield, Namsi, was at Panghyon, some
15 miles west of Taechon. If these airfields became operational, CPLAAF and KPAAF
aircraft would be able to reach as far south as Pyongyang and the airspace north of the
city would become as hotly contested as that in MiG Alley.

Given the threat of MiG-15s during daylight hours, the initial plan to neutralize the
airfields was to bomb them at night using the Short-Range Navigation (SHORAN)
system of radio beacons to ensure bombing accuracy. Unfortunately, the night
raids against Saamchan on 13 and 14 October were not a success and it was clear
that daylight attacks would be necessary. These were mounted between 18 and
23 October. B-29 raids were to be strongly escorted and timed to coincide with fighter-
bomber attacks on targets farther north, in order to ensure minimal attention from
MiG-15s. On 18 and 21 October the 98th BG missed its rendezvous with its escort
and diverted to secondary targets south of the Chongchon River. The 19th BG
carried out a successful mission against Saamchan on 18 October and was tasked
against Taechon on 22 October. On this day, a force of 12 B-29s with a close escort
of F-84s reached Taechon under an overcast at 10,000ft. Some 20 MiG-15s from the

17th IAP, 14 more from the 18th GvIAP and another 20 from the 523rd IAP had been scrambled from Tatungkao in response to the UNC raid. The 17th IAP and 18th GvIAP aircraft concentrated on the fighter-bombers in the north, while the 523rd IAP was vectored towards the B-29 raid. Descending in a mass formation through over 15,000ft of cloud, the MiG-15s burst out from the overcast and caught the B-29s just after they had dropped their weapons. Leading his regiment into the attack, Pplk A. P. Smorchkov emptied his cannons into one B-29 and shot it down.

The airfield at Namsi was attacked on 23 October, a day that became known as 'Black Tuesday'. Once again, the 19th BG was tasked for the mission and that morning, nine B-29s, in three flights of three, set out from Okinawa, bound for the target. After they crossed the frontlines, they linked up with their fighter escort of 24 F-84s. A fighter screen of 31 F-86s also patrolled a line between Sonchon and Kusong (Guseong), to keep MiG-15s away from the bombers. Despite the daylight and favourable weather conditions, the attack on Namsi had been planned using SHORAN, but this system led the bombers directly overhead the airfield of Taechon and its formidable anti-aircraft batteries. Some aircraft were damaged by anti-aircraft fire as they overflew, and after leaving the gun engagement zone they became vulnerable to MiG attack. Soviet radars had detected the raid the three regiments of the 303rd IAD were launched to intercept. Three regimental formations, consisting of 20 MiG-15s from the 17th IAP, 20 from the 18th GvIAP and 18 from the 523rd IAP, headed towards Namsi, with up to four miles between each formation. The two regiments of the 324th IAD launched with another 26 MiG-15s shortly afterwards as a second wave. Splitting the force to keep the F-86s tied up, the MiG-15s swept down through the F-84 escort and wreaked havoc amongst the B-29s. Three bombers were shot down and three more

By the end of 1951, most B-29 Superfortress-equipped units had been forced to operate at night. Here an aircraft from the 98th BG has been painted in a night camouflage scheme. (NARA)

were so badly damaged that they had to divert to Kimpo (K-14) to make emergency landings. The remaining three aircraft recovered to Okinawa, but two of them were also seriously damaged. One F-84 had been shot down, one MiG-15 was shot down north of the Yalu River as it recovered to base, and three more MiG-15s were damaged.

In the following days, there were three more daylight B-29 raids. On 24 October eight B-29s from the 98th BG escorted by 16 Meteors and ten F-84s bombed the highway bridge at Sunchon. Once again, the three regiments of the 303rd IAD launched en masse and 55 MiG-15s headed towards the bombers. The Soviet pilots repeated the tactics of the previous day, with the 20 MiG-15s of the 523rd IAP tasked with tying up the F-86 screen while the other MiGs attacked the B-29s. The MiGs only just caught up with the bombers before they crossed the coast near Wonsan and since the Soviet pilots were prohibited from flying over the sea, they only managed

Munsan in 1951: The Sikorsky H-19 Chickasaw was arguably the first production helicopter which could carry a useful load over a reasonable distance. In US Navy service it was designated the HOS4. (Joe Scherschel/The TIME LIFE Picture Collection via Getty Images)

one attacking pass. Nevertheless Pplk A. P. Smorchkov of the 18th GvIAP shot down one B-29, his third B-29 victory in three days, although in doing so he was wounded by the defensive fire from the bomber. Two other B-29s were also damaged. In the fight between the MiG-15s and F-86s, Col H. R. Thyng of the 4th FIG scored his first victory of the conflict by shooting down St Lt G. K. Dyachenko. The Soviet pilot successfully ejected from his aircraft, as did two F-86 pilots, Lt B. B. Irish of the 334th FIS and Lt F. T. Wickes of the 336th FIS, after they were both shot down by St Lt D. A. Samoylov. Three days later, another eight B-29s, accompanied once more by 16 Meteors and 32 F-84s, raided the railway bridge at Sinanju. This time one B-29 was damaged and had to carry out an emergency landing at Seoul (K-16) and two others were less seriously damaged. A raid against Songchon the next day was unchallenged, but the decision had already been taken to limit the B-29 to night operations in future.

During late October, US intelligence sources in North Korea, known as 'Unit Y', indicated that on 30 October, senior Chinese and North Korean military staff would be holding a conference at Kapsan, a small village in the mountainous area of northeast Korea. That morning eight Corsairs and eight Skyraiders launched from the USS *Essex* and flew to Kapsan at low-level to avoid detection. Just after 09:00hrs local time, they carried out an intensive attack on the compound, leaving it a smoking ruin. It was later reported by 'Unit Y' agents that over 500 senior personnel had been killed in the compound and that the records of the North Korean Communist Party had been destroyed.

In mid-October, there was a changeover in the CPLAAF units at Antung: the 4th HS withdrew to Shenyang for a rest from combat operations and their place was taken by the 3rd HS, comprising the 7th FT, 8th FT and 9th FT. Between 12 September and 19 October, the 4th HS had had ten engagements with UN fighters and had lost 14 MiG-15s. Learning from the experience of their predecessors, the 3rd HS adopted the tactic of avoiding combat with F-86s and concentrating on small formations of UNC fighter-bombers.

More MiG-15s became available to the CPLAAF with the deployment of the 14th HS, reinforced by the 6th FT, to the new airfield at Takushan, almost 30 miles west of Antung. In addition, the newly trained KPAAF 60th JHY deployed to Uiju

A US Navy AD Skyraider diving to attack a railway bridge in North Korea, in October 1951. Spans of the main bridge have already been dropped but note the bypass bridge that has been constructed to the left of the main bridge and the craters left by previous attacks. (NARA)

An F-84G Thunderjet of the 8FBS/ 49FBW in Korea during 1952. (USAFM)

airfield in early November. At the same time, the KPAAF command was merged into the CPLAAF command responsible for operations over Korea to form the Unified Air Army (UAA).

The first week of November was a time of many combats in MiG Alley, both between the MiG-15 and F-86 and between the MiG-15 and F-80 and F-84 fighter-bombers. Despite numerous claims by both sides, honours remained evenly matched at only two or three losses, plus two Meteors that were severely damaged by MiG-15s of the 523rd IAP on 3 November. Two days later, four MiG-15s from the CPLAAF 9th FT bounced a formation of F-84s near Sinanju. The number four pilot, Luō Cānghǎi, claimed the destruction of three F-84s in one pass, and the loss of one F-84E from the 136th FBG was confirmed on that day. That same day saw the commencement of night raids by B-29 bombers against the airfields at Saamchaan, Taechon, Namsi and Uiju. These were carried out by bombers operating singly, each following a SHORAN arc to their designated target. Darkness offered protection against fighters because the MiG-15 units only flew by day and the Lavochkin La-11 flown by the 351st IAP night-fighter regiment lacked the performance to catch the B-29. Raids continued through the winter months.

Some of the islands in the Pansong archipelago, some 50 miles off the Chongchon estuary, had proved a thorn in the side of the CPLAAF over the summer because of UNC intelligence troops based there. These included personnel serving a radar site which had been established on Taehwa Island to assist UNC fighter aircraft operating in MiG Alley. The CPVA started an operation to retake the island chain on 6 November and the CPLAAF was tasked to provide air support for the operation. On that morning, nine Tupolov Tu-2 bombers from the 22nd FT escorted by 16 La-11s from the 4th FT bombed UN positions on Taehwa. Echoing UNC tactics, a screen

Groundcrew prepare the La-11 night fighter allocated to Major Dushin of the 351st IAP (credited with one victory in China and 2 victories in Korea) for a night combat sortie. The cowling is painted red, the upper surfaces light grey and the lower surfaces are black. (Krylov & Tepsurkaev)

of 24 MiG-15s from the 7th FT patrolled a line between Sunchon and Sinmi Island. The air operation was successful, but despite the efforts of the CPVA, UN positions remained on the island. Taehwa was revisited a week by KPAAF Yak-9Ps, which strafed the UN installations, and Po-2s also attacked at night.

Clashes between Soviet and UNC jets continued through November, causing small but steady attrition on both sides. Large air battles took place on 18 November in which both Soviet and Chinese MiG-15s were involved and during which both sides claimed kills. In the early afternoon, Wáng Hǎi led 16 MiG-15s of the 9th FT to intercept UNC fighter-bombers and they located a flight of F-84s bombing a bridge over the Chongchon River near Sunchon. The Chinese claimed to have shot down five F-84s, including two by Wáng Hǎi. UNC losses on that day amounted to one F-80 and one F-84, while the 64th IAK lost two MiG-15s.

Seven days later, the Chinese flight leader Liu Yüti claimed to have destroyed four F-84s in a single engagement, although no UNC aircraft losses are recorded on that date. The seemingly inflated claims by Chinese pilots are quite understandable given their extreme inexperience in comparison to Soviet and UNC pilots, especially given the over-claiming even by those combat-experienced pilots. In fact, the greatest destruction of aircraft on that day was of KPAAF MiG-15s on the ground at Uiju.

They had been spotted by F-86 pilots Capt K. D. Chandler and Lt D. W. Ragland, who swept down and strafed the aircraft, destroying four and damaging four more.

On 30 November the CPLAAF was tasked to attack the UNC intelligence facilities on Taehwa Island once more, while CPVA troops landed on nearby Sinmi Island. This time the mission was carried out by Tu-2s of the 24th FT escorted by La-11s of the 4th FT. After the success of three weeks earlier, the Chinese 24th FT led by Gāo Yuèmíng decided to repeat the effective tactics of its sister regiment. Unfortunately, UNC air command had received prior intelligence about the mission and the Chinese formation was met by 31 F-86s of the 4th FIG led by Col B. S. Preston. Four Tu-2s,

Two F-86 Sabres from the 4th FIG take-off for a patrol in MiG Alley. (USAFM)

including one flown by the formation leader Bì Wǔbīn, were destroyed and another two were seriously damaged. Credit for three of the kills was claimed by Maj G. A. Davis. Three La-11s and a MiG-15 were also shot down. However, the La-11s fought fiercely and although no UNC fighters were actually lost during the engagement, Wàng Tiānbǎo inflicted serious damage on an F-86 flown by Maj W. W. Marshall.

The following day, it was the turn of the Soviet MiG-15 pilots to hand out a crushing defeat to 77 Sqn RAAF. That morning, 14 Meteors carried out a fighter sweep at 19,000ft in the Sunchon area, when they were bounced by 20 MiG-15s from the 176th GvIAP. Attacking in pairs, the MiGs shot down three Meteors and seriously damaged another. Gun camera film from Fg Off B. Gogerly indicated hits on one MiG-15 and he was awarded a confirmed kill, but all the Soviet aircraft had successfully recovered to Antung. The action on this day demonstrated the shortcomings of the Meteor in air combat and 77 Sqn subsequently switched to ground-attack operations, a role for which the Meteor was much better suited.

The F-86 force in Korea was considerably strengthened with the conversion of 51st FIG to the aircraft. After passing its F-80s to the 8th FBG, the 51st FIG moved to Suwon (K-13) and flew its first operational F-86 sortie on 1 December. The increased number of F-86s available to fly into MiG Alley made it more difficult for Soviet and UAA MiG-15s to break through the fighter screen to attack fighter-bombers. Nevertheless, combats continued over North Korea throughout the month. The 5th AF night-bombing campaign against the North Korean airfields proved to be successful. Saamchan, Taechon and Namsi were kept out of operation, while the damage to Uiju caused the KPAAF to withdraw the depleted 60th JHY across the Yalu River to Antung on 15 December. The PLAAF, too, had experienced a setback two days previously, when MiG-15s of the inexperienced 14th HS had been caught by F-86s from the 4th FIG, which shot down seven MiGs for no loss to themselves.

In December the 60th JHY had lost three MiGs-15s in combat, while in the same period the 303rd IAP and 324th IAP had between them lost six aircraft and the 3rd HS and 14th HS had both lost some 12; four Tu-2s and three La-11s had also been destroyed, making approximately 28 Soviet and UAA aircraft shot down during the month. On the UNC side, four F-86s, three Meteors, one F-84 and one F-80 had been shot down, making a total of nine, although at least some of another ten losses attributed to ground fire may also have been air combat losses. Thus, the comparative kill ratios between the sides in the month was approximately 2.5:1 in favour of the UNC. However, discounting the inexperienced Chinese and Korean pilots, Soviet-UNC kill ratio favoured the Soviet pilots.

The close of 1951 marked the halfway point in the Korean War. In 18 months, the ground war had transformed from a series of campaigns of rapid movement to a static war with entrenched frontlines. For the first year of the conflict, UN aircraft had enjoyed complete freedom of operation in the skies over the whole of Korea, but this air superiority had been challenged by Soviet pilots who at one stage took back command of the airspace of MiG Alley. However, the perennial challenge to fighter-bombers and light bombers was anti-aircraft fire. KPA and CPVA rear echelons were well protected by guns and cleverly sited 'flak traps' took their toll of the unwary. Although the Chinese and North Koreans had amalgamated their air assets in the UAA, the command and control of these forces and of the Soviet 64th IAK remained disjointed, whereas the command of UN air forces under the FEAF and TF77 was virtually seamless after lessons had been learned in the early days of the war. All the belligerents were very keen to contain the war: UNC aircraft were prohibited from crossing the Yalu River and Soviet pilots were not allowed to cross the coast or venture south of the Pyongyang-Wonsan line. Although these restrictions were sometimes ignored, they did serve to limit the scope of the war.

Four F-86 Sabres fly in a classic 'finger four' formation over South Korea. (Michael Rougier/ The TIME LIFE Picture Collection via Getty Images)

CHAPTER 6

A STATIC WAR

1 JANUARY–31 DECEMBER 1952

As 1952 began, the war over Korea rolled on against a background of continuing armistice negotiations. On the ground, the frontlines had stabilized not far from where they had been when the war started some 18 months previously. In the air, UNC aircraft enjoyed air supremacy south of a line between Pyongyang and Wonsan, but north of that the skies were patrolled by 12 MiG-15 regiments, or approximately 350 fighter aircraft, flown by Soviet, Chinese or North Korean pilots. Control of this airspace was contested by five UNC F-86 squadrons, numbering around 100 aircraft. A large force of UNC fighter-bombers and bomber aircraft, both land- and carrier-based, carried out interdiction and CAS sorties all over North Korea.

MIG-15 VERSUS F-86

The first months of 1952 were a period of change for many of the fighter pilots operating over Korea. The wholesale rotation of both Soviet and Chinese units took place, while the UNC units also had an intake of newcomers to replace tour-expired pilots. The Soviet 303rd IAD was replaced at Antung in late January by the 97th IAD (16th IAP and 148th GvIAP) and the following month the 324th IAD was relieved at Tatungkao by the 190th IAD (256th IAP, 494th IAP and 821st IAP). The Chinese 4th HS (10th FT and 12th FT) moved to Antung in January, taking the place of the 3rd HS, while the 15th HS (43rd FT and 45th FT) replaced the 14th HS at Takushan in the same month. The North Korean 60th JHY remained at Antung. New pilots arriving at the USAF 4th FIG, based at Kimpo (K-14) included Flt Lt R. E. Lelong, an RAF World War II night-fighter ace, who was detached from his exchange posting with the air gunnery school at Nellis AFB, Nevada. However, many replacement pilots were far less qualified, some of them having only previously flown transport aircraft. Thus, there was a dilution of experience on both sides of the Yalu River, although it was more marked on the 64th IAK-UAA side.

The MiG-15 and the F-86 were well-matched adversaries, with similar performance. At high level, the MiG-15bis had the edge over the F-86E: it had a higher ceiling and a better rate of turn than the F-86, which it could also out-climb. MiG-15 formations

A flight of four North American F-86 Sabres of the 51st FIG, which was based at Suwon. (Michael Rougier/The TIME LIFE Picture Collection via Getty Images)

would often fly as high as 50,000ft, some 5,000ft higher than the F-86 could manage, so the MiGs frequently had the advantage of altitude and could also break off an attack by climbing steeply back up beyond the reach of the F-86. Below 30,000ft, the F-86 was the more manoeuvrable aeroplane, although the MiG retained its superior rate of climb. Thus, while the MiG could disengage by climbing, the preferred defensive manoeuvre by the F-86 would be a tight descending turn. A sustained turn of around six G was usually enough to escape from a MiG-15, not least because one advantage of the F-86 over the MiG-15 was that it provided anti-G protection for the pilot, whereas the MiG did not. Soviet, Chinese and Korean pilots found the effects of high G manoeuvring to be extremely fatiguing, so the lack of protection also affected the long-term alertness of MiG-15 pilots.

The difference in tactics employed by each side reflected their different roles and experience levels. The role of the MiG-15 was to prevent UNC ground-attack and bomber aircraft from attacking their targets, either by destroying them or making them jettison their weapons. With a massive number of aircraft available but many inexperienced pilots, Soviet and UAA MiG-15s flew in large numbers so that overwhelming force could be applied against their targets. MiG-15s would expect to fight any and all aircraft types operated by the UNC, from the F-86 to the F-51 to the B-29. MiG-15s were usually seen in large regimental-sized formations, called 'trains' by UNC pilots. These would be made up of flights of four to six aircraft stepped at different altitudes, with each formation covering the one beneath it. Soviet pilots, who included a number of World War II veterans, tended to be confident and aggressive, but they were constrained to remain north of the Pyongyang-Wonsan line, though they rarely flew south of the Chongchon River and they were prohibited from flying over the sea. Soviet MiG-15 regiments tended to be launched specifically to intercept incoming raids and they were vectored to their targets by GCI radar control. In contrast to the Soviets, the Chinese and Korean pilots were semi-trained and many of them had fewer than 50 hours of jet flying. In general, they did not understand enough Russian to be able to use the Soviet GCI radar service, so they tended to fly standing patrols and rely on visual sightings to locate their adversaries. The MiG-15 operators were aware that UNC aircraft were prohibited from crossing the Yalu, so they would climb to their operating altitude in the sanctuary area to the north of the river before setting off into MiG Alley. Chinese and Korean 'trains' would often fly from the Suiho (Supung) Reservoir on the Yalu River to Pyongyang and then turn northwards back towards Antung. Many F-86 pilots often commented that some MiG pilots seemed reluctant to engage in combat and this was probably the case for two reasons. Firstly, by flying high above UNC aircraft, the pilots might often simply not see other aircraft, and secondly, being aware of their own inexperience, the Chinese pilots in particular might not wish to engage unless they had a clear advantage. UNC pilots had noticed the cyclical pattern in the aggression and ability displayed by the MiG-15 pilots, which corresponded to the changeover of MiG-15 units in-theatre.

The role of the F-86 in Korea was to establish a fighter screen between the MiGs and the large number of UNC fighter-bombers flying daily low-level interdiction

LEFT:
Ground crews at Antung
readying MiG-15bis night
fighter No. 53210546
of the 351st IAP for
a sortie. Note the
camouflage finish on
the upper surfaces.
(Krylov & Tepsurkaev)

BELOW:
St Lt Yakhya Zaliusizovich
Iskhangaliev (one victory
in Korea) of the 351st
IAP getting into the
cockpit of the MiG-15bis
No. 2915376.
(Krylov & Tepsurkaev)

A poor quality but nevertheless rare image of a line-up of CPLAAF MiG-15s. CPLAAF units operating over Korea carried North Korean markings. (Cooper/ Grandolini)

missions against the MSRs running from Antung and Manpojin southwards through Sinanju to Pyongyang. By early 1952, the F-86s regularly launched in group strength, operating in flights of four. Take-off times would be staggered three minutes apart between flights, so launching a maximum effort sweep from Kimpo, using three squadrons of 16 aircraft, would take around 33 minutes. This ensured that MiG Alley was well saturated by F-86s patrolling at varying altitudes and also that there were fresh F-86 flights available to intercept the MiGs which had been scrambled against earlier flights. In the operating area, some flights would be at 42,000ft to 45,000ft while others would fly below the contrails. While staying beneath the contrails surrendered some altitude advantage, it meant that pilots knew that any aircraft leaving trails were hostile; it also meant that MiGs diving down from above the contrail level would become easily visible as they made their attack. Once it was apparent that combat would be joined, the F-86s would jettison their wing tanks and accelerate to fighting speed around 0.95 Mach. The F-86 flights would remain on patrol until the first aircraft in the element reached their 'bingo' or minimum fuel. This was enough to return from the Yalu River to Kimpo or Seoul, but it was not unusual for pilots to run short of fuel and there was usually one flame-out landing at Kimpo each week.

The first serious clashes of the year took place on 6 January. A number of engagements took place throughout the day, after which F-86 pilots claimed to have shot down five MiG-15s and Soviet MiG-15 pilots claimed to have shot down nine F-86s. The Chinese pilot Fan Wanzhang of the 7th FT also claimed to have shot down an F-86 that attempted to bounce his formation leader. In fact, on that day the UNC recorded the loss of just one F-86 and no Soviet MiG-15s were lost in combat. However, St Lt V. G. Stepanov, who had six kills to his name, was killed in a landing accident at Tantungkao, when his aircraft overran the runway, possibly as a result of battle damage. During the month, two more Soviet aces were shot down in combat, Kpt L. K. Shchukin (15 victories in Korea) on 7 January and Kpt S. M. Kramarenko (13 victories in Korea) four days later. Both pilots ejected from their aircraft but were injured and took no further part in the conflict. The 5th AF also lost its highest scoring ace pilot on 10 February when Maj G. A. Davis, commanding the 334th FIS (of the 4th FIG), with 14 victories in Korea, was shot down in combat. There is still controversy over who killed Davis: the Chinese maintain that it was the Chinese pilot Zhāng Jīhuì from the 12th FT, while the Soviets assert that St Lt M. Averin of the 148th GvIAP did so. The Chinese were not without their high-profile losses, too: Meng Jin, commander of the 7th FT, failed to return from a combat with F-86s over Taechon on 11 January.

Two F-86 Sabres of the 335th FIS/ 4th FIG on strip alert at Kimpo (K-14) in April 1952. The aircraft on the left is an F-86A while that on the right is an F-86E, which was shot down by a MiG-15 on 4 July 1951; Capt Clifford C. Jolley ejected successfully. Note the yellow recognition bands which replaced the previous black and white stripes. (USAFM)

A MiG-15 framed at close range in the gun camera of an F-86. (USAFM)

GROUND-ATTACK OPERATIONS

While air defence and air-to-air combat were the priorities for Soviet and UAA aircraft, the primary role of UNC air power in Korea was support of the ground forces by the interdiction of enemy MSRs and close support of friendly troops. In January 1952, most of the UNC ground-attack units, with the exception of the B-29 medium bombers and carrier-borne aircraft, were based in South Korea. Closest to the frontlines were the F-80s of the 8th FBG based at Suwon (K-13) in the west and the Corsairs and Tigercats of MAG-12 at Kangnung (Gangneung – K-18) in the east. MAG-33, comprising the Skyraiders of VMA-121 and the Panthers of VMF-311, was based farther south at Pohang (K-3). The F-51s of the 18th FBG and 2 Sqn SAAF were also based in the far south at Chinhae (K-10), although they made daily use of Hoengsong (K-46) for refuelling and re-arming between sorties. Hoensong was also the home of the F-51s of 10th *Jeontu Bihaengdan* (JB Fighter Group) of the ROKAF, commanded by *Daelyeong* (Colonel) Kim Yong Hwan. Taegu (K-2) was home to the F-84s of the 49th FBG and 136th FBG and it was also used as a forward operating base by the F-84s of the 116th FBG, whose home base was at Misawa. The B-26s of the 3rd BG flew from Kunsan (K-8). Still based at Kimpo (K-14), the Meteors of 77 Sqn RAAF switched from the air-defence role to ground-attack operations at the start of the new year.

After snow at Kimpo caused a 24-hour delay, Wg Cdr R. T. Susans, the new commanding officer, led 77 Sqn RAAF on its first Meteor ground-attack sortie on 8 January. The four Meteors were armed with full loads of 20mm ammunition and eight 60lb rockets for an attack on the water tower at Chongdan (ten miles northwest of Yonan). The aircraft flown by Flt Lt J. T. Hannan was hit by ground fire in the ventral fuel tank, which proved to be the Achilles heel of the Meteor in the ground-attack role: although Hannan recovered safely to Kimpo, there would be many instances in the future when the tank would explode on being hit, causing the loss of the aircraft. The Meteor proved to be an excellent rocket platform, but less suitable for strafing using the cannons. The high control forces made it difficult to adjust tracking in the much shorter ranges involved in using a gun rather than a rocket. One tactical innovation designed by 77 Sqn was the napalm rocket, made by filling the warhead of a 60lb rocket with napalm; where US aircraft had to overfly targets at very low-level to drop napalm bombs, the Australians had a stand-off capability with the new weapon.

In the first few days of the year, the 77 Sqn aircraft were also used for 'strip alert', at readiness on the ground to launch in the fighter role in case of intruders. However, Wg Cdr Susans persuaded HQ 5th AF that it would be far more effective to use the aircraft in a standing patrol and, subsequently, during daylight hours the Meteors operated a continuous combat air patrol between Haeju and Singye at 20,000ft; each pair would remain on task for an hour before being relieved by the next pair.

Off the west coast of Korea, HMS *Glory* and the USS *Bairoko* (CVE-115) took over from HMAS *Sydney* and USS *Badoeng Strait* in TE95 at the end of January, while on the east coast the TF77 strike force was made up of the carriers USS *Essex*, USS *Antietam* and USS *Philippine Sea*. The former two would be relieved by USS *Boxer* and USS *Valley Forge* at the end of February. The carrier aircraft were tasked with interdiction sorties against the railway systems and CAS sorties for ground forces.

Winter conditions once again, this time on USS *Essex* (CV-9) on 18 January 1952. F4U-5N Corsairs, F2H-2 Banshees, F9F Panthers and AD Skyraiders of the carrier air group are on deck. (US Navy)

On 12 January, aircraft from USS *Essex*, taking advantage of good moonlight shining on the snow-covered landscape, flew a pre-dawn armed reconnaissance sortie. Under these conditions the black railway tracks stood out well against the snow and the steam plumes from locomotives made them easily visible. During the sortie, the aircraft found two trains and destroyed both locomotives as well as 36 railcars. While snow cover could make target acquisition easier, the frozen ground was so hard that sometimes bombs bounced off it and then exploded underneath the aircraft. One solution used by B-26 crews was the para-munition, a 500lb bomb suspended below a parachute. The weapon could be dropped from around 100ft above the target, ensuring its accuracy, while its nearly vertical descent ensured that it did not bounce. The corollary was that the aircraft had to overfly the target at low-level and was thus exposed to anti-aircraft fire; and it was anti-aircraft fire, not the MiG-15, that remained the main threat to ground-attack aircraft.

For example, USN and USMC units lost 25 aircraft to anti-aircraft fire and none to air combat during the month of January 1952. Partly, of course, this was because the MiG-15s very rarely operated over the eastern part of the country, but even in the west, the anti-aircraft gun proved to be the most effective weapon against UNC fighter-bombers: 2 Sqn SAAF lost six F-51s in January, all to ground fire. Another victim claimed by anti-aircraft fire on 2 January was Flt Lt D. Hinton RAF who had deployed to Korea while serving on an exchange posting with the 20th FBG at

An F4U-5N Corsair night fighter of VC-3 ready for a catapult launch from USS *Essex* (CV-9), during operations off Korea, January 1952. The fairing on the port wing houses the APS-6. In the background, the HO3S-1 helicopter stands by in case of an emergency during launch and take-off. (US Navy)

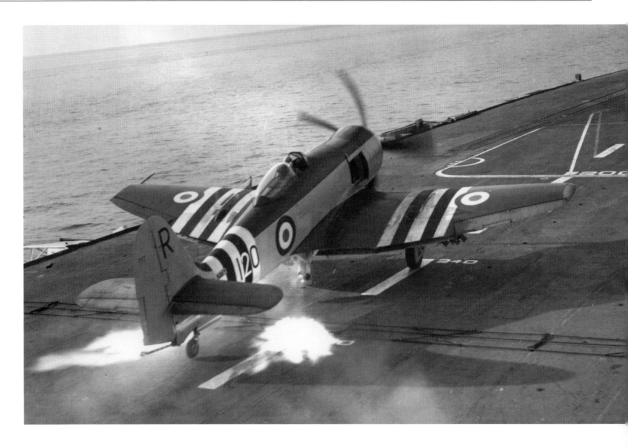

A Sea Fury FB11 of No.804 NAS carrying out a RATOG take-off from HMS *Glory* (R-62). The tails of the rocket armament under the wings are also just visible. HMS *Glory* carried out three deployments to Korea, in 1951, 1952 and 1953. (Jarrett)

Shaw AFB. Flying an F-84E with the 49th FBG, Hinton was bombing the railway track just north of Sunan when he was shot down and killed. The concentration of anti-aircraft artillery south of the Chongchon River had become so intense that in January 1952, 5th AF switched to attacking interdiction targets north of the river, since there were fewer guns there and the threat from the MiG-15 was deemed to have reduced. The F-84 groups were given targets on the rail line between Sinanju and Sonchon, while the F-80s were tasked against the stretch between Kaechon to Huichon.

It was a matter of principle in the US air services that every effort would be made to rescue downed airmen, no matter the cost. The helicopter came to play the most important part in this role. Off the east coast, each of the carriers of TF77 had its own helicopters aboard and the cruiser USS *Rochester* also acted as a helicopter support ship. These aircraft covered all naval operations along the eastern littoral. In the west and centre of the country, the responsibility for search and rescue fell to Detachment 1 of the 3rd Air Rescue Squadron (ARS) based at Seoul (K-16), which flew a number of different aircraft types. By the spring of 1952, the unit had eight Sikorsky H-19 Chickasaw helicopters and a similar number of the earlier H-2 Dragonfly. Although the primary role of these aircraft was the rescue of downed aircrew, 66 percent of the tasking involved casualty evacuation (Casevac) missions from the frontlines to the Mobile Army Surgical Hospitals (MASH), a job shared with US Army Bell H-13

Sioux helicopters. From mid-1951, Detachment 1 had kept two helicopters based on Paengnyongdo Island (Baengnyeongdo), also known as 'P-Y Island', off the western tip of the Ongjin Peninsula. Each day one helicopter was deployed to Chodo Island in order to be far enough forward to reach into North Korea. From February 1952, both helicopters were permanently based at Chodo, where the beach on the island was also usable as an emergency landing strip for damaged fighter-bombers. Apart from the helicopters, L-5 light aircraft were frequently used for rescue missions and the 3rd ARS also operated three Grumman SA-16 Albatross amphibians from Seoul. These aircraft were well suited to water pick-ups. During all fighter-bomber operations, a Rescue Combat Air Patrol (ResCAP) of F-51s was positioned close to the frontlines, so that it could locate the downed airman and clear the way for a rescue aircraft. A flight of F-86s was also held at strip alert to act as top cover for the ResCAP.

Despite the best efforts of the bomber and fighter-bomber crews, the UNC interdiction campaign was not delivering the anticipated results. Aircraft were effective in cutting rail tracks, dropping bridge spans and closing off tunnels, but the Chinese and North Koreans proved to be ingenious and resourceful in effecting repairs. The rail routes could be repaired almost as quickly as they could be cut and Operation *Strangle* did not appreciably affect the fighting capabilities of the CPVA or KPA.

One attempt to produce better results was the campaign by B-26 and B-29 against the 'Wadong chokepoint'. Near the village of Wadong, ten miles northwest of Yangdok, the main highway from Wonsan to Pyongyang crossed the lateral railway line in a deep gorge. Target planners at the FEAF believed this to be the ideal point to cut off both road and rail communications. In a sustained effort in the 44 days between 26 January and 11 March, the FEAF medium and light bombers dropped nearly 4,000 500lb bombs into the gorge, but at best the railroad was unusable for seven days and the highway for just four days. The bombs had done little but churn up the surrounding countryside. Realising that a different approach was needed, The FEAF unveiled a new interdiction campaign code-named Operation *Saturate* on 3 March. The new strategy was for round-the-clock strikes against small sections of rail track using 500lb or heavier bombs. The whole campaign was tightly controlled with US 5th Air Force operations staff choosing exact targets and defining the attack direction as well as the routes to and from the target, including altitudes to be flown. Each day around 600 fighter-bomber daylight sorties would be tasked and these would be followed up by B-26 strikes at night. The B-29 force was to be directed primarily against bridges.

On 11 March a special task was ordered against a CPVA/KPA supply depot at Mulgae-ri, five miles northwest of Pyongsan. During the day, the 8th FBG mounted 254 sorties against supply stores that had been dispersed and camouflaged in the area. Each of the F-80s flew five missions during the day to achieve the task. There were similar logistical targets across the CPVA/KPA rear areas, but the new interdiction campaign against the rail infrastructure took priority over the next months. Operation *Saturate* opened with a night attack by B-26s of the 3rd BG on 15 March and in the first weeks the results seemed inconclusive. However, 460 fighter-bomber attacks over the two days of 25 and 26 March were enough to close a section of the Chongju-Sinanju line

In the centre of this photograph, the Meteor F8 flown by Wg Cdr R.H. Susans, commanding 77 Sqn RAAF, can be seen firing rockets at a CPLA/ KPA barracks on 8 February 1952. (State Library of Victoria)

for five days. In the same timescale, B-29s took down bridges at Pyongyang, Sinanju and Sinhung. The effort continued through April and was very effective in closing off the rail line between Sinuiju and Sinanju, but despite this success, the 5th AF lacked the strength to keep up the pressure. The railway attacks of Operation *Strangle* had cost 243 fighter-bombers destroyed and another 290 aircraft damaged, but replacement aircraft only numbered 131 and by the end of April the fighter-bomber groups were running short of aircraft.

THE MIG ALLEY CONFLICT CONTINUES

Daily battles continued in MiG Alley. The Chinese MiG-15 force had been bolstered by the arrival in March of the 12th HS (34th FT and 36th FT) at Takushan and the 17th HS (49th FT and 51st FT) at Tatungkao, making four Chinese air divisions based within the 'Antung Complex'. On the UNC side, a search radar had been established on Chodo Island midway through January and although the radar post had no

height-finding capability, it could give some warning of MiG activity. In the first months of the year the inexperience of the new Soviet and Chinese units in theatre was noticeable: they tended to remain in large formations and to avoid engagement if they could. By January the pilots of the 303rd IAD and 324th IAD had been exhausted both physically and psychologically by weeks of high-altitude high-G combat, but the effectiveness of the 64th IAK was hardly improved by replacing combat-hardened veterans by the very inexperienced pilots of the 97th IAD and 190th IAD. These units were from the PVO-Strany air-defence service, rather than the Soviet air force and they were trained to be interceptor pilots rather than air combat pilots. Nor were the Soviets helped by Chinese anti-aircraft gunners who, for example, shot down St Lt A. P. Fedoseev on 24 March, as a formation of MiG-15s from the 148th GvIAP manoeuvred near the coast. Two more Soviet MiG-15s were also lost that day, and so was one F-86. UAA MiG-15s were active during the month and on 20 March five UAA MiG-15s bounced six F-51s from 2 Sqn SAAF as they pulled off from an attack on the rail track to the north of Sonchon. The MiGs shot down one of the South African F-51s.

The 3rd Air Rescue Group operated an interesting mixture of aircraft for combat rescue, including the Grumman SA-16 Albatross amphibian and Sikorsky H-5G helicopter shown here. (USAFM)

In March, UNC F-86 pilots claimed to have destroyed 39 MiG-15s, although the actual losses of Soviet aircraft stood at only 16; in turn the Soviets claimed to have shot down 43 F-86s and four F-84s, against actual figures of six F-86s, two F-84s and an F-80. Unfortunately, the loss figures for UAA MiG-15s in the period are not recorded, but are thought to be in the region of 20, which would tend to corroborate the USAF figures. One factor in the success of the F-86s was the relaxation of the ban on crossing the Yalu River. UNC pilots were now permitted to cross the river into Manchuria if they were in 'hot pursuit' of enemy aircraft, although the definition of 'hot pursuit' was open to interpretation: Soviet pilots reported frequent attacks by F-86s while making approaches to the airfields of the 'Antung Complex'.

A team of four pilots from the RAF Central Fighter Establishment (CFE), led by the well-respected World War II Hawker Typhoon pilot Wg Cdr J. R. Baldwin, arrived in Korea in February to gain jet combat experience. The pilots were split evenly between the 4th and 51st FIGs. Before they were cleared for operational flying, the RAF pilots underwent the short in-theatre training course, which was mandatory for all new pilots and was known colloquially as 'Clobber College'. During a week's flying, they were shown how to fight the F-86 at the extremes of its manoeuvre envelope so that they had the confidence to extract the best performance from the machine; they also practised flying in two-, six- and eight-aircraft tactical formations. The thorough tactical grounding provided by 'Clobber College' was undoubtedly another factor in the success of the F-86 groups in Korea. The RAF pilots were quickly integrated into the operational flying and Wg Cdr Baldwin, who was acting as the group operations officer, was awarded the US Distinguished Flying Cross (DFC) for his 'outstanding airmanship and tactical skill' while leading a flight on 6 March. Unfortunately, however, he did not return from a weather reconnaissance sortie in the Pyongyang-Chinnampo area nine days later, possibly the victim of spatial disorientation.

From March, the RCAF was also represented on the F-86 squadrons, as Canadian pilots were detached to them for 50-mission operational tours. The first RCAF pilot on this programme was Fg Off W. G. Nixon, who actually flew over 70 missions with the 51st FIG. In all, 17 more RCAF pilots would fly the F-86 over Korea between March 1952 and the end of hostilities.

During late March the Soviet units exchanged their battle-weary aircraft for factory-new MiG-15bis fighters. The change was noted by UNC pilots, since in contrast to the previous aircraft which were finished in a highly polished clear varnish, the new machines were painted in a dull silver-green to make them less visible. The red-painted noses which the Soviets had previously used as an aid to identification were also discontinued. The arrival of the new aircraft coincided with some changes in tactics as the Soviet regiments gained in experience and confidence. The regimental-sized formations were replaced by smaller, more flexible sections of four to six aircraft and some formations flew purposefully in the contrail level to advertise their presence and attract F-86s; meanwhile more MiG-15 sections would lurk either above or below the contrails to catch the F-86 flights as they prepared to engage the decoys.

Both sides hailed the battle of 1 April as being an important victory. On that day MiG-15s of the 494th IAP and 821st IAP tangled with F-86s from both the 4th FIG

A MiG-15 of the CPLAAF - note the nine stars under the cockpit indicating the kills credited to this aircraft. (Cooper/ Grandolini)

and 51st FIG during battles in the sky between Pakchon and Sonchon. During a day of combat, ten MiG-15 kills were claimed by UNC pilots, while Soviet pilots claimed nine F-86 kills, but only one F-86 and two MiG-15s were actually lost on that day. In addition, one more MiG-15 was seriously damaged by a pair of F-86s while it was in the landing pattern at Tatungkao.

There was a further re-shuffle of Chinese MiG-15 units in May 1952. The 6th HS replaced the 15th HS at Tatungkao, while the 4th HS left Antung in the same month. On 8 May four Meteors were covering a maximum effort strike by 485 fighter-bombers against a storage depot at Suan, south of Pyongyang, when they were bounced by two MiG-15s. The number three Meteor was hit by a 23mm cannon shell, but as the MiGs flew past, Plt Off W. H. Simmonds, flying number four, fired on the MiG. The aircraft was seen to pull up and enter a spin, at which point the pilot ejected. These MiG-15s reportedly had red-painted noses, which makes it likely that they were KPAAF aircraft, hand-me-downs from the Soviets. Three days later, a US Navy patrol aircraft was attacked by two MiG-15s off Takushan. Again, given the prohibition of Soviet over-sea flight and the reluctance of Chinese pilots to do so, it seems likely these aircraft were also from the KPAAF.

The Soviet 64th IAK was particularly successful on 17 May, when Pplk G. F. Dmitriuk led 20 MiG-15s of the 821st IAP below the F-86 screen to intercept a large formation of 24 F-84s from the 49th FBG. Achieving complete surprise, the MiGs bounced the F-84s near Sonchon and were able to make two firing passes as they ran through the formation. Three F-84s were shot down and another was so badly damaged that it crashed while attempting to make an emergency landing. After this episode, the F-86s began to post some flights at lower levels. Another

F-86 tactic was known as 'hawking' and involved placing a CAP over the mouth of the Yalu River, ready to dive down and attack any MiG-15s attempting to land or take off from airfields in the Antung Complex. Although this practice stretched the definition of the 'hot pursuit' rule, it proved to be very effective.

The UNC, the Soviet 64th IAK and the UAA all improved their night-fighter capability in the first half of 1952. The US 68th FIS had started its conversion from the F-82 to the Lockheed F-94B Starfire in December and the 319th FIS, which also operated the F-94, deployed from McChord AFB, Washington, to Suwon (K-13) on 22 March. The other UN night asset was VMF(N)-513, which was operating a depleted number of Tigercats from Kunsan (K-8) but awaiting the arrival later in the year of the Douglas F3D Skyknight. The CPLAAF converted the La-11 regiment from the 2nd HS to the night role and moved the unit to Antung. The KPAAF, too, recognized the need to establish a specialist night-fighting unit and the 56th JHY took on the role. The unit started to patrol the night skies from mid-May, attacking B-26s on 25 and 26 May. Yak-9Ps also stalked B-26s on 29 May and 2 June, but on each occasion, they were unable to achieve a firing solution. Then, on the night of 7 June, two aircraft from VMF(N)-513 were attacked by Yak-9Ps in two separate incidents. In the first, a Tigercat flown by Capt R. R. Scott and Tech Sgt H. Dudugjan was fired

Maj. Harry Bailey briefing B-29 Superfortress crews at Yokota Air Base near Tokyo for a bombing raid against Sinuiju, North Korea. (USAFM)

on as it pulled off an attack on a convoy near Haeju. Scott fired at the enemy fighter as it flew past but did not observe any hits. A little later, a Yak-9P fired on a Corsair flown by Lt J. W. Andre as he recovered from a bombing pass in a similar area. As the fighter flew past Andre, it was silhouetted against the sky; he fired two bursts at it, after which the Yak was seen to catch fire and crash into the hillside.

For their part, the Soviets recogniszd that while the La-11 could catch a B-26, it did not have enough performance to challenge the B-29 successfully. As a result, the 351st IAP had started flying the MiG-15 at the beginning of the year and from February it operated a mix of 12 MiG-15s and 18 La-11s. The Soviet night-fighting capability was further enhanced by the arrival in May of the 147th IAP, another dedicated night-fighter regiment. On the night of 10 June, 11 B-29s from the 19th BG were tasked to carry out a SHORAN bombing attack on the rail bridge at Kwaksan. The bombers set off in a loose stream a few minutes apart and as they started to follow the SHORAN arc towards the target, they were picked up in turn and illuminated by searchlights. Four MiG-15s were scrambled from Antung to intercept them, using GCI control co-ordinated with the searchlight batteries. The first bomber was engaged by Pplk M. I. Studilin, commander of the 147th IAP, who set its port engines on fire, while Kpt A. M. Karelin of the 351st engaged three of the following bombers, one of which exploded in mid-air. Between them, the two Soviet pilots destroyed two B-29s and damaged another so badly that it only just limped into Kimpo.

In daylight on 20 June, Maj Baek Gi-Rak led four KPAAF La-9s on a training flight from Antung. Unfortunately for the Korean pilots, the formation was seen by F-86s from the 4th FIG, which were carrying out a fighter sweep along the Yalu River. Col R. N. Baker led his flight into attack and two La-9s were swiftly shot down, but the other two aircraft proved to be difficult adversaries. In particular, Baek Gi-Rak manoeuvred expertly, defeating high speed passes by the F-86 pilots. However, he was finally killed by Capt F. C. Blesse of the 4th FIG, who out-manoeuvred him in an unexpected slow-speed attack.

AIR PRESSURE

After Operation *Saturate* ground to a standstill at the end of April, the pre-operation logistical target list was resurrected in light of the success of the Mulgai-ri raid on 11 March. During May, three large-scale fighter-bomber attacks were mounted against targets around Pyongyang. In the first one, on 15 May, 256 sorties destroyed a vehicle repair facility at Tang-dong, just north of Pyongyang. On 22 May, 472 sorties were tasked against an ammunition factory in an industrial complex at Kijang-ni, to the southwest of Pyongyang, and the next day 275 sorties were flown against a steel fabrication factory in the same area.

Meanwhile, after a year of negotiations, the armistice talks at Panmunjom were still deadlocked. In an attempt to break the impasse by exerting pressure on the North Korean industrial base, the UNC leadership decided to target the electrical

F-51D Mustangs of the 12th FBS/ 18th FBG (foreground) and 67th FBS (background) at Hoengsong (K-46) in 1952. (USAFM)

(NARA)

FÀN WÀNZHÀNG, CPLAAF
MiG-15, 7th Regiment, 6 January 1952

While the four US planes were circling and searching, he used the sun as a cover and dived to attack from a height of 10,000 metres. The US pilots never expected that a single machine would suddenly dare to engage a formation. He took the opportunity to shoot the last US plane. When the US aircraft almost filled the entire gunsight, he opened fire and a cannon shell hit the enemy aircraft which exploded with heavy black smoke. The other three US planes realised their poor predicament and slipped away like dogs. He levelled off and continued to catch up with the formation, scanning the skies as he went. Soon, he spotted four more American planes. He carried out a split-S and dived down from the height of 9,000 metres, firing his cannons at the enemy leader. The enemy aircraft immediately shuddered twice and started to smoke. He quickly closed in, as three tongues of fire licked the enemy and it finally fell away. The other three US planes were angered when their leader was shot down and took advantage of the three-to-one advantage. They flipped up and down around him, trying to push him down to gain a high advantage. He was very calm, and skillfully out-manoeuvred the enemy. Just as enemy plane was about to fire, he kicked the rudder bar and the aircraft immediately skidded up to the left... The gunfire from the three enemy planes came close to the aircraft. He reversed in a barrel roll and came down behind the US machine. He fired at the last US plane which exploded in a volley. The other two US planes saw their companions shot down and accelerated away, desperately fleeing to the sea.

power supplies in the country. During their years of occupation, the Japanese had built a robust and efficient hydro-electric power generation system that fed into a grid providing electricity to all of North Korea and much of southern Manchuria. The generation plants were integrated with the Suiho, Changjin, Fusen (Pujon) and Kyosen (Pungsan) Reservoir systems. The Suiho dam generating station on the Yalu River, some 40 miles upstream of Sinuiju, was the fourth largest in the world, with four generators powered by water taken directly from the dam wall. The other three reservoir systems, set in the mountainous east of the country, were differently arranged. In each case, water was led from the reservoir through tunnels to a powerhouse at the head of a valley. After powering this set of generators, the water was then directed downstream through penstocks to three more generating stations. Thus, each generator complex at Changjin, Fusen and Kyosen comprised four separate sub-stations.

A co-ordinated mass attack by navy and air force aircraft was planned for the morning of 23 June. It was hoped that the large numbers of aircraft would completely overwhelm the defences. Because of the proximity of Typhoon Dinah, the morning of 23 June was dull and cloudy, and the mission was delayed until 16:00hrs. By the afternoon, the weather had cleared sufficiently for the four carriers of TF77, USS *Boxer*, USS *Princeton*, USS *Philippine Sea* and USS *Bonne Homme Richard*, to launch their air wings. Meanwhile, a fighter screen of 84 F-86s from both the

Groundcrew from 2 Sqn SAAF re-arm a North American F-51D Mustang (NARA)

Loaded with 1,000lb bombs, this F-80C Shooting Star 35th FBS/ 8th FBG taxies over PSP matting in late 1952. This aircraft was shot down by ground fire on 17 January 1953; the pilot Lt Edward L. Stickels ejected safely. (USAFM)

4th and 51st FIGs was established on the Yalu, including some 20 aircraft in a 'hawking' CAP directly above Antung and Tatungkao. The first aircraft in the attack against Suiho were from USS *Boxer*: Panthers concentrated on suppressing the anti-aircraft defences, while Skyraiders bombed the generator house. Aircraft from USS *Princeton* and USS *Philippine Sea* followed and the whole strike was completed within a few minutes. The naval aircraft were followed by 45 F-80s from the 8th FBG and 79 F-84s from the 49th FBG and 136th FBG. Further east, simultaneous strikes were being carried out against the other three systems. Aircraft from USS *Boxer*, USS *Princeton* and USS *Bonne Homme Richard* struck the Fusen 1 and 2 and the Kyosen 1 and 2 stations, while F-51s from the 18th FBG bombed the Fusen 3 and 4 stations and 1st MAW aircraft attacked the Changjin 3 and 4 stations. Throughout the attack, the MiG-15s remained on the ground at Antung and Tatungkao: with low cloud preventing aircraft from more westerly airfields from neutralising the threat from the 'hawking' CAP overhead, the commanders believed that the risk to aircraft taking off from the two clear airfields was too high.

From the UNC perspective the operation was a complete success. At a stroke, the electrical supplies to North Korea and southern Manchuria had been cut by 90 percent, and despite the scale of the operation, there had been no aircraft losses. Follow-up attacks on Changjin, Fusen and Kyosen continued over the next four days to ensure that the generators remained off-line.

Another success came on 4 July, when UNC fighter-bombers attacked the North Korean military academy at Sakchu, seven miles southeast of the Suiho dam. Intelligence sources had indicated that some 2,000 North Korean officer cadets were undergoing training there and a force of 70 F-84s was tasked to destroy the establishment. As the raid developed, a regimental-sized formation of MiG-15s from the 494th IAP was vectored towards the fighter-bombers, but in their haste to attack, the MiG-15s failed to notice the high escort of F-86s and they paid dearly for their mistake. In the initial engagement, seven MiG-15s were shot down by the F-86s for the loss of one F-86; and when further MiG-15s from the 821st IAP arrived on the scene to support their comrades, another three MiG-15s were shot down. In a third engagement by the 256th IAP, Lt V. M. Mitin destroyed an F-86, but another MiG-15 was lost in the combat; however, the bombing at Sakchu that followed this tactical success was mostly inaccurate.

CAS missions also continued through the summer months with around 100 sorties launched each day in direct support of UNC ground forces. Following the established procedures, these missions were directed by Mosquitoes that by now were flying the upgraded AT-6 Texan, which could fire smoke rockets to indicate targets. The fighter-bombers were generally tasked against enemy bunkers and artillery positions.

To ease the crowding at Antung and Tatungkao, and no doubt mindful also of the vulnerability of aircraft operating from the airfields closest to the Yalu River, the Chinese opened a new airfield at Dabao, on the banks of the Aihe River, some ten miles northeast of Fengchen. The airfield was known as Dapu by the Soviets and Fengchen by the UNC. The first units to move there were the Soviet 256th IAP at the

This F-86E Sabre of the 51st FIG, seen at Suwon (K-13), was shot down on 1 May 1952. The pilot Col Albert W. Schinz, the deputy commander of the 51st FIG, ejected successfully and landed on Taehwa-Do Island, where he evaded capture for several weeks before being rescued. (USAFM)

A flight of F-86E Sabres of the 51st FIG on patrol in early 1952. (Jarrett)

Lt (JG) G.W. Stinnett, Jr. at the controls of an F9F-2 Panther of VF-24 from USS *Boxer* (CV-21), over Kojo Island, South Korea on 27 June 1952. (US Navy)

end of June and the Chinese 12th HS in early July. Another rotation of Chinese units in July brought the 18th HS to relieve the 6th HS at Takushan, and in a changeover of Soviet forces the 216th IAD arrived from the Azerbaijan SSR to replace the 97th IAD at the end of the month. The 518th IAP and 878th IAP went to Tatunkao, while the 676th IAP moved to Dabao. The 133rd IAD also arrived from Kaliningrad to reinforce the 64th IAK in July; the 415th IAP and 726th IAP moved to Antung and Dabao respectively during the month, before swapping over in August. The USAF also changed over fighter-bomber units in July: the 58th FBG replaced the 136th FBG at Taegu (K-2) and the 116th FBG was withdrawn. Its place was taken by the 474th FBG, another F-84 unit, which moved to Kunsan (K-8). Meanwhile, a second team from the RAF Central Fighter Establishment, led by Sqn Ldr J. R. H. Merrifield, had arrived to fly the F-86 with the 4th and 51st FIGs in late June.

The UNC fighter groups had begun to receive the F-86F during the summer. The new variant was fitted with a more powerful engine, giving it the ability to match the ceiling of the MiG-15bis. From late summer the new aircraft were also fitted with the '6-3' wing. The chord of the wing had been extended along the leading edge by six inches at the root, reducing to three inches at the wingtip. This configuration gave the aircraft much better handling qualities during high-Mach, high-altitude manoeuvring, though the removal of the leading-edge slats meant that improvements at high speed were bought at a cost to low-speed handling.

Another new aircraft to join the UNC order of battle during the summer of 1952 was the Douglas F3D Skyknight jet-powered night fighter. These aircraft were destined for VMF(N)-513 and arrived at Kunsan (K-8) at the end of June. Among the crews who deployed with the aircraft were two RAF officers, Sqn Ldr J. R. Gard'ner and Sqn Ldr N. Poole from the CFE, who were tasked to carry out a combat evaluation of the Skyknight. The first operational mission by VMF(N)-513 with the Skyknight in Korea was flown by Gard'ner with Staff Sgt R. G. Kropp, on 11 August. Unfortunately, the squadron commander, Col P. D. Lambrecht and his navigator 2Lt J. M. Brown were killed when they crashed into the sea some 30 miles south of Antung four nights later.

The summer monsoon brought thick clouds over Korea and Manchuria, limiting air operations and, since half of the CPLAAF pilots were not qualified in instrument flying, the number of MiG-15s flying over Korea dropped markedly. In any case, the CPLAAF units were withdrawn from combat operations for much of July while their commander, Liu Yalou, carried out a review into the high losses being experienced by the service. Despite sometimes inclement weather, UNC ground-attack missions continued. On 11 July, Operation *Pressure Pump* involved over 1,200 sorties flown in three waves against 30 individual targets in Pyongyang. Almost every UNC flying unit in theatre participated, although the naval aircraft only took part in the morning

The Douglas F3D Skyknight all-weather fighter joined VMF(N)-513 at Kunsan (K-8) in the summer of 1952. Known to its crews as 'Willie the Whale' the Skyknight was equipped with a AN/APQ-35 radar/ fire control system. (US Navy)

wave as weather conditions in the Sea of Japan precluded launching in the afternoon. Later in the month, on 19 and 20 July, aircraft from TF77 attacked the Changjin power stations once more, with follow-up attacks each night by 44 B-29s. Naval aircraft mounted more attacks on industrial facilities in the following week: on 27 July aircraft from USS *Bonne Homme Richard* bombed the zinc and lead mill at Sindok (north of Tanchon) and the next day 13 Skyraiders and 25 Corsairs from USS *Princeton* attacked the magnesite plant at Kilchu (Kilju).

Although poor weather may have limited the number of Chinese pilots who could fly, the UAA MiG-15s still ranged south of Pyongyang and KPAAF aircraft patrolled over the sea. On 27 July four MiGs bounced a flight of Fireflies from HMS *Ocean* as they pulled off a target near Kangso, damaging one Firefly enough to make it force-land on Chodo Island. Four days later two MiG-15s attacked a USN Mariner flying boat over the Yellow Sea between Port Arthur and Tatungkao. Two crew members were killed, two were seriously wounded and the aircraft made an emergency landing at P-Y Island. Then on the morning of 9 August two formations of MiG-15s intercepted three separate formations of Sea Furies from 802 Sqn to the southwest of Sariwon. In the first combat, eight MiG-15s closed on a flight of four Sea Furies from their five o'clock. The Sea Furies turned into the attack, meeting the MiGs head-on. After the first pass, the MIG-15s attempted to re-attack and once again the Sea Furies met them head-on, firing on one of the MiGs as it passed the formation. The MiG was then seen to crash. The victory was credited to the flight leader, Lt P. Carmichael, although he stated in his combat report that the MiG-15 had crashed after 'all the flight having a shot [at it]'. Lt P. S. Davis, in the number two aircraft, also stated that 'it was impossible to see who destroyed the aircraft, as it crashed after it had been fired on by all members of the flight in quick succession.'

During August, UNC ground-attack aircraft continued the campaign against North Korean industrial sites. On 5 August, 111 sorties were launched against tungsten mines at Kusong and on 11 August 145 sorties were flown against a chemical plant at Inhungni (ten miles southwest of Sinuiju). Daylight attacks were complemented with night-bombing raids by B-29s against the Nakwon munitions plant, southeast of Sinuiju on 18 August and the Suiho dam five days later. During this latter mission, defensive fire from one B-29 shot down a MiG-15 flown by Kpt G. M. Poltavets, killing the pilot. There were few combats in MiG Alley during the month, but on 6 August around 50 Soviet MiG-15s of the recently arrived 518th IAP and 676th IAP engaged a force of 35 F-86s, while UAA MiGs intercepted a formation of F-84s.

Previously that morning, two MiG-15s from the 878th IAP had been shot down by F-86s in the landing pattern at Tatungkao. Neither side scored kills during the combat, but despite top cover from two more Soviet MiG-15 regiments over Antung, another MiG-15 from the unit was shot down as it recovered to Tatungkao. Meanwhile, the UAA MiGs had shot down one F-84E.

Another large-scale bombing raid against Pyongyang was mounted on 29 August. Through the day, UNC ground- and carrier-based aircraft flew 1,403 sorties in three waves against government offices as well as factories, warehouses and barracks.

(Jarrett)

Lt R.D.R. HAWKEWORTH RN
Firefly, HMS *Ocean*, 27 July 1952

Having led a steep R/P attack on two large buildings in the town of Kangso, I heard my No.3 report a large coolant leak in his port radiator, possibly caused by a detached R/P fin. We were already heading west towards the coast, so I levelled off at about 5,500 ft and weaved to let him catch up. I had seen three bogies to the northward, high and very distant and when my observer reported Sea Furies at five o'clock low, I assumed that they were the same aircraft. I then heard 'Look out, MiGs, I've been hit' – recognised No 4's voice, then my observer 'Yes, dead astern, Jink!' I jinked starboard and down, saw a silver swept wing jet pass below and to starboard with large slow firing flashes coming from each wing. The jet put himself in my sights which were unfortunately set for R/P and 'dim' but I fired a short burst on reversing my bank, then banked again to starboard and dived under a convenient cloud just astern of my No.4 (at the time I thought he was No.3 but it was No.4 overshooting). The MiG on my tail had been very close when I jinked and was presumably too fast to follow and broke away to port and up without firing. My No.2 had a non-vital hit by small calibre shell (23mm?) in his starboard wingtip, which he wisely did not report until the excitement had abated. Apparently, the Sea Fury flight had been bounced by four MiGs and had unwittingly led them to us and been unable to switch R/T channels in time to warn us. My No.4 had been hit in the starboard tailplane by what I reckoned to be a 30mm shell. I watched No.3 carry out a copybook ditching near HMAS *Bataan* due to his coolant leak. I detached No.2 to return to the ship with two Furies; I then flew south in time to watch No.4 carry out a wheels up flapless landing on the beach at Paengyong-do.

Before each wave, Sabres and Meteors established a defensive screen along the Chongchon River and F-80s of the 8th FBG and F-84s of the 474th FBG attacked anti-aircraft batteries. The following night, 11 B-29s from the 19th BG attacked the remaining targets in the city. In another large-scale raid on 1 September, aircraft from the USS *Essex* and USS *Princeton* bombed the oil refinery at Hoeam, three miles west of Aoji in north-eastern Korea, while the air group from USS *Boxer* took on mining installations at Musan. During clashes between F-86s and MiG-15s over the Suiho Reservoir three days later, two MiG-15s were shot down, but the bulk of the air-to-air kills that day were scored by F-86s 'hawking' over Dabao: two Soviet aircraft were shot down as they took off, while two more Soviet MiGs and another six Chinese MiGs were shot down as they recovered to Dabao short of fuel. However, three F-86s were lost that day and a further one was damaged.

On 9 September, 82 F-84s attacked the military academy at Sakchu once again. This time, the MiG-15 pilots were more successful in intercepting the fighter-bombers, shooting down three F-84s and causing many others to jettison their ordnance before they could complete their attack. But success came at a cost: six MiG-15s were shot down by the F-86 screen and three pilots were killed. Two MiGs were credited to Canadian F-86 pilots: Flt Lt E. A. Glover and Flt Lt J. C. A. LaFrance, who were both RCAF officers flying operational tours with the USAF, claimed kills that day. On the same day, KPAAF MiG-15s were active in the Chinnampo area where four MiG-15s approached a flight of six Corsairs from VMA-312 operating from USS *Sicily*. On

Loaded with four 1,000-lb bombs, this F-80C Shooting Star of the 35th FBS/ 8th FBG is in an unusual configuration. Lt William B. Slade was killed when the aircraft was shot down by anti-aircraft fire on 12 May 1952. (USAFM)

this occasion the MiGs did not fire on the UN aircraft, but on the next day, there were two combats between MiG-15s and USMC Corsairs over the Taedong estuary. The first engagement, between three Corsairs from VMA-323 and four MiG-15s, lasted ten minutes, but neither side scored a kill. In the second engagement, four MiG-15s attacked a pair of Corsairs from VMA-312 at 8,000ft. The Corsair leader, Capt J. G. Folmar, shot down one of his attackers but was then shot down himself, although he was rescued within minutes by an SA-16 amphibian.

After reports that two generators at the Suiho dam were still operational, another attempt was made to neutralize the power station, this time by B-29s. Just before midnight on 12 September, six B-29s dropped aluminium foil strips to jam the enemy radars while six B-26s attacked searchlights, successfully extinguishing 30. However, some searchlights were based on the northern side of the Yalu River and were therefore immune from attack and, though deprived of their radar, the anti-aircraft batteries continued to fire a heavy box-barrage. Two MiG-15 night fighters were scrambled to intercept the bombing force and St Lt Y. Dobrovichan fired on a B-29, which exploded over the target area. Despite causing extensive damage to the complex, the bombers failed to hit the generator building.

The weather was poor for much of the rest of September and air operations were limited during the last week of the month. Weather conditions caused the loss of four MiG-15s and one F-86 on 15 September, a day in which another four MiG-15s were shot down while taking off from Dabao and three F-86s were lost in air combat. The poor weather at the end of September provided ideal cover for a B-29 nighttime SHORAN attack on the Namsal-li chemical plant on the banks of the Yalu River near the Suiho Reservoir. Three B-29s dropped proximity-fused bombs over anti-aircraft positions and then orbited the area while jamming enemy radar signals, while seven B-26s attacked searchlights. The main force of 45 B-29s then dropped their bombs, successfully destroying the plant.

Late summer and autumn saw another changeover of Soviet and Chinese units. The Soviet 216th IAD had deployed the 518th IAP and 878th IAP to Tatungkao and the 676th IAP to Dabao in July, and in late August, the 32nd IAD commenced longer-range operations with the 224th IAP and 535th IAP from Mukden-West (Shenyang) and the 913rd IAP from Anshan. These divisions replaced the 97th IAD and 190th IAD in theatre. In addition, a Soviet naval fighter regiment, the 578th IAP from the Pacific Fleet, took over aircraft left by the 97th IAD at Antung in September. In the CPLAAF, the 15th HS returned to the frontline at Takushan in late October, where it was joined by the 12 HS, which moved back there from Dabao. The British presence in Korea was increased in the autumn of 1952 after Australians had begun to run short of pilots to reinforce 77 Sqn RAAF and volunteers were sought from RAF squadrons. The first five RAF pilots started flying from Kimpo in September, with five more arriving in October and another five in November; over the course of the conflict some 30 RAF pilots flew combat tours with 77 Sqn. RAF pilots on exchange postings to USAF units also continued to rotate through Korea for combat tours: in September, Flt Lt G. S. Hulse, a wartime Spitfire pilot, joined the 4th FIG at Kimpo.

ABOVE:
The black-and-white checkerboard on the tail of this F-86F Sabre indicates that it is from the 51st FIG based at Suwon (K-13). This aircraft was later transferred to the Republic of China Air Force. (USAFM)

LEFT:
The ungainly lines of an F3D Skyknight of VMF(N)-513 in flight over Korea. (US Navy)

An F9F-3 Panther of
VF-24 armed with bombs
launches from USS Boxer
(CV-21) in the summer
of 1952. This aircraft was
damaged beyond repair
when it crashed on
deck on 6 August 1952
and it was subsequently
jettisoned overboard.
(US Navy)

An F2H-2 Banshee
of VF-11 from
USS Kearsarge (CVA-33)
flown by Ensign
Buffkin in flight over
Wonsan airfield,
North Korea on
20 October 1952.
(US Navy)

A factory rebuilt LT-6G Texan of the 6147th Tactical Control Group used for 'Mosquito' FAC duties. The group initially used light liaison aircraft but switched to hastily modified T-6D and T-6F. (USAFM)

On 2 October a pair of MiG-15s from the 518th IAP led by St Lt F. P. Fedotov bounced a formation of four Meteors returning from an attack against a target near Sinanju. The MiGs closed rapidly from behind and beneath the Meteors, firing on the number 3 and number 4 aircraft, seriously damaging them. Sgt K. J. Murray managed to nurse his aircraft back to Kimpo where he made a dead stick landing after both engines flamed out, but Fg Off O. M. Cruickshank, an RAF pilot, was killed when he ejected from his aircraft. The pilot of the lead Meteor had shut down an engine, believing it to have failed, so the number 1 and number 2 Meteors landed on the beach at Chodo Island, although both aircraft were subsequently found to be undamaged. While Soviet MiG-15s restricted their activity to the confines of MiG Alley, UAA aircraft continued to range farther afield. In particular, in early October the KPAAF 60th JHY was tasked against UN naval aircraft operating in the east of the country. These aircraft had hitherto been safe from MiG attacks because they lay beyond the range of GCI radar cover, but this had been extended. The first mission by four KPAAF MiG-15s was led on 4 October by *Daewi* (Senior Lieutenant) Gan Gyong-Duk. North Korean GCI directed the four MiGs towards seven Corsairs from VF-884, which were returning from an airfield target at Yonpo to USS *Kearsarge* (CV-33), which had joined TF77 in mid-September. The MiGs caught the Corsairs just off Wonsan and in one swift but deadly high-speed pass they shot down one Corsair into Wonsan Bay, killing the pilot, Lt E. F. Johnson. Three days later, KPAAF MiG-15s bounced four Corsairs from USS *Princeton* near Hungnam, but this time they did not make a kill. In a second engagement that day with aircraft from USS *Princeton*, one pair of MiG-15s took on eight Skyraiders with no success, but the other pair, led once more by Gan Gyong-Duk, intercepted four Corsairs, shooting down Lt J. R. Shaughnessy. Panther escorts for subsequent naval strikes were enough to deter further interference by KPAAF MiG-15s, but on 12 October three F-51s from 2 Sqn SAAF were unlucky. As they approached Kowon on an armed reconnaissance sortie, they were attacked by four KPAAF MiG-15s that shot down Lt T. R. Fryer on their first pass. The two remaining F-51s fought off the MiGs, which disengaged to the north after two more firing passes.

The KPAAF MiGs were not in evidence on 8 October during a co-ordinated USAF/USN airstrike on the important rail junction at Kowon (Gowon). Ten B-29s escorted by Banshees from VF-11 (USS *Kearsarge*) bombed the anti-aircraft batteries in the area, after which naval aircraft from USS *Kearsarge*, USS *Essex* and USS *Princeton* attacked bridges and railway installations.

During October and early November, battles raged over the high ground in the Iron Triangle at Triangle Hill near Kumhwa and White Horse Hill in the Chorwon Valley. Now that UNC ground-attack aircraft were no longer committed to the interdiction campaign, there could be a greater emphasis on CAS missions. The number of CAS missions flown by UNC aircraft rose from 2,900 in September to nearly 4,500 in October. In addition, the US Navy commenced a new BAI campaign against supply dumps close behind the CPVA/KPA frontlines, but which were beyond the range of UNC artillery. Known as 'Cherokee' strikes, the naval air attacks were intended to be pre-planned operations against known targets, which would be carried out typically by some 50 aircraft. This concept differed markedly from the extant system of CAS, which entailed small formations of up to eight aircraft, whose targets would be chosen by a

A pair of Meteor F8s of 77 Sqn RAAF on patrol over Korea.
(77 Sqn RAAF)

The nose of an RB-26C
Invader reconnaissance
aircraft of the 12th TRS/
67th TRG based at
Kimpo (K-14) (USAFM)

Mosquito FAC, who would, in turn, closely control all aspects of the sortie near the frontlines. The Cherokee strike highlighted the fundamental differences in CAS and BAI doctrine between the USN and USMC on the one hand and the USAF on the other, but both sides were keen to make the system work. A compromise was found in the use of a Mosquito to clear the naval aircraft into the area and mark the target with smoke. This new system also coincided with a new army tactic of using artillery to suppress known anti-aircraft sites: co-ordinating with the Mosquito, the artillery would fire air-burst shells over known enemy anti-aircraft batteries just before UNC aircraft arrived overhead. The first Cherokee strike was mounted on 9 October and thereafter they accounted for almost half of the missions flown by aircraft from TF77.

There was a diversion for TF77 and some 5th AF units in mid-October, when preparations were made for an amphibious landing at Kosong (Goseong), some 50 miles south along the coast from Wonsan. After two days of intensive 'softening up' operations in the landing area by naval gunfire and by both naval and air force aircraft, 32 C-119s flew to the frontline near Chorwon at dawn on 15 October. Instead of dropping paratroops, they turned back to Taegu. Meanwhile, a vast assault force was waiting off the coast, but the weather forced a delay in the landings until afternoon. The landing craft were launched, but after sailing towards the coast, they turned back to their ships: unknown to all the participants, the whole operation had been an elaborate hoax, designed to draw CPVA/KPA troops away from the frontline. Unfortunately, the Chinese and North Koreans had not been taken in and the only forces diverted by the 'Kojo Feint' were those of the UNC.

Poor weather continued to hamper air operations over Korea in early November, but the Skyknight crews of VMF(N)-513 began to enjoy some successes by night. In the early hours of 3 November, a Skyknight flown by Maj W. T. Stratton and Sgt H. C. Hoglind was vectored by the 'Dutchboy' GCI controller towards a contact at 14,000ft over Sinuiju. Closing to within a third of a mile, Stratton caught sight of the target, which he identified as a Yakovlev Yak-15 (although it was most probably a UAA La-11). He fired three bursts at it and saw three explosions on the aircraft, which dived away on fire and smoking heavily. Late on 7 November, another Skyknight, flown this time by Capt O. R. Davis and W/O D. F. Fessler, destroyed a MiG-15 flown by Lt Kovalev of the 351st IAP over Sonchon.

On 10 November a four-ship of F-51s from 2 Sqn SAAF led by 2 Lt J. Moir was tasked against artillery positions and infantry trenches east of Kumsong (Kimhwa). During the attack, 2Lt B. M. Forsythe, in the number three aircraft, suffered a weapons hang-up on the first pass and had to re-attack, during which both he and his wingman, 2Lt P. Maxwell, suffered battle damage. There was a large reception party to meet them

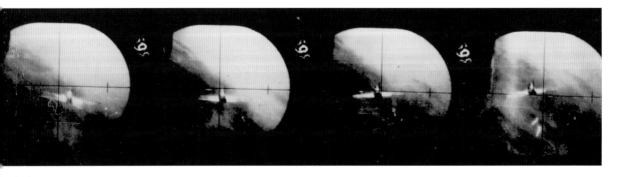

F-86F Sabre of the 39th FIS/ 51st FIG at Suwon (K-12) flown by Lt Jim S. Thompson with colourful artwork along the fuselage. (USAFM)

on their return to Hoengsong (K-46), which Forsythe took to be due to their emergency landing; however, the gathering was there to celebrate the 50,000th operational sortie flown by the 18th FBG, which he had just completed.

The aircraft carrier USS *Oriskany* (CVA-34) joined TF77 on 31 October, relieving USS *Essex*. By mid-November the ship was in the north of the operating area in the Sea of Japan, just 100 miles south of Vladivostok. As a precaution against attack by Soviet aircraft, the ship mounted a CAP of eight Panthers from VF-781 over the fleet. During the morning of 18 November, a number of radar contacts were observed at a distance from the fleet, but early in the afternoon a group of contacts began to approach the ships. Four of the Panthers were dispatched to intercept and identify them. Meanwhile, four MiG-15s of the 781st IAP led by Kpt N. M. Beliakov had taken off from Unashi (Zolotaya Dolina) Air Base to patrol the area and monitor US military activity. The Panther pilots reported seeing seven MiG-15s and it seems that as each side positioned to investigate the other, the US pilots interpreted the Soviet manoeuvring to be hostile. Lt E. R. Williams leading one pair of Panthers opened fire and shot down one MiG-15 immediately. Despite the clearly superior performance of the MiG-15 over the Panther, two more MiGs were shot down in the ensuing mêlée and all three Soviet pilots were killed: only St Lt B. V. Pushkarev returned to Unashi.

An RF-86A reconnaissance aircraft of the 15th TRS/ 667th TRG. This aircraft was shot down by ground fire on 27 June 1952, killing the pilot Maj Jack P. Williams. (USAFM)

During the combat, one MiG-15 hit Williams, causing severe damage to the flying controls of his Panther, but with great skill he managed to land back on USS *Oriskany*. While the engagement was a demonstration of the fighting prowess of the US Navy, an open confrontation between US and Soviet aircraft constituted a serious international incident, but both sides decided that news of it should be suppressed.

Night raids by B-29s against industrial targets continued. On 19 November, St Lt Dobrovichan of the 147th GvIAP was airborne on night patrol. He was vectored onto a contact that he identified as a B-29 and which he was able to follow thanks to the light of flares; these were probably released by MiG-15s from the 523rd IAP, which were also patrolling the area. Over a five-minute period, Dobrovichan fired four bursts of cannon fire into the bomber, which caught fire and crashed, becoming the second B-29 he had brought down.

At the end of November, the CPLAAF 14th HS replaced the 12th HS at Takushan. Earlier, an La-11 unit from the 9th HS had moved to the airfield at Kuandian, 25 miles northwest of the Suiho dam, to bolster the defences of the dam facilities. This was a temporary measure until work at the airfield to make it suitable for jet aircraft operations could be completed in the new year. In comparison to US, Soviet and Chinese commitments, the part played by the UK and Canada in the air war was very small, but it was nonetheless effective. In December 1952, four RCAF pilots were serving with F-86 units and a further eight had completed 50-mission operational tours over the summer and autumn months. The second attachment of pilots from the RAF CFE was also nearing the end of its duty, with another four pilots from the CFE waiting to take their place. British and Canadian officers had held executive positions in the F-86 units to which they had been attached and they had also been credited with successes against MiG-15s during air combat. Some 33 percent of the pilot strength of 77 Sqn RAAF was made up of RAF officers and negotiations were also in place to allow RAF pilots to be seconded to USAF F-86 and F-84 units from early 1953. Both RAF and RCAF transport aircraft were involved in the supply and movement network to and from Korea, and RAF Sunderland flying boats continued to patrol the seas around Korea. Off the west coast, HMS *Glory* had started her third operational cruise.

One RAF Meteor pilot, Flt Lt O. M. Bergh, was a prisoner of war, having been shot down by ground fire in August, and one Canadian F-86 pilot, Sqn Ldr A. R. MacKenzie, was also shot down and captured. MacKenzie was lost during a combat near the Suiho dam on 5 December between F-86s of the 51st FIG and MiG-15s of the 518th IAP, when he was shot down by Kpt Fedotov.

The KPAAF had resumed its night heckling attacks with raids on Chodo Island in late November. Then, on 5 December, it mounted a two-hour raid by 11 aircraft on the Seoul area. The slow-moving aircraft, with small radar cross-sections, proved

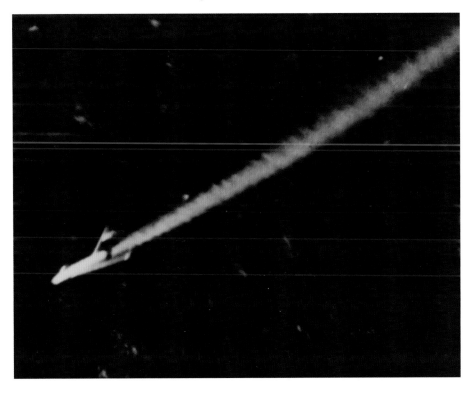

A MiG-15 trailing smoke after being shot down by a US Navy fighter over Korea, possibly one of two MiG-15s shot down by F9F-5 Panthers of VF-781 from USS *Oriskany* (CVA-34) on 18 November 1952. (US Navy)

Part of the tailfin of F-86F Sabre No. 51-12906 which was shot down on 5 December 1952 by Kpt Fedor P. Fedotov (3 victories in Korea) of the 518th IAP/ 216th IAD. The pilot, Sqn Ldr Andrew R MacKenzie, an RCAF pilot flying with the 39th FIS/ 51st FIG ejected and was taken prisoner. (Krylov & Tepsurkaev)

A US Marine Corps
F4U Corsair pulls up
after dropping napalm
on CPLA positions in
the Imjin River sector
of the Korean front lines,
October 1952.
(US Navy)

difficult to intercept, but on the night of 10 December a Skyknight flown by Lt A. J. Corvi and Sgt D. R. George destroyed a Yak-18 as it returned at 2,000ft from bombing Chodo Island. Night-time raids by B-29s on industrial targets continued, along with B-26 and Tigercat night interdiction missions and occasional MPQ-directed B-29 operations near the frontlines. On most days, UNC aircraft mounted around 700 combat missions.

Combats in MiG Alley continued daily through the middle of the month. During a number of separate engagements over Pakchon on 22 December, two MiG-15s and one F-86 were shot down. The F-86 pilot, Lt D. R. Reitsma, attempted to make for Chodo Island before ejecting and two H-19 helicopters were launched from Chodo to rescue him. The crew of the second H-19 included Sqn Ldr W. S. O. Randle, an RAF pilot on secondment to the USAF. Unfortunately, despite the efforts of the helicopter and Corsair ResCAP pilots, Reitsma could not be recovered.

In the last major action of the year on the night of 30 December, six B-29s from the 19th BG bombed the Choak-Tong ore processing plant to the east of Sinuiju and another 12 B-29s were tasked against targets in the Pakchong area. It was a clear night with bright moonlight and contrails above 25,000ft. When the bombers were detected by radar, five MiG-15s were scrambled. The first MiG airborne was flown by Mr A. M. Karelin of the 351st IAP, who was instructed to hold over the Suiho Reservoir. He was then given radar vectors to intercept the bombers, which he was able to locate thanks to the contrails. After closing on one B-29, Karelin fired six separate bursts at it

and saw the aircraft break up in front of him. On his return to Antung, parts of the B-29 were found embedded in the MiG-15. The other four pilots also carried out successful intercepts, damaging two more B-29s sufficiently to force them to make emergency landings at Suwon (K-13). Two of the B-29s in the Pakchon area were also fired on.

As the year ended, the pilots of the 18th FBG looked forward to re-equipment with the F-86F, which would replace the F-51 in the ground-attack role. Conversion to the F-86F also extended to 2 Sqn SAAF and the unit was withdrawn from the frontline on 28 December to train on the new aeroplane. So ended a year of conflict that, unlike the previous 18 months, had been static and, in many ways, routine. And, against a backdrop of the third harsh winter of the conflict, armistice negotiations seemed to be similarly deadlocked.

CHAPTER 7

TOWARDS AN ARMISTICE

I JANUARY–27 JULY 1953

The third winter of the war was another hard one with harsh weather and freezing conditions. The average daily temperature in January was -1°C and there was snow on the ground. As the new year opened, each side was seeking ways of strengthening its bargaining position in the armistice negotiations, so there was no let-up in hostilities. The airspace above North Korea continued to be hotly disputed by Soviet, Chinese, North Korean and UNC airmen.

By January 1953, the CPLAAF had a large fighter force operating over North Korea: four CPLAAF air divisions, each containing two MiG-15 regiments, were based in the Antung complex (the 1st HS at Antung, the 6th HS and 17th HS at Tatenkou and the 12th HS at Takushan) and another two were based close by in Manchuria (the 3rd HS at Mukden and the 4th HS at Laioyang). As they had gained more experience, the CPLAAF MiG-15 pilots had become more confident and aggressive and UAA MiGs occasionally ranged south almost as far as the battlefield itself. The strength of the Soviet 64th IAK in theatre remained at three air divisions, each of three regiments. Two of these were based forward in the Antung complex and the other was at Mukden. While the Soviet and Chinese MiG-15 units in the Antung complex fought the daily battles in MiG Alley and beyond, the task of those based at Mukden and Liaoyang was to patrol over Antung to secure the airfields against 'hawking' by F-86 flights.

NIGHT TACTICS

As the war progressed, night operations had taken on more importance. For the B-29 force, darkness offered some protection against high-performance jet fighters and as a result of the move to night bombing, the Soviet and UAA night-fighter force also gained in prominence. In addition, darkness provided the KPAAF with cover for their guerrilla-style attacks on UNC airfields and radar installations. In turn, the increased threat from these aircraft, as well as that from enemy fighters over North Korea, had led

Waves breaking on the bow of USS *Oriskany* (CVA-34) during heavy winter weather off the Korean coast, 10 January 1953. A number of Vought F4U-5N Corsairs have been lashed-down on the flight deck. (US Navy)

Snow covered Hawker Sea Fury FB11s on the flight deck of HMS *Glory* (R-62) during the winter of 1952/53. (Jarrett)

to the introduction of the Skyknight and F-94 Starfire into the theatre to bolster the UNC night-fighter capability. However, the main driver towards the UNC evolving a coherent night-fighting capability was the fact that almost all CPVA/KPA resupply and logistics movement was carried out at night; attempting to stop or limit this traffic was the primary role of the B-26 force. In the autumn of 1952, B-26 missions had become more closely integrated with fighter-bomber missions. The fighter bombers would cut roads or drop bridges just before dark, so that the B-26s could hunt for vehicles that had been held up by each obstruction. In another tactical variation known as 'Spotlight', an RB-26 would search for railway targets and when it found them it would call in a B-26, illuminating the target with flares so that the interdictor could attack. Using these tactics, 5th AF interdictors claimed the destruction of over 2,500 vehicles and 33 locomotives in January and similar figures in February. Yet another tactic was to use jet-powered fighter bombers on clear nights: taking off in ten-minute intervals they would be vectored to fly along the MSR at around 15,000ft. If the pilots saw vehicle lights, they would glide down towards the target and bomb it; since CPVA/ KPA were expecting low-level attacks by propeller-driven aircraft, the swift but quiet approach of a jet took them by surprise, before they could disperse off the road. The technique was reasonably successful but was limited by the comparatively small bombload of the F-80 or F-84.

In addition to USAF assets, VMF(N)-513 dispatched between two and four Tigercats each for night interdiction sorties, often working with 'Lamplighter'-equipped Privateers. Naval aircraft from TF77 aircraft carriers also launched regularly on 'night heckler' sorties at dusk and just before dawn, searching for vehicle convoys or trains in the eastern part of the country. In the winter conditions, vehicles and trains often stood out well against the snow.

Night-time CAS operations had also become an essential component of the battlefield: CPVA and KPA forces frequently assembled for attacks or attempted to infiltrate in the hours of darkness and night bombing of enemy positions could prevent an assault before it started. For UNC air forces, MPQ radars offered a means of mounting CAS missions in darkness or poor weather by B-26s, Tigercats, Skyraiders and Corsairs, as well as B-29s and, on occasions, jet fighter-bombers. Meanwhile, the night-bombing campaign by B-29s against the industrial targets in North Korea continued through the winter, using the SHORAN navigation system. Typically, the bomber force would be preceded by a fighter sweep of two Tigercats and would also be escorted by four Skyknights. The tactics used by the Skyknights varied: sometimes they would follow the bomber formation, while at other times they would establish a CAP near Antung and be directed by GCI toward any hostile contacts. When the F-94B had arrived in theatre the previous March, the aircraft was restricted to operating over South Korea, for fear that if an aeroplane was lost over North Korea, its state-of-the-art fire control system might fall into Soviet hands. The restriction was lifted in the winter and in January 1953, the 319th FIS began to operate patrols of between four and six F-94s flying some 30 miles ahead of the bomber force.

The Soviet and UAA night-fighter force consisted of two Soviet regiments (the 351st and 298th IAPs) plus an extra squadron (from the 147th GvIAP) with the MiG-15 based at Antung and Tatungkao, and a composite Chinese unit, made up of experienced pilots from the 2nd and 4th HS, which flew eight MiG-15s and eight La-11s from Antung. In addition, an La-11-equipped night-fighter squadron had joined the KPAAF 3rd YPY at Anshan. While the La-11 lacked the performance to tackle the B-29, it could successfully take on the B-26. The other two regiments of the 3rd YPY flew the Yak-18 and Po-2LSh.

The MiG-15 night fighters, operated under GCI control and also used the ground-based searchlights to help them intercept B-29s. With the advent of UNC fighter escort, MiG-15s sometimes acted in a co-ordinated pincer attack on the Skyknight or F-94: one MiG-15 would present itself ahead of the escort fighter and act as a decoy while another MiG-15 approached from behind. In these circumstances, the Skyknight had an advantage over the F-94 because it was fitted with a rear warning radar. The first night engagement of the year was on 10 January during a raid by ten B-29s on the bridges across the Chognchon River at Anju and simultaneously by four more B-29s against the railway marshalling yard at Chongju. Soviet radars were jammed, and a defensive CAP was established on the Cholsan area. However, despite these measures, three MiG-15s from the 351st IAP intercepted the B-29s over Chongju, destroying one bomber of the 307th BG. Another B-29 was lost the

ABOVE:

MiG-15 pilots of the KPAAF. By early 1952, the KPAF had four fighter regiments equipped with the MiG-15, two of which were based at Kuandian to defend the Suiho dam. (Cooper/Grandolini)

RIGHT:

Major Kultyshev (one victory in Korea), commander of the 1st AE/ 351st IAP on the stepladder, assisting his ground crew to prepare his MiG-15bis for a sortie. (Krylov & Tepsurkaev)

following night, an RB-29 of the 91st Reconnaissance Squadron, which was shot down near Antung by St Lt Y. Khabiev while dropping propaganda leaflets along the Yalu River. That same night, a Skyknight flown by Maj E.P. Dunn and M Sgt L.J. Fortin shot down a hard-manoeuvring MiG-15 over Sinanju. Seven nights later, it was the turn of a Skyknight to carry out some evasive manoeuvring, when Capt G. Kross and M Sgt J. A. Piekutowski were fired on by a MiG-15 while they were escorting B-29s close to the Yalu River. After overspeeding the Skyknight in a vertical dive to escape, they nursed it back to Kunsan (K-8) where they discovered numerous cannon holes in the airframe.

There were more night engagements at the end of the month. One B-29 was shot down on the night of 28/29 January and another was severely damaged two nights later. Both of these aircraft were accounted for by Mr A. M. Karelin, who became the first 'night ace' of the Korean War after being credited with six B-29 kills, all of which had been at night. However, the exchange was not one-sided: Karelin had to carry out an engine-out landing at Antung because of the damage caused by defensive fire from the last B-29. There were other MiG losses on those nights, too: Capt J. R. Weaver and M Sgt R. P. Becker claimed a MiG-15 on the night of 28 January and Col R. F. Conley with M Sgt J. N. Scott claimed another on 31 January. In the intervening nights, Capt B. L. Fithian and Lt S. R. Lyons scored the first F-94 kill of the conflict, claiming the destruction of an La-11 on 30 January.

An experimental infrared detection device fitted to the nose of a B-26C of the 13th BS/ 3rd BG. Although crude, the equipment was used with some success to locate heat sources such as locomotives at night. (USAFM)

DAYLIGHT OPERATIONS

On 10 January, UNC fighter-bombers began a six-day campaign against the bridges over the Chongchon River. Over 1,100 sorties were mounted, of which over 700 were directed against the anti-aircraft batteries in the target areas. On 13 January, 96 MiGs, all from the CPLAAF, engaged the UNC F-86s and F-84s, claiming to have shot down two F-86s (though none were lost) and to have prevented most of the F-84 formations from delivering their attacks. In return, UNC pilots claimed to have downed two MiG-15s. In air-to-air engagements the following day, this time involving Soviet MiG-15s, F-86 pilots claimed another eight MiG-15s destroyed, two more probably destroyed and eight damaged, while Soviets claimed the destruction of three F-86s with another damaged. The actual losses on the day were just two MiG-15s. The pilot of one of those MiG-15s, St Lt N. P. Solokov, lost his life after he had safely ejected from his aircraft. He landed on the ice on the Suiho Reservoir but crashed through it and was drowned when the weight of his parachute dragged him down.

At least part of the combat success of the F-86 groups was due to their aggressive leadership. Perhaps none were more aggressive than Lt Col E. L. Heller, who commanded the 16th FIS of the 51st FIG. Like many other squadron commanders, Heller used a loose interpretation of the 'hot pursuit' rules of engagement for crossing the Yalu River and on 23 January he led a flight of four aircraft, including Capt D. D. Overton, who had recently scored his fifth MiG kill, over the river and

The pilot of an F-86F Sabre of 2 Sqn SAAF carries out his external pre-flight check of the aircraft. The unit converted to the type in the first months of 1953. (SAKWVA)

well into Manchuria. Both Heller and Overton were alleged to have shot down two MiG-15s each, but during the combat some 50 miles north of the Yalu River, Heller was shot down by Lt I. I. Karpov of the 913rd IAP, who was himself then shot down, probably by Overton. Heller was captured by the Chinese, and unfortunately, the combat had also been witnessed by delegates travelling to the armistice negotiations in Panmunjom. Their subsequent report caused considerable diplomatic embarrassment for the US and as a result, the rules for crossing the Yalu River were, in the short term at least, enforced more vigorously.

The Suiho dam was revisited on 15 February by 22 F-84s from the 474th FBG, which were escorted by 82 F-86s, while they carried out a low-level bombing raid on the generator house at the base of the dam wall. The anti-aircraft defences were taken by surprise, not least because heavy guns had been deployed there to counter any raids from medium-level by B-29s. There were no losses that day and the bombing was accurate, too, successfully shutting off the generators for several days. Three days later the F-84s attacked a KPA tank training and repair facility at Kangso, some 12 miles southwest of Pyongyang. This was the 49th mission for Flt Lt R. Watson, one of the RAF pilots attached to the 58th FBG, who scored direct hits with his two 1,000lb bombs. The target was revisited by F-84s, as well as naval and 1st MAW aircraft the following day and more than 240 buildings within the complex were destroyed.

The first sortie flown by 2 Sqn SAAF with its new F-86 on 22 February was not a fighter-bomber mission, but a fighter sweep over the Yalu. On this sortie, the 2 Sqn SAAF CO, Cmdt Gerneke, flew as wingman to Maj J. P. Hagerstrom from the 51st FIG. This expansion of the role of the squadron reflected the wider concern

A Lockheed F-94B Starfire night fighter of the 319th FIS, Suwon. After claiming a MiG-15 on the night of 8 June 1953 Lt Col Robert V. McHale and Capt Samuel Hoster were lost in this aircraft five nights later when they collided with their intended quarry near Cho Do Island on west coast of North Korea. (USAFM)

An F-86F Sabre ground-attack variant in the short-lived markings used by the 18th FBG at Osan-ni (K-55) in early 1953; the tail markings were soon changed to red/white/blue vertical stripes. (USAFM)

regarding the numbers of aircraft becoming available to the Soviet and UAA forces and, in particular, the substantial number of Ilyushin Il-28 bombers that had entered service. The CPLAAF 8th HS was known to have converted to the Il-28 and to have 100 of the bombers based at Tsitsihar (Qiqihar), some 400 miles north of Mukden. In addition, intelligence sources reported Il-28s flying from Kunchuling (Gongzhuling) near Changchun, which was known to be the base of the KPAAF 4th *Hang-gong Sadan* (Aviation Division). For this reason, the F-86F fighter-bomber units were now expected to assume the air-to-air role as well as the ground-attack role, so that they could be used against both ground- and air-based threats. The first combat-ready F-86 pilots from the 18th FBG followed suit on 25 February, with a four-ship flight joining a fighter sweep. However, some of the F-51 pilots experienced difficulty in converting onto the F-86, so the group would not be fully combat ready until the beginning of April. The 8th FBG pilots encountered fewer difficulties in their transition from the F-80C to the F-86F and that unit, which had started its conversion a month after the 18th FBG, flew its first operational sortie with the new type on 7 April.

POLITICAL CHANGES

The election of Dwight D. Eisenhower as president on 20 January and the death of Soviet leader Josef Stalin on 3 March 1953 brought a different dynamic to the negotiations at Panmunjom. There was a new urgency on both sides to find a solution to an ongoing conflict that benefitted neither of them. Nevertheless, the negotiations remained tortuous and regardless of the strategic situation, the war remained 'business as usual' at a tactical level for those involved in the fighting. Two Soviet

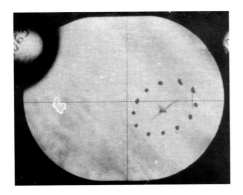 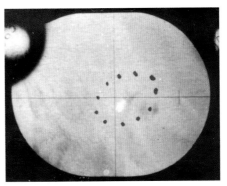

Frames of gun camera film of Kpt Nikolay M. Zameskin supporting his sixth kill claim against F-86E No. 51-2749 on 4 February 1953. The Sabre appears to explode, but there is no corresponding loss recorded by the USAF on this date. (Krylov & Tepsurkaev)

MiG-15 regiments began their tour of operations with the 64th IAK in February: the 298th IAP night-fighter regiment took the place of the very successful 351st IAP which returned to the USSR and a naval unit, the 781st IAP, deployed to Tatungkao, to replace the 578th IAP, which rejoined the Pacific Fleet. A squadron from the 913rd IAP also moved to the airfield at Kuandian in mid-March. The CPLAAF made changes in March, when the 17th HS replaced the 12th HS at Takushan, where it was joined in April by the 14th HS.

Daily battles continued in MiG Alley throughout February and March. During one of these encounters, Flt Lt G. S. Hulse, an RAF pilot flying with the 4th FIG, lost his life in an incident which illustrates the split-second hazards of aerial combat. Over Cholsan, Hulse, covered by his wingman Maj E. M. Sommerich, closed on a MiG-15 from behind and scored hits. The MiG began to smoke and decelerated rapidly, perhaps as a result of the damage inflicted by Hulse. Suddenly faced with a huge overtake, Hulse was forced to pass down the right-hand side of the MiG-15. Apparently believing that the MiG had been disabled, Hulse then turned left across the nose of the MiG, which then opened fire on him. Hulse was hit by a 37mm shell that tore off the outer portion of his port wing and sent his F-86 spinning out of control. The MiG-15 was finished off by Sommerich.

Weather forced a lull in the air combats in the second half of the month, but night raids by B-29s continued. On 17 March the bombers ventured back into MiG Alley, targeting the industrial complex at Ponghwa, some eight miles east of Sinuiju. Four B-29s attacked the anti-aircraft positions, after which another 21 bombers bombed factory buildings. No enemy night fighters attacked and nor were there any losses to anti-aircraft fire. Four nights later, the targets were the bridges over the Taeryong River at Yongmi (Unjon): 18 B-29s successfully knocked down spans on two bridges, but by the time the bombers returned the following evening, one of the bridges had already been repaired. The bridge campaign continued on 6, 7 and 11 April, concentrating on the bridges over the Chongchon River at Sinanju, but once again, despite accurate and successful bombing, the bridges were never out of service for more than 24 hours. The remarkable ability of the North Koreans to repair damage was matched by their ingenuity and determination in building 70 miles of railway track in just 14 weeks to bypass the Chongchon estuary.

On 7 April Capt H. E. Fischer of the 51st FIG, who had been credited with the destruction of ten MiG-15s, was shot down over Manchuria. He had legitimately pursued a MiG over the Yalu River and then seen the opportunity to attack another in the vicinity of Dabao airfield. During this second engagement he was shot down by another MiG-15. His capture was a major propaganda opportunity for the CPLAAF, which identified 20-year-old Han Dechai as the pilot who had shot down Fischer. However, this is disputed by the Soviets, who claim that St Lt G. N. Berelidze of the 224th IAP in fact shot him down. Five days later two more aces, USAF Lt J. C. McConnell of the 51st FIG and Soviet Kpt S. A. Fedorets of the 913rd IAP, were also shot down in combat, although they both ejected successfully to fly and fight again. McConnell, who was one of three F-86 pilots shot down that day, was swiftly

LEFT:
A F4U Corsair armed with rockets taking off from USS *Kearsarge* (CVA-33) in late 1952 or early 1953. (US Navy)

LEFT:
An F2H-2 Banshee from USS *Kearsarge* (CVA-33) releases a 250-lb bomb on a target in North Korea, early in 1953. (US Navy)

A controller using semaphore flags to signal to a (probably CPLAAF) regiment of MiG-15s as it prepares for a mass take-off. (USAFM)

picked up by a Sikorsky H-19 Chickasaw helicopter of the 3rd ARS. Once again, there is a question as to who shot down the USAF pilot, with both the Soviet and Chinese claiming to have done so; the CPLAAF gives credit to Jiang Daoping. At the time, the Soviets were content to let the Chinese take public credit for aerial victories, since their participation in the war was secret, but that has made it more difficult to ascertain the exact circumstances.

The 8th and 18th FBGs flew their first F-86 ground-attack missions on 12 and 13 April respectively and the first CAS mission by the F-86 was flown by the 18th FBG on 27 April. Meanwhile, at nighttime, the KPAAF 3rd YPY continued its bombing raids against UNC installations. On 15 April KPAAF Po-2LSh and Yak-18 aircraft subjected Chodo Island to a two-hour attack and in the early hours of 23 April they bombed and strafed Kimpo airfield (K-14) damaging five RF-80s. On the night of 3 May an F-94 flown by Lt S. G. Wilcox and Lt I. L. Goldberg intercepted a slow-moving hostile contact and radioed 'I've got him', only for the F-94 radar trace to fade from the GCI screen: it seems that the F-94 crew had misjudged the closure rate and the fighter had collided with its target. The 319th FIS had better luck in the early morning of 10 May when an F-94 flown by Capt J. R. Phillips and Lt B. J. Atto claimed a MiG-15 kill over Chongju.

The increasing presence of the CPLAAF was apparent in April and May, but so too were the shortcomings of its relatively inexperienced pilots. On 16 May F-86 pilots claimed a record of 11 MiG-15 kills, all of them against CPLAAF, for no loss. The rising CPLAAF losses caused concern in Beijing. During the month of April 1953, the UNC had lost six F-86s and one F-84 in air combat, while the Soviets lost four MiG-15s – but the CPLAAF lost 15 MiGs; in May the figures were two F-86s, one F-84 and one F-94 against just two Soviet MiG-15s and 27 Chinese MiGs. These figures do not include aircraft damaged during air-to-air engagements. Thus, Soviet and UNC losses were broadly similar, but the Chinese losses stood out as being greater by an order of magnitude. An enquiry into the reasons for this difference by the deputy commander of the CPLAAF, Wang Bingzhang, found, perhaps unsurprisingly, that

ABOVE: Meteor F8 'Halestorm' of 77 Sqn RAAF armed with napalm rockets at Kimpo (K-14). The aircraft was flown by Sgt George S. Hale, who claimed the destruction of a MiG-15 on 27 March 1953. (State Library of Victoria)

LEFT: An aerial view, taken by a 'Mosquito' FAC, of the front lines on the 'Old Baldy' position which was the scene of heavy fighting in 1952 and 1953. The trench lines and treeless landscape are reminiscent of a World War 1 battlefield. (USAFM)

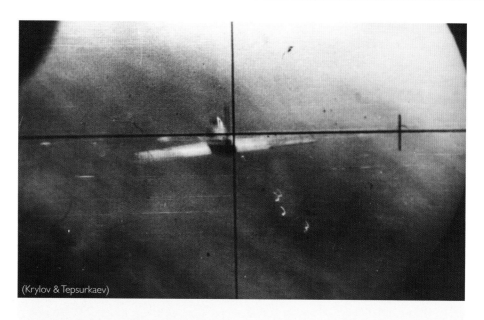

(Krylov & Tepsurkaev)

Mr S.A. FEDORETS, VVS
MiG-15bis, 32nd IAD, 3 March 1953

We took off, climbed to 14,000 metres and arrived in an area east of the hydro-electrical station. There we encountered a group of F-86s on an interception course at almost the same altitude. The dogfight began in spirals, but with tighter turns and increase in G-loads, everyone descended to medium and low altitudes. Everything was going well: we were pressing the enemy, when suddenly Sergei Tiurin, the tail end pilot in our squadron's formation, radioed: 'Look right – a Sabre has got behind me.' I swung around to the right and gave it a burst to drive it away. The Sabre reacted by rolling over into a dive, while Tiurin headed back to base in a climb. I looked around and saw that I was now alone. I shoved my control stick forward and went into a dive at a 60–70° angle. In the dive I found what I thought to be a Sabre directly in front of me. However, against the background of the terrain at such a dive angle it was possible to be mistaken. I continued to close and from a range of 300–400 metres I fired a short burst which stitched the Sabre, but only after making sure that it was an F-86 and not a MiG. From its jet pipe I saw a white emission and the F-86's speed sharply dropped – his engine had lost thrust. I decided to give him another short burst from a range of 100 metres and barely had time to bank my aircraft to the left, so the belly of my MiG's fuselage didn't impale itself on the Sabre's tailfin. My aircraft slipped past beneath the Sabre's left wing by just 3 to 5 metres and by some miracle I avoided colliding with it (my gun camera footage showed that I had fired my final burst at a range of just 3 metres).

ABOVE:
An F-86E Sabre of the 4th FIG in a sandbagged revetment at Suwon (K-13). This aircraft was an ex-RCAF Sabre Mk2. (Jarrett)

LEFT:
Fg Off Roy Watson (second left), an RAF pilot flying with the 311th FBS/ 58th FBG from Taegu (K-2), clutches a bottle of fizz after completing his 100th operational mission on 16 April 1953. (Watson)

Future astronaut 2nd Lt Edwin 'Buzz' Aldrin, serving with the 51st FIG, in the cockpit of his North American F-86E Sabre after scoring a MiG-15 kill in early 1953. A number of the early astronauts had combat experience in the Korean War. (NARA)

it was down to inexperience and to poor proficiency in co-ordination, tactics and marksmanship. Certainly, Soviet pilots considered that although the Chinese pilots were aggressive and courageous to a fault, they were also prone to being target-fixated and often rushed into the attack without checking their surroundings for other hostile aircraft. Furthermore, UNC pilots frequently commented on the poor shooting of MiG pilots. In the last weeks of May, the inexperience of some MiG-15 pilots had also been clearly illustrated by at least seven cases where the MiG-15 entered a spin while manoeuvring and the pilot had ejected almost immediately.

THE IRRIGATION RESERVOIRS

At the end of April, the armistice negotiations once again became deadlocked and the UNC commanders looked for a means of applying strategic pressure on the DPRK leadership. It was decided that attacks on the dams controlling the irrigation system in the Haeju Peninsula would affect the rice production in the region and thereby demonstrate that the UNC could, if necessary, destroy the means of food production in North Korea. As a secondary effect, destruction of the dams would also lead to flash floods, which would wash away roadways and railway lines.

The first strike was against the Toksan dam on the Kyollyong Reservoir, five miles north of Sunan. On the afternoon of 13 May, 20 F-84s from the 58th FBG bombed the dam but were unable to determine the results. However, a follow-up mission the next morning found that the dam had collapsed during the night and the Potong River valley had flooded all the way to Pyongyang, washing away the main road and rail links between Pyongyang and the Yalu River. At a stroke the attack had achieved what numerous interdiction sorties over the previous months had been trying to do. On 15 May, 24 F-84s attacked the Chasan dam on the Chamo Reservoir, six miles southwest of Suncheon, but both this attack and another the following morning did not puncture the dam wall. However, a third attack that afternoon by 24 F-84s breached the dam and once again, flood waters cut off communication routes and damaged the rice crop.

After a pause of a week, on the night of 22 May, a force of seven B-29s dropped 56 2,000lb bombs on the Kuwonga dam on the Imwon Reservoir, seven miles north of Pyongyang. Despite accurate bombing, both this attack and another a week later were unsuccessful because the North Koreans had pre-emptively drained the reservoir.

The Suiho dam was also attacked twice during May, when it became clear that the two generators were back on line. On 10 May, Col V. E. Warford led eight F-84s from the 474th FBG on a low-level attack on the generators' house. Despite intense anti-aircraft fire, the F-84 pilots bombed accurately without loss, but their efforts were in vain and the generators continued to run. On 30 May it was the turn of 12 F-86Fs from the 8th FBG, which approached the area at medium-level, mimicking the fighter groups, before diving towards the dam and dropping their 1,000lb bombs. The tactic kept them safe from the anti-aircraft gunners, who took them to be fighter aircraft and ignored them, but once again seemingly accurate bombing did not interrupt the power generation at the dam.

A MiG-15 pilot ejects from his stricken aircraft. The sequence was captured, on 14 May 1953, by the gun camera in the F-86 flown by Aldrin. (PhotoQuest/ Getty Images)

A flight of four F-86E Sabres of the 25th FIS/51st FIG over Korea on 22 May 1953. (USAFM)

A breach in the Chasan
dam on the Chamo
reservoir, six miles
southwest of Sunchon,
which was attacked
by three waves of
24 F-84s on 15 May
1953. (USAFM)

Taxying over PSP matting
at Kimpo (K-14), this
Meteor F8 of 77 Sqn
RAAF is loaded with
sixteen napalm rockets.
(RAF Museum)

The summer monsoon arrived in mid-May, bringing with it poor weather that lasted into mid-June. The activities of TF77 were also limited by Typhoon Judy, which struck Japan on 7 June. Despite the weather, the KPAAF 3rd YPY carried out a raid over Seoul on the night of 26/27 May, scattering the city with small bombs and artillery shells. Guerrilla-style night raids continued into June and the elusive nature of the Po-2s and Yak-18s rendered them immune from the UNC defences. Chinese night fighters also had success on the night of 30 May when a MiG-15 flown by Hou Shujun shot down a Skyknight flown by Capt J. B. Brown and Sgt J. V. Harrell. Some degree of revenge was extracted a week later by Col R. V. McHale and Capt S. Hoster in an F-94B, who claimed the destruction of a MiG-15 on 8 June. This aircraft was probably also a Chinese night fighter. Unfortunately, the same crew was lost four nights later, while intercepting a slow-moving target: they collided with their intended victim and it seems that once again an F-94 crew was caught out by high closure rates against a slow mover.

On the ground, the CPVA and KPA took advantage of the low clouds to mount offensives along the frontlines in the area of the Hook, to the east of Kaesong, Finger Ridge in the centre of the country, and to the northeast of the Punchbowl. Whenever the weather permitted, aircraft from the 5th AF, 1st MAW and TF77 carried out CAS missions. Between 3 and 6 June, 19 B-29s mounted MPQ-2 CAS missions on the CPVA positions near the Kumsong Bulge. A clearance in the weather in the middle of the month gave UNC aircraft the opportunity to concentrate on CAS missions and on 15 June TF77 carriers launched record numbers of sorties: USS *Princeton* launched 180, while USS *Boxer* and USS *Lake Champlain* (CVA-39) both launched 147 sorties. USMC aircraft flew 285 sorties that day, of which 163 were CAS missions, while 5th AF flew a total of 1,833 operational sorties.

The improvement in the weather had also enabled the campaign against the irrigation dams to continue, with strikes against the Kusong and Toksang dams on 13 June. The Kusong dam, five miles west of Kusong, was attacked by 54 F-84s late in the afternoon and another 40 F-84s bombed the Toksang dam, six miles west of Taechon, 40 minutes later. Both dams were attacked again the next day, but any damage to them had already been repaired. A further raid against Kusong badly damaged the dam, but it still held; however, when seven F-84s and 16 USMC Corsairs arrived for a final attack on 18 June, they found that the reservoir had been drained. Similarly, attacks on Toksang by ten B-29s on 14 June, and by eight F-84s, 16 Corsairs and 16 B-29s on 18 June, were unsuccessful because the damage was quickly repaired; and the water level had been lowered to reduce the vulnerability of the dam wall. The middle of June had also seen the start of a campaign to neutralize all the airfields in North Korea, to deny their use to the KPAAF after the imminent signing of the armistice. Sinuiju and Uiju were bombed by B-29s on the night of 10 June and the airfields at Pyongyang, Namsi and Taechon were attacked on 4 and 9 July.

The cult of the 'ace', a pilot credited with five or more air-to-air kills, had led to some pilots taking arguably unjustifiable risks in order to increase their own score. On 18 June, Capt L. R. Moore of the 4th FIG led his four-ship of F-86s across the

(C. Granville-White)

Flt Lt J.H. GRANVILLE-WHITE, RAF
F-86E, 51st FIG, 17 May 1953

I returned westwards and spotted two contrails heading north. I suspected them to be MiGs heading for the 'fence' [the Yalu River], so I set up a 'bounce' on the farthest contrail, leaving my numbers 3 and 4 men to take the nearest. I was right: they were MiGs. At this moment my number 2 called 'Bingo – 200lbs.' I found two Sabres hot on the trail of the MiG, so moved into a firing position on the left of the firing Sabre. At this point we were heading down in a medium dive at Mach 0.96 towards the fence, so I sent my number 2 man home to get out of the area with the highest Mach possible. The first Sabre fired out on the MiG, so the number 2 man moved in to fire at 15,000ft and broke off at 7,000ft. I then moved over to the right side of the Sabre firing. These two Sabres fired at 3,000ft to 4,000ft. When the second Sabre had fired out, we were heading for a valley running north-south. I then moved in and fired one burst which seemed to hit the MiG in the engine section, as he slowed up and allowed me to close. By this time, we were down to 4,000 ft and I was in his slipstream being thrown around the cockpit like a ping pong ball. My 'uncaged sight' flew off the screen, so I caged it and continued firing at 1,500ft, when the filament in my sight went out. I then closed to 300ft and continued firing, using the tracers for direction; most of my shots went over his canopy. I was out of ammunition, so broke to the left and last saw the MiG heading north-east up a valley... I put in a claim and was awarded a 'probable' as my film showed the first burst which got a few lucky hits on the MiG's tail section.

ABOVE:
A pair of F2H-2 Banshee catapulted from USS *Lake Champlain* (CVA-39) making the first Korean War strikes by the carrier on 15 June 1953. (US Navy)

LEFT:
An F9F-5 Panther of VF-111 based aboard USS *Boxer* (CVA-21) in flight over North Korea, 14 June 1953. (US Navy)

This F-86F Sabre of 2 Sqn SAAF was written off on 19 May 1953 while being flown by 2Lt J.H. Coetzee, after the undercarriage collapsed on landing. (SAKWVA)

Yalu towards the airfield at Kuandian, looking for 'trade'. Two of the F-86s returned to base short of fuel, but Moore and his wingman, RAF pilot Flt Lt C. B. W. Downes, pressed on and bounced a formation of MiG-15s that was recovering to Dabao. Moore scored his fifth victory, but the two F-86s became separated and Moore returned alone to Kimpo where he carried out a dead stick landing after running out of fuel. Meanwhile, Downes was pursued by a MiG-15 at low-level over Dabao airfield. He eventually escaped from it, but he did not have enough fuel to reach Kimpo and landed on the beach at Chodo Island instead.

Nightly raids by KPAAF aircraft over Seoul and the surrounding area, including UNC front-line positions, continued to be a source of irritation. Large raids against Seoul on the two nights of 15 and 16 June caused fires in Seoul and set 5,000,000 gallons of fuel ablaze at Inchon. Propeller-driven aircraft, including Skyraiders and Fireflies, had been brought in to stop the raids, but this measure was only partially successful: a Skyraider flown by Maj G. H. Linemeier and CWO V. Cramer from VMC-1 brought down a Po-2 in the early hours of 16 June, but the raids continued. Better results were obtained by US Navy pilot Lt G. P. Bordelon of VC-3 from the USS *Princeton*. Flying a Corsair, Bordelon shot down two Yak-18s on 30 June, two La-11s on 5 July and another Yak-18 near Pyongyang on 16 July, becoming the only US Navy ace of the war. The activities of the 3rd YPY were also severely curtailed by attacks on potential bases. The B-29 raid on the night of 3 July had destroyed the runway at Pyonggang (K-21) and on 16 July F-86s from the 8th FBG destroyed two 'night hecklers' stranded there. Two Skyknights (one USN and one USMC) were lost in this period, on 2 and 4 July, while operating near Chinnampo. Both aircraft were probably lost to Chinese MiG-15s.

ABOVE:
An F9F Panther of the USMC armed with napalm cannisters delivers an attack on CPLA/KPA positions on 10 June 1953. (NARA)

LEFT:
KPAAF ground crew refuelling and re-arming a MiG-15. (Cooper/ Grandolini)

Lt (JG) Hugh N. Batten of VF-91 lands his severely damaged F9F-2 Panther aboard USS *Philippine Sea* (CVA-47) after it was hit by anti-aircraft fire on 12 July 1953. (US Navy)

Poor weather over North Korea curtailed flying for the first week of July, but there was a period of heavy fighting in MiG Alley between 11 and 22 July. Maj J. Jabara scored his 15th confirmed kill on 15 July, shooting down St Lt Gagarinov. The improved weather enabled the 5th AF to resume attacks on airfields and bridges in North Korea, although operations by TF77 were still limited by weather in the Sea of Japan. Bridges at Sinanju were bombed by 16 B-29s from the 98th BG on the night of 10 July and the next night another 16 B-29s, this time from the 307th BG, bombed the bridges at Yongmi. Daylight attacks by fighter-bombers the following day targeted the major crossing points over the Chongchon River as far upstream as Huichon. At nighttime, B-26s kept up harassing attacks on repair parties. Between 18 and 23 July daily attacks were flown by fighter-bombers against Sinuiju and Uiju airfields. The CPLAAF launched 20 MiGs to counter the raid on 19 July and claimed to have shot down two F-86s and damaged another; in fact, three F-84s were lost on that day, but it is unclear whether they were lost to anti-aircraft fire or fighter attack.

All of this frenzied aerial activity took place at the same time as a breakthrough on the ground by CPVA in the ROKA 2 Corps area near Kumhwa on the night of 13 July.

In the first few days, the focus of UNC aircraft became CAS sorties flown in support of UNC troops, with 28 Mosquito aircraft co-ordinating airstrikes. By 20 July the ground situation was stabilized.

Soviet pilots fought their last combat on 20 July and during the day Kpt B. N. Siskov and St Lt V. I. Klimov both shot down F-86s of the 4th FIG which attempted to engage MiG-15s in the landing pattern at Dabao. That night a large raid by B-29s revisited the airfields at Uiju, Sinuiju, Namsi, Taechon, Pyongyang and Saamcham, all of which had been repaired since the previous raids. The last engagements between UAA MiG-15s and F-86s took place on 22 July. In the final combat, Lt S. P. Young of the 51st FIG chased Lt Su Chul-Ha of the KPAAF 60th JHY as he headed back towards Antung, eventually shooting down the MiG-15 close to Antung.

The armistice was signed at 10:00hrs on 27 July 1953, declaring a ceasefire from 22:00hrs Korean time, giving the 5th AF 12 hours to complete its campaign against airfields. A strike by 24 F-84s from the 58th FBG attacked Kanggye and simultaneously 23 F-84s from the 474th FBG hit Chunggangjin (Chunggang), approximately 50 miles further north on the Yalu River. In the afternoon, a third strike by 24 F-84s of the 49th FBG plus another 12 from the 58th FBG and 474th FBG bombed Sunan. Earlier in the day, a patrol of F-86s from the 4th FIG led by Capt R. S. Parr came across an Ilyushin Il-12 transport aircraft and shot it down, making it the last aeroplane to be shot down during the war. Just 37 minutes before the ceasefire, Capt W. I. Armagost of VMF-311 dropped 500lb bombs on a CPVA/ KPA supply dump, but the final bombs dropped in the Korean War were delivered at 21:36hrs by a B-26 of the 3rd BG on a radar-directed CAS mission.

At 22:00hrs both sides ceased combat operations.

The MiG-15 flown by KPAAF pilot No Kŭm-sŏk when he defected to South Korea, landing at Kimpo (K-14) on 21 September 1953. (USAFM)

CHAPTER 8

IN RETROSPECT

The Korean War was a baptism of fire for the newly independent US Air Force and for the recently formed CPLAAF. Also, it represented a combat debut for the KPAAF. The conflict demonstrated the remarkable flexibility of air power and offered many lessons to those wishing to study it objectively.

THE AIR FORCES

Perhaps the most remarkable aspect of the Korean War was the transformation of the CPLAAF from a small cadre of trainees in late 1949 to a large, modern, jet-equipped air force with recent combat experience in just under four years. To have achieved this in such a short timescale is impressive; to have done so from a population consisting mainly of rural peasants with little or no formal education is almost miraculous. CPLAAF pilots may have been criticized for their lack of skills, but as the war progressed, so the Chinese pilots gained in flying and tactical skill. To an extent, the CPLAAF leadership sacrificed short-term tactical success for longer-term strategic gain: by rotating all the MiG-15 units through the combat zone, they exposed the maximum number of pilots to combat flying. One lesson learned in World War I and re-learned in almost every aerial conflict since then is that if a crew survives its first ten missions, its chance of completing the next 90 missions is improved exponentially; the CPLAAF leadership was successful in giving that experience to the maximum number of its pilots. But the success of the CPLAAF must be weighed against its failure to defend its ground troops against UNC aircraft, or to carry out the CAS mission itself. Having ceded the initiative over North Korea to the UNC in 1951, it was faced with an impossible task to regain it.

The KPAAF is often derided as being ineffectual during the conflict, but that is a simplistic assessment. Like the CPLAAF, the KPAAF had expanded rapidly in a short time and at the start of the war it was a small but effective fighting force. In the first days of the conflict, the KPAAF destroyed the ROKAF, and established air superiority over its own troops and supported them directly. It was only the intervention of the much larger and vastly more powerful US air arms that stopped it in its tracks. Fighting the USAF was an unequal war of attrition that the KPAAF could never win. Instead, the KPAAF commanders sought to rebuild their air force while waging a guerrilla-style campaign to wear down the opposition.

The Torii gate leading to the Sabre flight line at Kimpo (K-14). Jet-versus-jet combat over MiG Alley stole the headlines during the Korean War, but arguably it was the unglamorous work of the UN ground-attack aircraft that proved to be the critical factor in the overall air campaign. (USAFM)

A detail from a DPRK propaganda poster illustrating the Yak-9P and MiG-15 with which the KPAF was first equipped. By the end of the war it was a considerably more effective air force than it had been in 1950. (Cooper)

It is true that the efforts of the KPAAF 3rd YPY were never a decisive factor in the conflict, but they undoubtedly affected the morale of UN forces, not least because they proved so difficult to counter, even with the most modern weapons systems. In the meantime, the KPAAF built up three air divisions of MiG-15s, leaving them with a modern and well-equipped air force at the end of the war. Again, one could argue that the KPAAF played the long game of strategic gain.

Perhaps the most under-rated services involved in the Korean War were the Soviet VVS and PVO, which provided the fighting units to the 64th IAK. This is largely because the Soviet involvement in the conflict was kept secret. Bizarrely, though, it seems that the CIA was fully aware of Soviet commitments even though the USAF pilots believed that they were fighting the Chinese with only a few Soviet 'honcho' instructors. The Soviet pilots were, in general, well-trained and capable pilots and many of the more senior ones had combat experience from World War II. The error made by the Soviets was to rotate entire aviation divisions en masse through the combat theatre, which meant that each new division had to start the learning phase afresh, while recent and hard-won combat experience was lost. UNC pilots noticed the cyclical performance of both Soviet and Chinese pilots, which enabled them to take the tactical initiative. The Soviets had been charged with the defence of Chinese airspace and the bridges across the Yalu River. In this they were broadly successful: Soviet pilots drove away the medium bombers, forcing them to operate by night, and were also successful in spoiling the attacks of fighter-bombers. But Soviet political constraints, restricting the activities of the 64th IAK to the area of MiG Alley, also limited their effectiveness.

From the very start of the conflict, the USAF demonstrated its amazing flexibility and an impressive ability to adapt to the tactical conditions. In the first days of the war, F-82 night-interceptor pilots became daytime fighter pilots, while F-80 fighter pilots swiftly converted to become F-51 ground-attack pilots, and B-29 strategic bomber crews became tactical bomber crews. Indeed, it was really only the courage and firepower of these pilots that stopped the KPA from pushing the ROKA and US troops into the sea near Pusan. But even so, these early armed reconnaissance operations were the short-term measures of crisis management rather than a properly planned interdiction campaign which might have been even more effective. One of the major obstacles to the air campaign was meddling by army commanders who did not understand air power and who did not approve of an independent air force; perhaps the greatest achievement of the USAF during the Korean War was that of finally breaking free from the influence of the army. After the introduction of the F-86, the USAF counter-air operations were extremely effective and in particular the 'hawking' (although theoretically illegal) proved the best way to limit the effectiveness of the MiG-15. The prohibition of operations north of the Yalu River may have seemed arbitrary, but it was a necessary measure to keep the war from escalating beyond the Korean Peninsula. However, the degree to which political constraints can undermine military effectiveness appeared to have been lost by the time of the Vietnam War in the following decade.

The success of USAF counter-air operations, both through air-to-air combat and the neutralisation of North Korea airfields, must be contrasted against the failure of the interdiction campaigns. Although the campaigns undoubtedly caused vast damage to infrastructure and thereby hindered the resupply and reinforcement of the field armies,

The CPLA/KPA proved to be ingenious in building replacement bridges swiftly, so that the efforts of UN ground-attack aircraft were quickly negated. (NARA)

they never stopped the flow of supplies. The problem was that the supply network was so vast and widespread that it was a massive undertaking to stop it and neither the USAF nor the USN/USMC had the resources to do so. Operation *Saturate* had come close to success, but in the end the USAF did not have enough aeroplanes to maintain the pressure for long enough for it to take effect. Furthermore, the UNC commanders completely underestimated the resolve, ingenuity and sheer determination of the North Koreans in repairing rail tracks, roadways and bridges. This lesson, too, was forgotten by the time of the 'Ho Chi Minh trail' in Laos and Vietnam.

For the USN and USMC, the Korean War was a very different prospect to their experience of mobile amphibious warfare during World War II. In particular, the aircraft carriers were no longer the centre of blue water operations against enemy capital ships, but simply off-shore airfields used for mounting air-to-ground missions. The co-ordination of naval air operations with those of the USAF also proved problematic: each service had its own air warfare doctrine and the USN was reluctant to put itself under USAF control. At a tactical level, the greatest difference in doctrine was that of Close Air Support. The naval and USMC understanding of the term CAS was very different from that of the USAF and the difference was never fully resolved. One practical difficulty was that the aircraft carriers of the day could either launch or recover aircraft but could not do both simultaneously. Thus, carrier air wings launched in one large deck launch and arrived over their target en masse. This worked well for saturating the defences around interdiction targets, but it simply swamped the Mosquito control system used by the USAF for CAS operations in Korea. The 'Cherokee' strikes were an effort to get around the problem, but in the end they, too, were compromised by USAF doctrine. Nevertheless, the experience of the USN/USMC in Korea of off-coast operations and of working closely with the USAF proved useful in Vietnam.

Both the RAAF and SAAF deployed single squadrons to Korea, making the air war a UN, rather than simply US, effort. Both units were respected for their professionalism and fighting prowess and they gained political leverage for their respective nations. However, the RAAF almost squandered its reputation when 77 Sqn attempted to convert from being a piston-engined ground-attack unit to a jet-powered air-defence unit. It would be easy to blame its failure entirely on the performance of the Meteor, but in reality, it was unwise to expect the squadron to become an instantly successful fighter unit when none of its pilots had any previous air-to-air experience. The return to the air-to-ground role restored the high esteem that 77 Sqn had enjoyed as an F-51 unit. The Australian participation in the Korean War cemented their position as one of the major powers on the Pacific Rim and also staked their claim to pre-eminence in the British Commonwealth; the South Africans established their military credentials amongst the nations in Sub-Saharan Africa and also signalled their independence from British influence. The completion of 50-mission F-86 tours by 19 Canadian pilots gained valuable combat experience for the RCAF, which became in Cold War years a small but universally well-respected service.

As one of the major world powers at the time, Britain was in many ways under-represented in the Korean war. The demands of Europe and the last vestiges of the empire called heavily on the resources of the RAF and RN and there was little left to commit to a conflict in Korea. The FEFBW provided a handful of Sunderland flying boats, which played a vital but unglamorous part in the war, and the aircraft carriers of the RN also contributed to offensive operations on the western seaboard. However, the limitations of British-built World War II piston-engined fighters soon became apparent: they had neither the range nor the performance to be truly effective and

TA Hawker Sea Fury FB11 of No.807 NAS making a RATOG take-off from HMS *Ocean* (R-68) on 1 June 1953; during the Korean War the Fleet Air Arm was handicapped by the limited range and performance of its aircraft. (Thomas)

the lack of jet aircraft relegated the Fleet Air Arm to a minor role. Despite the many difficulties, the RAF was able to make a significant contribution to fighter and fighter-bomber operations, both in advisory and practical capacities. The RAF and USAF enjoyed a close relationship, sealed by the many exchange postings where officers from each nation filled important posts in the air force of the other, and the advice of Gp Capt Wykeham-Barnes and Wg Cdr Johnson in the first months of the war was both sought after and well received. Later in the war the little-known participation by over 70 RAF pilots – equivalent to the strength of five squadrons – in air operations with USAF and RAAF units was notable for its professionalism, aggression and effectiveness. The tactical lessons of Korea were eagerly studied and applied in the RAF jet fighter force.

ROLES AND EQUIPMENT

The aerial war over Korea is often typified as the conflict between the F-86 and the MiG-15, and a kill ratio in the order of 10:1 in favour of the F-86 is often quoted. In fact, the claim of such a high kill ratio does not stand up to scrutiny and in any case a direct comparison between MiG-15 and F-86 is akin to comparing apples to pears. While the F-86 exclusively fought against the MiG-15, the MiG-15 fought against the F-51, F-80, F-84, F-86, F-94, Corsair, Banshee, Panther, Skyknight, B-26 and B-29, thus any comparison of air-to-air kills must include these types. Furthermore, the role of the MiG-15 was to defend specific targets from bombers, and that could be achieved as much by making a bomber miss its target as it could by destroying the bomber. In any case, the loss figures from all sides, which provide a more realistic and reliable statistic than the kill claims, tend to indicate almost parity between UNC and Soviet aircraft. Indeed, in a lecture to the RAF Central Fighter establishment on 10 March 1952, Maj Jabara, the leading USAF jet ace at the time, stated that losses to date averaged one US jet for every MiG-15 destroyed. That said, F-86 pilots undoubtedly improved their kill rate in late 1952 and early 1953 by the tactic of 'hawking' and shooting down MiG-15s as they took off or landed. While this was a sound tactic for destroying aircraft, it is hardly indicative of the relative performance of aircraft and pilots in air combat. It is difficult to determine the losses incurred by the CPLAAF both in air combat and in flying accidents, but it seems likely, because of the relative inexperience of Chinese pilots, that the comparative loss rate for the CPLAAF was higher than the UNC or Soviet figures.

Although air-to-air combat attracts much interest, the main role of the UNC air forces was the support of ground troops, either directly through CAS missions or indirectly by interdiction of the enemy resupply and reinforcements. The success or otherwise of the UNC interdiction campaigns has already been addressed and the difficulties of co-ordinating naval and air force CAS missions have also been mentioned. However, despite those difficulties, the CAS efforts of the UNC were very effective and played an important part on the battlefield. Streamlining of USAF and USN/USMC CAS doctrine was several years away, but the process started in Korea; the Mosquito techniques were also adapted successfully in Vietnam. One of the main lessons to be drawn from air-to-ground operations in Korea was the vulnerability even of fast jet aircraft to ground fire: most of the combat losses over Korea were due to anti-aircraft fire rather than action by enemy fighter aircraft.

The introduction of jet aircraft exposed pilots to higher speeds, altitudes and G-forces, but the basic tenets of air combat remained unchanged. What had changed was the rate of closure of aircraft and therefore the need to see an opponent sooner, and this in turn generated the need for air-to-air radar even in day fighters; better weapons in the form of air-to-air missiles were needed, too, in order to engage enemy aircraft at greater ranges. But greater performance was bought at a cost of shorter range and the need for longer runways. The former handicap would be overcome by the technique of air-to-air refuelling, which also served to offset the lack of flexibility incurred by the latter.

The speed of the jet aeroplane was in contrast to the performance of the helicopter, which also proved its worth in Korea. Previously the helicopter had been seen by many as something of a gimmick, with little practical use, but helicopters soon showed their value in being able to reach places that other aircraft could not. In particular, the role of Combat Search and Rescue (CSAR) had its genesis in Korea and has formed a central part of US air operations ever since.

If the Korean War saw the rise of the jet aircraft and the helicopter, it also saw the rise of the USAF and the CPLAAF. It also established the template for a number of 'limited' wars during the Cold War years and beyond. And almost 70 years since the signing of the armistice, the continued tension along the Demilitarized Zone (DMZ), which almost coincides with the pre-1950 border between North and South Korea, demonstrates that military aggression rarely solves political problems.

Many of the participants in the Korean War later rose to influential positions in their respective services. Lt Denis Earp (far right), who was a F-51 Mustang pilot, is seen here on the on the day of his release from captivity in North Korea. Earp later became the chief of the SAAF. (SAKWVA)

REFERENCE NOTES

CHAPTER 1

Geographic details from lecture at the RAF Central Fighter Establishment by Sqn Ldr Wright at TNA Air 20/7798 and Futrell (pp 62–66).

Comments on air-to-air gunnery scores from Mansell/ Champneys letter 27 March 1953 at TNA Air 20/7798

Details of Jabara/ Frailey shoot down from 'Richard Frailey: The Air War Over Korea' by John C. Hughes, 2017 Washington State Archives.

CHAPTER 2

All KPAAF information, including pilots' names, from Dildy (pp 4–26). KPAAF aircraft identification follows Dildy's interpretation, although I have also interpreted any radial-engined type (eg Lavochkin La-5/7) mentioned in other sources as being a Yak-11 and any bomb-dropping types such as Il-10, in accordance with the AoB by Dildy (p 9).

Destruction of the convoys on 9 July is described in Appleman (p 90) and Hess p 101) and that on 10 July by Appleman (p 95), Cull and Newton (p 20) and Futrell (p 91) although Y'Blood, 'Down in the Weeds' (p 11) maintains that the incident occurred on 11 July. The latter three sources make no mention of the event of 9 July and it is possible that they (and Hess) have amalgamated the two events into one.

'USS *Valley Forge* (CV-45): Report of Operations 16 July to 31 July 1950' gives targets on 18 and 19 July as Pyonggang – not Pyongyang (Cull and Newton p 261; Dildy p 22, Futrell p 99).
HMS *Black Swan* report at TNA ADM 116/ 6212.

CHAPTER 3

USMC – details from Montross and Canzona; US Army and ground dispositions from Appleman; USAF from Futrell (including RAZON); US Navy carriers from respective 'Reports of Proceedings'; KPAAF from Dildy.

Comments on napalm from Johnson in TNA Air 20/7796.

Wykeham-Barnes report on B-26 night-intruder operations at TNA Air 20/7796.

HMS *Comus* report at TNA ADM 116/6215.

Boxer citation in Air 2/12421.

HMS *Jamaica* report at ADM 116/6218.

Inchon details by Bouchier at TNA DEFE 33/1.

CHAPTER 4

Air-to-air engagements in early November are drawn from Seidov (pp 46–64), Futrell (pp 243–250), and Dildy (pp 28–31). I have discounted kill claims that are not substantiated by the other side. According to Seidov (pp 56–7) Soviet pilots intercepted F-51s and F-80s on 10 November, but it seems more likely that these were a misidentification of ADs and F9Fs since these types were in the area at that time (USS *Leyte* Pt IIa, USS *Philippine Sea* Pt IIa) and Soviet pilots misidentified naval aircraft on other occasions (Cleaver pp 129–30, Seidov p 54).

Comments about Soviet pilots opening out of range when attacking B-29s from Krylov and Tepsurkaev, 'Last War of the Superfortress' (p 23).

Comments about F-80 survivability from *Flight*, 17 August 1950, also Stewart (pp 116–8); also, Bailey at TNA ADM 1/23259.

Seidov states (p 46) that 7th FT/3rd HS replaced 10th FT/4th HS at the beginning of February, but Xiaoming Zhang (Appendix D) gives 12th FT/4th HS, with 3rd HS not in theatre until October 1951.

CHAPTER 5

MiG-15 vs B-29 accounts details from Leonid Krylov, Yuriy Tepsurkaev,
Kpt B. S. Abakumov's account of combat in both Seidov and Yefim Gordon (MiG-15) on 12 April exactly matches the damage reported in Korean War Air Losses Database.

Adderley DFC citation reads 'Moqal-li' but as this cannot be found, I have assumed it to be the place 'Mugŏl-li' which would have been on or near the UN frontlines on 21 May.

The MiG-15 vs B-29 engagement on 1 June is described by Seidov (pp 145-7) as well as Krylov and Tepsurkaev, 'Last War of the Superfortress' (p 47) and there are further details in TNA Air 20/7313.

Chinese MiG Zhao Dahai – Seidov (p 129) records as 31 May, but Krylov and Tepsurkaev state the date as 9 July, which accords with Futrell (p 312). The date, crash position (offshore when Soviet airmen did not fly over the water) and early mark of the aircraft that was recovered by the UN (Hallion pp 144–5) all point to the aircraft being that of Zhao Dahai rather than a Soviet machine.

Seidov's account (pp 169–170) of the engagement between MiG-15 and Panther on 21 July closely matches the description of events in the 1st MAW Historical Diary.

Details of Meteor engagements and Steege's concerns from 77 Sqn combat reports in TNA Air 20/10167, report by AVM Bouchier on 19 September at TNA Air 20/7611 and correspondence in the Sir John Slessor papers at TNA Air 75/108.

Accounts of CPLAAF sorties from Zhang and Communist Party of China – some detail on the action of 30 November from Bruning (p 177).

Details of the Namsi raid are mainly from McGill but I have used the figures for numbers of escorting fighters from Bouchier's contemporary report in TNA Air 8/1708.

CHAPTER 6

Comparison of F-86 and MiG-15 in combat and details of respective tactics are from reports by Lelong (TNA Air 20/10169), Bailey (TNA ADM 1/23259) and CFE teams at TNA Air 20/10168, Air 20/10169, Air 64/169, Air 20/7798.

Comments about Meteor from Wg Cdr Susans lecture to CFE at TNA Air 20/10167 plus 77 Sqn reports in TNA Air 8/1709, Air 20/7798 and Air 20/10167. Dispositions of Chinese units from CIA Korea Daily Reports and also Zhang (Appendix D).

8/1709, Air 20/7611, Air 20/7313. First Meteor ground-attack mission given as 7 January by Wilson (p 105) but 8 January by Odgers (p 222).

Details for the Wadong Chokepoint from the CIA report 'The Korean War – Lessons for Vietnam.' (CIA-RDP78S02149R000100040010-5) and Futrell (p 450).

Tigercat and Corsair night combats on 7 June are described in the 1st MAW Historical Diary.
Gard'ner and Poole report on early F3D Skyknight operations is at TNA Air 20/7638.

2 October – Australian Hughes account in Wilson (p 127) closely matches Soviet Fedotov account in Seidov (p 435).

The night fighter attacked by Stratton/Hoglind on 3 Nov was probably an La-11, since no Yak-15s were known to be in theatre, whereas the Soviets, CPLAAF and KPAAF used the La-11 as a night fighter; the La-11 is similar in size and configuration to a Yak-15, including having a long nose with a blunt front (the radial engine) and the two types could be easily confused in a dark sky. No Soviet La-11 losses are recorded for that night.

The Davis/Fessler MiG-15 kill is recorded by Krylov and Tepsurkaev, 'Soviet MiG-15 Aces of the Korean War' (p 75) on the night of 6/7 November and in USMC records as 8 November; however, the first USMC report is timed at 01:30hrs local time, making it most likely that the engagement took place late on 7 November.

CHAPTER 7

CPLAAF dispositions from the USMC 'Estimate of the Enemy Air Situation 1-53'. Fithian/Lyons actually claimed an La-9, but the type known to be in theatre was in fact the La-11 (Dildy p 58).

Kross /Piekutowski combat from Dorr, Lake and Thompson (p 66).

Some detail on the Heller shoot-down from the Spinetta article, 'MiG Madness: The Air War over Korea', Aviation History, 2008 and Seidov (p 472).

Hulse details from Higson/Grandy letter 8 April 1953 at TNA Air 20/7798 and *Sabrejet Classics*, Vol 17, No 1, spring 2009.

Futrell (p 625) places Ponghwa industrial site three miles south of Sinuiju, but the map shows it to be eight miles east of Sinuiju.

F-94 claim on 10 May from TNA Air 20/7798 'Air Activity in Korea' report dated 15 June 1953 and Dorr, Lake and Thompson (p 66).

Aircraft loss figures from Xiaoming (p 193), Krylov and Tepsurkaev (p 83), Seidov (pp 510–1, 521), Korean War Air Losses Database.

Report of MiG-15 pilots entering spins and ejecting from TNA Air 20/7798 'Air Activity in Korea' report dated 1 July 1953.

Irrigation dam raids are described in Stewart (pp 166–188).

GLOSSARY

5th AF	5th US/UNC Air Force
AFB	Air Force Base
AN/MPQ-2	Narrow beam radar for directing CAS missions
ARS	USAF Air Rescue Squadron
BAI	Battlefield Air Interdiction attacks within the Bomb Line against targets not in contact with friendly troops
Bde	Brigade
BG	USAF Bombardment Group
Bomb Line	UNC – line beyond which aircraft could operate without Mosquito/TACP contro
Bout One	The first ROKAF F-51 unit
BS	USAF Bombardment Squadron
CAP	Combat Air Patrol
Capt	Captain (USAF/USMC/SAAF rank)
CAS	Close Air Support
CFE	RAF Central Fighter Establishment
Col	Colonel (USAF/USMC/SAAF rank)
CPLA	Chinese People's Liberation Army
CPLAAF	Chinese People's Liberation Army Air Force (*Zhōngguó Rénmín Jiěfàngjūn Kōngjūn*)
CPVA	Chinese People's Volunteer Army
CVG	Carrier Air Group
Daelyeong	Korean rank equivalent to Colonel
Div	Division
DPRK	Democratic People's Republic of Korea
Ens	Ensign (USN rank equivalent to 2nd Lt)
FAC	Forward Air Controller
F(AW)S	US Fighter (All-Weather) Squadron
FBG	USAF Fighter Bomber Group
FD	PLAAF Flight Brigade of eight to ten aircraft (*Fēixíng Dàduì*)
FEAF	US Far East Air Force (also an RAF formation)
FEFBW	RAF Far East Flying Boat Wing
FEG	USAF Fighter Escort Group
Fg Off	Flying Officer (RAF/RAAF/RCAF rank equivalent to Lt)
FIG	USAF Fighter Interceptor Group

FIS	USAF Fighter Interceptor Squadron
Flt Lt	Flight Lieutenant (RAF/RAAF/RCAF rank equivalent to Capt)
FT	PLAAF Flight Regiment (*Fēixíng Tuán*)
G	force of gravity
GCI	Ground Controlled Intercept
Gen	General (USAF/US Army/USMC rank)
GvIAP	Soviet Guards Fighter Aviation Regiment (*Gvardeyskiy Istrebitel'nayy Aviatsionnyy Polk*)
HHY	KPAAF Mixed Aviation Regiment (*Honhab Hang-gong Yeondae*)
HS	PLAAF Aviation Division (*Hángkōng shī*)
HVAR	High Velocity Aircraft Rocket
IAD	Soviet Fighter Division (*Istrebitel'naya Aviatsionnaya Diviziya*)
IAK	Soviet Fighter Aviation Corps (*Istrebitel'naya Aviatsionnaya Korpus*)
IAP	Soviet Fighter Aviation Regiment (*Istrebitel'nayy Aviatsionnyy Polk*)
JATO	Jet Assisted Take-Off
JHY	KPAAF Fighter Aviation Regiment (*Jeontugi Hang-gong Yeondae*)
Jung-wi	KPAAF rank equivalent to Lieutenant
KMAG	US Korea Military Advisory Group
KPA	Korean People's Army
KPAAF	KPA Air Force
Kpt	Kapitan (Soviet rank equivalent to Capt)
Lt	Leytenant (Soviet rank equivalent to 2nd Lt)
Lt	Lieutenant (USAF/USN/USMC/SAAF rank; USN rank equivalent to Capt)
M Sgt	Master Sergeant (USAF/ USMC rank)
Mach number	Relationship between airspeed and the local speed of sound
MAG	US Marine Aircraft Group
Maj	Major (USAF/USMC rank)
MATS	US Military Air Transport Service
MAW	US Marine Aircraft Wing
Mosquito	USAF Airborne FAC
Mr	Mayor (Soviet rank equivalent to Major)
MSR	Main Supply Route used by CPVA/KPA
Plt Off	Pilot Officer (RAF/RAAF/RCAF rank equivalent to 2nd Lt)
Pplk	Podpolkovnik (Soviet rank equivalent to Lt Col)
PRC	People's Republic of China
PSP	Pierced Steel Planking
PVO	Soviet Air Defence Service (*Proti-Vovozdushnaya Oborona*)
RAAF	Royal Australian Air Force
RAN	Royal Australian Navy
RCAF	Royal Canadian Air Force

ResCAP	Rescue Combat Air Patrol (defensive air cover for air rescue operations)
RN	Royal Navy
ROK	Republic of Korea
ROKA	Repulic of Korea Army
ROKAF	Republic of Korea Air Force (*Daehanmingug Gong-gun*)
SAAF	South African Air Force
Sgt	Sergeant (USAF/USMC/RAF/RAAF rank)
SHORAN	Short-Range Navigation system of radio beacons for blind b g
Sojwa	KPAAF rank equivalent to Major
Sqn	Squadron
Sqn Ldr	Squadron Leader (RAF/RAAF/RCAF rank equivalent to Maj)
St Lt	Starshiy Leytenant (Soviet rank equivalent to Senior Lt)
TACP	US Tactical Air Control Party
TF77	USN Task Force 77
UAA	Unified Air Army (of the KPAAF and CPLAAF)
UN	United Nations
UNC	UN Command
USAF	United States Air Force
USMC	US Marine Corps
USN	US Navy
VF	USN Fighter Squadron
VHF	Very High Frequency (radio)
VMF	USMC Fighter Squadron
VMF(N)	USMC Night-Fighter Squadron
VVS	Soviet Air Force (Voyenno-Vozdushnye Sily)
Wg Cdr	Wing Commander (RAF/RAAF/RCAF rank equivalent to Lt Col)
WO	Warrant Officer (RAAF rank broadly equivalent to M Sgt)
YPY	KPAAF Night Bomber Regiment (Yagan Poggyeoggi Yeondae)

An AD-4N Skyraider of
VF-194 from USS *Boxer*
(CVA-21) carrying a full
load of bombs towards
a target in North Korea,
early 1953. (US Navy)

APPENDIX 1

Pilots credited with five or more confirmed air-to-air kills over Korea

Note: 'confirmed kills' do not necessarily reflect the actual outcomes of aerial combat.

Name	Rank	Service	Group/Regt	Claims
Sutyagin, N.V.	Mr	Soviet VVS	17th IAP	22
Pepelyayev, Y.G.	Plk	Soviet VVS	196th IAP	19
McConnell J.C.	Capt	USAF	51st FIG	16
Jabara, J.	Maj	USAF	4th FIG	15
Os'kin, D.P.	Mr	Soviet VVS	523rd IAP	15
Shchukin, L.K.	Kpt	Soviet VVS	18th GvIAP	15
Fernandez, M.J.	Capt	USAF	4th FIG	14.5
Davis, G.A.	Maj	USAF	4th FIG	14
Baker, R.N.	Col	USAF	48th FBG	13
Kramarenko, S.M.	Kpt	Soviet VVS	176th GvIAP	13
Sheberstov, K.Y.	Mr	Soviet VVS	176th GvIAP	12
Smorchkov, A.P.	Pplk	Soviet VVS	18th GvIAP	12
Bakhayev, S.A.	Mr	Soviet VVS	523rd IAP	11
Milaushkin, P.S.	Kpt	Soviet VVS	176th GvIAP	11
Okhay, G.U.	Kpt	Soviet VVS	523rd IAP	11
Blesse, F.C.	Maj	USAF	4th FIG	10
Fischer, H.E.	Lt	USAF	51st FIG	10
Garrison, V.	Lt Col	USAF	4th FIG	10
Johnson, J.K.	Col	USAF	4th FIG	10
Moore, L.R.	Capt	USAF	4th FIG	10
Parr, R.S.	Capt	USAF	4th FIG	10
Ponomarov, M.S.	Mr	Soviet VVS	17th IAP	10
Samoylov, D.A.	St Lt	Soviet VVS	523rd IAP	10
Suchkov, I.A.	Kpt	Soviet VVS	176th GvIAP	10
Dokashenko, N.G.	Kpt	Soviet VVS	17th IAP	9
Foster, C.G.	Capt	USAF	51st FIG	9
Low, J.F.	Lt	USAF	4th FIG	9
Mikhin, M.I.	Kpt	Soviet VVS	518th IAP	9

Subbotin, S.P.	Mr	Soviet VVS	176th GvIAP	9
Zabelin, V.N.	Mr	Soviet PVO	821st IAP	9
Wáng Hǎi		CPLAAF	9th FT	9
Ges, G.I.	Kpt	Soviet VVS	176th GvIAP	8
Hagerstrom, J.P.	Maj	USAF	18th FBG	8.5
Pulov, G.I.	Pplk	Soviet VVS	17th IAP	8
Risner, J. R	Maj	USAF	4th FIG	8
Ruddell, G. I	Lt Col	USAF	51st FIG	8
Buttelmann, H.	Lt	USAF	51st FIG	7
Alfeyev, V.I.	Kpt	Soviet VVS	196th IAP	7
Antonov, P.N.	Mr	Soviet VVS	18th GvIAP	7
Fedorets, S.A.	Mr	Soviet VVS	913rd IAP	7
Ivanov, L.N.	Kpt	Soviet VVS	196th IAP	7
Jolley, C.D.	Capt	USAF	4th FIG	7
Karasev, A.N.	Pplk	Soviet VVS	523rd IAP	7
Lilley, L.W.	Capt	USAF	4th FIG	7
Mitusov, A.I.	PPK	Soviet VVS	196th IAP	7
Shulev, V.F.	Kpt	Soviet VVS	17th IAP	7
Volkov, N.S.	Kpt	Soviet VVS	17th IAP	7
Zameskin, N.M.	Mr	Soviet VVS	878th IAP	7
Zaplavnev, Y.M.	Kpt	Soviet VVS	196th IAP	7
Zhào Bǎotóng		CPLAAF	7th FT	7
Adams, D.E.	Maj	USAF	51st FIG	6.5
Gabreski, F.S.	Col	USAF	4th FIG	6.5
Jones, G.L.	Lt Col	USAF	4th FIG	6.5
Marshall, W.W.	Maj	USAF	4th FIG	6.5
Artemchenko, S.S.	Mr	Soviet VVS	17th IAP	6
Bokach, B.V.	Kpt	Soviet VVS	196th IAP	6
Bolt, J.F.	Maj	USMC	51st FIG	6
Boytsov, A.S.	Mr	Soviet PVO	16th IAP	6
Fàn Wànzhāng		CPLAAF	7th FT	6
Kalyuzhnyy, A.A.	Mr	Soviet VVS	HQ 303rd IAD	6
Karelin, A.M.	Mr	Soviet VVS	351st IAP	6
Kasler, J.H.	Lt	USAF	4th FIG	6
Liú Yùdī		CPLAAF	7th FT	6
Love, R.J.	Capt	USAF	4th FIG	6
Shebanov, F.A.	St Lt	Soviet VVS	196th IAP	6
Sūn Shēnglù		CPLAAF	9th FT	6
Vyshnyakov, S.F.	Plk	Soviet VVS	176th GvIAP	6

Name	Rank	Service	Group/Regt	Claims
Whisner, W.T.	Maj	USAF	4th FIG	5.5
Abakumov, B.S.	Kpt	Soviet VVS	196th IAP	5
Baldwin, R.P.	Col	USAF	51st FIG	5
Bashman, A.T.	Mr	Soviet PVO	148th GvIAP	5
Becker, R.S.	Capt	USAF	4th FIG	5
Berelidze, G.N.	Kpt	Soviet VVS	224th IAP	5
Bettinger, S.L.	Maj	USAF	4th FIG	5
Bordelon, G.P.	Lt	USN	VC-3	5
Bychkov, S.S.	Kpt	Soviet VVS	17th IAP	5
Cleveland, C.G.	Lt	USAF	4th FIG	5
Creighton, R.D.	Maj	USAF	4th FIG	5
Curtin, C.A.	Capt	USAF	4th FIG	5
Dmitryuk, G.F.	Mr	Soviet PVO	821st IAP	5
Gibson, R.D.	Col	USAF	4th FIG	5
Goncharov, N.M.	Kpt	Soviet VVS	196th IAP	5
Hán Décǎi		CPLAAF	43rd FT	5
Jiǎng Dàopíng		CPLAAF	45th FT	5
Kincheloe, I.C.	Capt	USAF	51st FIG	5
Kolyadin, V.I.	Pplk	Soviet VVS	28th GvIAP	5
Korniyenko, N.L.	Kpt	Soviet VVS	18th GvIAP	5
Latshaw, R.T.	Capt	USAF	4th FIG	5
Lǔ Mín		CPLAAF	36th FT	5
Moore, R.H.	Capt	USAF	51st FIG	5
Muravyov, V.G.	Kpt	Soviet VVS	196th IAP	5
Naumenko, S.I.	Kpt	Soviet VVS	29th GvIAP	5
Olenitsa, A.A.	Mr	Soviet PVO	821st IAP	5
Overton, D.D.	Capt	USAF	51st FIG	5
Popov, V.P.	Kpt	Soviet VVS	523rd IAP	5
Shatalov, G.T.	St Lt	Soviet VVS	523rd IAP	5
Shelamonov, N.K.	Kpt	Soviet VVS	196th IAP	5
Sis'kov, B.N.	Kpt	Soviet VVS	224th IAP	5
Stepanov, V.I.	St Lt	Soviet VVS	18th GvIAP	5
Thyng, H.R.	Col	USAF	4th FIG	5
Wescott, W.H.	Maj	USAF	51st FIG	5

Meteor crew of
77 Sqn RAAF receive
a final briefing before
a combat patrol.
(77 Sqn RAAF)

APPENDIX 2

British and Canadian aircrew who flew operational tours with US and Australian units

Name	Rank	Service	Type	Unit	Service	Notes
Adderley M.C.	Sqn Ldr	RAF	F-84	27th FEG	USAF	
Almond J.C.C.	Flt Lt	RAF	F3D-2	VMF (N) 513	USMC	
Arnott D.A.	Fg Off	RAF	Meteor	77 Sqn	RAAF	
Babst E.F.	Flt Lt	RAF	Meteor	77 Sqn	RAAF	
Bailey J.S.	Lt Cdr	RN	F-86	4th FIG	USAF	
Baldwin J.R.	Wg Cdr	RAF	F-86	51st FIG	USAF	KiA – 15.03.52
Ball B.J.	Flt Lt	RAF	Meteor	77 Sqn	RAAF	
Bayne T.N.M.	Flt Lt	RAF	F-86	unknown	USAF	
Bennett R.L.	Flt Lt	RAF	F3D-2	VMF (N) 513	USMC	
Bergh M.O.	Flt Lt	RAF	Meteor	77 Sqn	RAAF	PoW – 27.07.52
Bliss W.H.F.	Flt Lt	RCAF	F-86	4th FIG	USAF	
Blyth C.I.	Flt Lt	RAF	Meteor	77 Sqn	RAAF	
Bodien H.E.	Sqn Ldr	RAF	B-26	3rd BG	USAF	
Booth F.H.G.	Fg Off	RAF	Meteor	77 Sqn	RAAF	KiA – 27.01.53
Boxer A.H.C.	Wg Cdr	RAF	B-29	92nd BG	USAF	
Broad R.N.	Fg Off	RAF	F-84	58th FBG	USAF	
Burley B.M.	Fg Off	RAF	Meteor	77 Sqn	RAAF	
Carew R.D.	Flt Lt	RCAF	F-86	4th FIG	USAF	
Chandler E.S.	Flt Lt	RAF	Meteor	77 Sqn	RAAF	
Chick J.F.H.	Flt Lt	RAF	F-86	4th FIG	USAF	
Christie A.M.	Fg Off	RAF	Meteor	77 Sqn	RAAF	
Coleman J.R.	Fg Off	RAF	Meteor	77 Sqn	RAAF	
Collins G.A.	Fg Off	RAF	Meteor	77 Sqn	RAAF	
Cruickshank O.M.	Fg Off	RAF	Meteor	77 Sqn	RAAF	KiA – 2.10.52
Daniel S.W.F.	Flt Lt	RAF	F-86	4th FIG	USAF	
Davidson R.T.P.	Wg Cdr	RCAF	F-86	4th FIG	USAF	
Devine C.D.	Fg Off	RAF	F-86	4th FIG	USAF	
Dickinson R.J.F.	Flt Lt	RAF	F-86	51st FIG	USAF	

Dollittle G.P.	Fg Off	RAF	Meteor	77 Sqn	RAAF	KiA–17.05.53
Downes C.B.W.	Flt Lt	RAF	F-86	4th FIG	USAF	
Dunlop D.A.	Flt Lt	RAF	F-86	4th FIG	USAF	
Eades G.O.	Fg Off	RAF	F-84	58th FBG	USAF	
Easley F.	Flt Lt	RAF	Meteor	77 Sqn	RAAF	
Evans F.W.	Flt Lt	RCAF	F-86	4th FIG	USAF	
Fleming S.D.	Fg Off	RCAF	F-86	4th FIG	USAF	
Fox W.W.	Sqn Ldr	RCAF	F-86	51st FIG	USAF	
French R	Flt Lt	RAF	F-86	51st FIG	USAF	
Gard'ner J.R.	Flt Lt	RAF	F3D-2	VMF (N) 513	USMC	
Glover E.A.	Flt Lt	RCAF	F-86	4th FIG	USAF	
Gordon-Johnson I.	Flt Lt	RAF	F-86	8th FBG	USAF	
Granville-White J.H.	Flt Lt	RAF	F-86	51st FIG	USAF	
Hale E.B.	Gp Capt	RCAF	F-86	51st FIG	USAF	
Harbison W.	Sqn Ldr	RAF	F-86	4th FIG	USAF	
Higson E.M.	Sqn Ldr	RAF	F-86	4th FIG	USAF	
Hinton D.	Flt Lt	RAF	F-84	49th FBG	USAF	KiA – 2.01.52
Holmes W.G.	Fg Off	RAF	Meteor	77 Sqn	RAAF	
Hoogland A.J.	Fg Off	RAF	Meteor	77 Sqn	RAAF	
Hulse G.S.	Sqn Ldr	RAF	F-86	4th FIG	USAF	KiA –13.03.53
James R.L.	Fg Off	RAF	Meteor	77 Sqn	RAAF	KiA – 7.04.53
Jenkins A.F.	Flt Lt	RAF	F-86	51st FIG	USAF	
Johnson J.E.	Wg Cdr	RAF	B-26	3rd BG	USAF	
Johnston I. L. M.	Flt Lt	RAF	Meteor	77 Sqn	RAAF	
King J.E.Y.	Flt Lt	RAF	F-86	51st FIG	USAF	KiA – 4.05.53
Knight R.	Flt Lt	RAF	F-86	51st FIG	USAF	
LaFrance J.C.A.	Flt Lt	RCAF	F-86	51st FIG	USAF	
Lamb R.L.R.	Sgt	RAF	Meteor	77 Sqn	RAAF	KFA – 22.08.51
Lambros A.	Fg Off	RCAF	F-86	51st FIG	USAF	
Lelong R.E.	Flt Lt	RAF	F-86	4th FIG	USAF	
Levesque	J.A.O.	Sqn Ldr	RCAF	F-86	4th FIG	USAF
Lindsay J.D.	Sqn Ldr	RCAF	F-86	51st FIG	USAF	
Lovell J.H.J.	Flt Lt	RAF	F-86	51st FIG	USAF	
Lowry R.E.	Flt Lt	RCAF	F-86	51st FIG	USAF	

Name	Rank	Service	Type	Unit	Service	Notes
MacKay J.	Sqn Ldr	RCAF	F-86	51st FIG	USAF	
MacKenzie A.R.	Sqn Ldr	RCAF	F-86	51st FIG	USAF	PoW – 5.12.52
Maitland J.R.	Flt Lt	RAF	F-86	51st FIG	USAF	
Mansell J.A.	Flt Lt	RAF	F-86	51st FIG	USAF	
McElhaw T.J.	Flt Lt	RAF	F-86	51st FIG	USAF	
Mellers J.	Flt Lt	RAF	Meteor	77 Sqn	RAAF	
Merifield J.R.H.	Sqn Ldr	RAF	F-86	51st FIG	USAF	
Mollan P.F.	Fg Off	RAF	Meteor	77 Sqn	RAAF	
Murphy J.N.	Flt Lt	RAF	F-86	51st FIG	USAF	
Nicholls J.M.	Flt Lt	RAF	F-86	4th FIG	USAF	
Nichols G.H.	Flt Lt	RCAF	F-86	51st FIG	USAF	
Nixon W.G.	Fg Off	RCAF	F-86	51st FIG	USAF	
Patrick K.	Gp Capt	RCAF	B-29	unknown	USAF	
Poole N.	Sqn Ldr	RAF	F3D-2	VMF (N) 513	USMC	
Price J.W.	Flt Lt	RAF	Meteor	77 Sqn	RAAF	
Randle W.S.O.	Sqn Ldr	RAF	H-19	3rd ARG	USAF	
Rigby W.T.L.	Fg Off	RAF	F-84	49th FBG	USAF	
Rosser A.J.	Fg Off	RAF	Meteor	77 Sqn	RAAF	KiA – 28.03.53
Ryan J.L.	Flt Lt	RAF	F-86	51st FIG	USAF	
Sawyer P.G.	Flt Lt	RAF	F-86	4th FIG	USAF	
Scannell M.	Sqn Ldr	RAF	Meteor	77 Sqn	RAAF	
Schwaiger I.L.	Fg Off	RAF	Meteor	77 Sqn	RAAF	
Scott D.G.	Flt Lt	RCAF	WB-29	55th WRS	USAF	
Scott P.H.L.	Flt Lt	RAF	F-84	136th FBG	USAF	
Smith B.N.	Fg Off	RAF	F-84	58th FBG	USAF	
Smith D.S.	Fg Off	RAF	Meteor	77 Sqn	RAAF	
Smith E.G.	Sqn Ldr	RCAF	F-86	4th FIG	USAF	
Smith R.	Fg Off	RAF	Meteor	77 Sqn	RAAF	
Spragg B.J.	Sqn Ldr	RAF	F-86	4th FIG	USAF	
Spurr L.E.	Flt Lt	RCAF	F-86	51st FIG	USAF	
Walker J.J.	Fg Off	RAF	Meteor	77 Sqn	RAAF	
Watson R.	Flt Lt	RAF	F-84	58th FBG	USAF	
Whitworth-Jones M.E.	Flt Lt	RAF	Meteor	77 Sqn	RAAF	
Wilkinson G.C.	Fg Off	RAF	F-86	unknown	USAF	
Williamson K.A.	Flt Lt	RAF	Meteor	77 Sqn	RAAF	

| Wykeham-Barnes P.G. | Wg Cdr | RAF | B-26 | 3rd BG | USAF | |
| Yetman F.B. | Flt Lt | RAF | F-84 | 58th FB | USAF | |

KiA – Killed in Action
KFA – Killed in Flying Accident
PoW – Prisoner of War

BIBLIOGRAPHY

DOCUMENTS

CIA Records

The Korean War – Lessons for Vietnam (CIA-RDP78S02149R000100040010-5)
Daily Korean Bulletin July–September 1952, October–December 1952, January 1953

Communist Party of China

Chén Huī, 'Chinese Hero Fights the World's Most Powerful Enemy and Fights Against the United States and Aids North Korea'

RAF Museum

AC81/1, Whitworth-Jones papers
MF 10043/25, Nichols logbook
MF 10086/14, Burnside logbook
X002-5402/011, Poole logbook
X003-0352, Axton papers
X003-7892/001/002, Bird-Wilson logbook and papers
X003-7937/001, Kinch memoir
X006-0176, Scott papers
X006-0176/002, Scott papers
X007-5216/006, Blyth logbook
X007-9192/013, French logbook

UK National Archives

ADM 1/23259
    F-86 Sabre operations: report by Lt. Cdr. J.S. Bailey, OBE DSC of experiences with USAF fighter wing in Korea.
ADM 1/23260
    Air Combat reports from HMS *Ocean* Sea Fury and Firefly aircraft against enemy MIG15s.
ADM 116/6212
    HMS *Black Swan,* June 1950–November 1951; HMS *Cardigan Bay,* June 1951–April 1953; HMCS *Cayuga,* November 1950–February 1952.
ADM 116/6215
    HMS *Charity,* September 1951–July 1953; HMS *Cockade,* September 1950–July 1953; HMS *Comus,* August 1950–January 1953; HMS *Concord,* September 1950–July 1953

ADM 116/6218
HNMS *Evertsen,* January–February 1951; HMS *Glory*, March 1951– May 1953; HMS *Hart*, June 1950; HMNZS *Hawea*, May 1951–June 1953; HMCS *Huron*, June–July 1951; HMS *Jamaica*, July–October 1950; HMS *Kenya*, August 1950– August 1951.

Air 2/12421
Korea: principles governing honours and awards to British Nationals by foreign countries fighting in Korea and vice versa.

Air 2/16815
Awards for services in Korea: recommendations; December 1950 onward.

Air 4/177
Logbook Flt Lt J.C.C. Almond.

Air 8/1709
Korea – MiG-15/Meteor combats: progress and tactical, narrative reports; story of F86 v MiG-15 by Squadron Leader W. Harbison.

Air 8/1782
Korea: air action.

Air 16/1177
Tactical air operations in Korea: reports of interrogations by I.A.W.R. of United States Air Force F-86 pilots engaged in fighter operations.

Air 20/7313
Reports on operations in Korea: allied and enemy force tactics, techniques, weapon effectiveness and equipment.

Air 20/7412
Maritime warfare policy and Sunderland operations in Korea.

Air 20/7611
Korea: MIG-15/Meteor combats.

Air 20/7638
Exchange of officers, Dominion, USN, USAF and other British services: reports etc.

Air 20/7796
Korea: reports on tactical aviation.

Air 20/7798
Korea: miscellaneous reports.

Air 20/8007
Korea: military operations.

Air 20/8929
Korea: various analytical reports.

Air 20/10167
Fighter tactics in Korea 1952.

Air 20/10168
Fighter tactics in Korea 1952–53.

Air 20/10169
Air operations in Korea.

Air 23/8517
Operations in Korean War in support of United Nations Forces: policy.

Air 64/169
Combat characteristics of the North American F-86 aircraft compared with the Russian MiG-15 as demonstrated in NW Korea.

Air 75/108
Air Chief Marshal Sir John Slessor papers: Korea: 1950–1962.

Air 77/40
B-29 operations in Korea to February 1952.

Air 77/41
Fighter and light bomber operations in Korea to February 1952.

DEFE 33/1
Situation Reports from British Consulate, Tokyo, To Ministry of Defence.

University of South Africa, Pretoria

Moore, D.M. 'The Role of the South African Air Force in the Korean War 1950–1953'. Doctoral Thesis, 1982

US Defense POW/MIA Accounting Agency

Korean War Air Loss Database, 2015

US National Archives in College Park, Maryland

1st Marine Air Wing Records – Korean War

US Naval History and Heritage Command

Report of Operations (various dates):
USS *Boxer* (CV-21), USS *Leyte* (CV-32), USS *Princeton* (CV-37), USS *Kearsarge* (CV-33), USS *Lake Champlain* (CVA-39),

USS *Valley Forge* (CV-45), USS *Philippine Sea* (CV-47), USS *Sicily* (CVE-118), USS *Badoeng Strait* (CVE-116).

Washington State Archives

John C. Hughes, Richard Frailey, 'The Air War Over Korea', 2017

BOOKS

Anon, *Steadfast and Courageous*, USAF History & Museums Program, 2000

Appleman, R.E., *South to the Naktong, North to the Yalu*, U.S. Government 1961, reprinted 1992

Arthur, M., *There Shall be Wings*, Hodder & Stoughton, 1993

Blesse, F.C., *Check Six Champlin*, Fighter Museum Press, 1987

Bruning, J.R., *Crimson Sky*, Brassey's, 1999

Burgess, R.R. & Thompson, W.E., *AD Skyraider Units of the Korean War*, Osprey, 2016

Carver, R.M.P., *War Since 1945*, Weidenfield & Nicholson, 1980

Chinnery, P., *Combat Over Korea*, Pen & Sword Books, 2011

Cleaver, T.M., *Holding the Line*, Osprey, 2019

Cleaver, T.M., *MiG Alley*, Osprey, 2019

Cleaver, T.M., *The Frozen Chosen*, Osprey, 2016

Cull, B. & Newton, D., *With the Yanks in Korea*, Vol 1, Grub Street, 2000

Dildy, D.C., *Fury from the North*, Helion & Co, 2019

Dildy, D.C. & Thompson, W., *F-86 Sabre vs MiG-15*, Osprey, 2013

Dorr, R.F., Lake, J. &Thompson W.E., *Korean War Aces*, Osprey, 1995

Dorr, R.F. & Thompson W.E., *The Korean Air War*, Motorbooks International, 1994

Downes, C., *By the Skin of my Teeth*, Pen & Sword Books, 2005

Futrell, R.E., *The United States Air Force in Korea 1950–1953*, U.S. Government, reprinted 1983

Gordon, Y. & Rigmant, V., *MiG-15 Design Development and Korean War History*, Motorbooks International, 1993

Hallion, R.P., *The Naval Air War in Korea*, Nautical & Aviation Publishing Co, 1986

Hastings, M.H.M., *The Korean War*, Michael Joseph, 1987

Hess, D.E., *Battle Hymn*, Peter Davies, 1957

Jackson, R., *Air War Over Korea*, Ian Allan, 1973

Krylov, L. & Tepsurkaev, Yu, *The Last War of the Superfortresses*, Helion & Co, 2016

Krylov, L. & Tepsurkaev, Yu, *Soviet MiG-15 Aces of the Korean War*, Osprey, 2008

Marion, F.L., *That Others May Live*, USAF History & Museums Program, 2004

McGill, E.J., *Black Tuesday Over Namsi*, Heritage Books, 2008

Montross, L. & Canzona, N.A., *US Marine Operations in Korea*, Vol 1, Historical Branch, USMC, 1954

Montross, L. & Canzona, N.A., *US Marine Operations in Korea*, Vol 2, Historical Branch, USMC, 1955

Montross, L. & Canzona, N.A., *US Marine Operations in Korea*, Vol 3, Historical Branch, USMC, 1957

Montross, L., Kuokka, H.D. & Hicks, N.W., *US Marine Operations in Korea*, Vol 4, Historical Branch, USMC, 1962

Moore, D. & Bagshaw, P., *Flying Cheetahs in Korea*, Ashanti Publishing, 1991

Mossman, W.C., *Ebb and Flow*, US Government 1990, reprinted 2002

Odgers, G.J., *Across the Parallel*, William Heineman, 1953

Randle, W., *Blue Skies and Dark Nights*, Independent Books, 2002

Seidov, I., *Red Devils over the Yalu*, Helion & Co, 2013

Stewart, J.T., *Airpower – the Decisive Force in Korea*, D Van Nostrand Co Inc, 1957

Thomas, G., *Sea Furies and Seafires Over Korea*, Grub Street, 2004

Thompson, W.E., *F9F Panther Units of the Korean War*, Osprey, 2014

Thompson, W.E., *F-51 Mustang Units of the Korean War*, Osprey, 2015

Wilson, D., *Lion over Korea*, Banner
　　Books, 1994
Y'Blood, W.T., *Down in the Weeds*, USAF
　　History & Museums Program, 2002
Y'Blood, W.T., *MiG Alley*, USAF History
　　& Museums Program, 2000
Zhang, X., *Red Wings Over the Yalu*, Texas
　　A&M University Press, 2002

MAGAZINE ARTICLES

Anon, 'Shooting Stars in Korea', *Flight*,
　　17 August 1950
Anon, 'Naval Air in Korea', *Flight*,
　　31 October 1952
Granville-Wright, J.H., 'Fighting MiGs in
　　Korea', *Royal Air Force College Journal*,
　　March 1955
King, H.F., 'The Sharp End', *Flight*,
　　19 June, 26 June and 3 July 1953
Tuel, H., 'Sq/Ldr Graham Hulse DFC,
　　RAF, MIA', *Sabrejet Classics*, Vol 17,
　　No 1, spring 2009
Spinetta, L., 'MiG Madness: The Air War
　　Over Korea', *Aviation History*, 2008

INDEX

ACKNOWLEDGEMENTS

I am very grateful to the following people for their generous support during my research into the Korean War:

In the UK: Graham Pitchfork for his great help, advice and support, Andy Thomas and Phil Jarrett who provided a number of photographs. To Bob Broad, who arrived to fly the F-84 in the last days of the conflict, to Chris Granville-White for photographs and details of his brother John, to Phil Watson, for photographs and details of his father Roy, to Tony Adderley for details of his father Michael and to Charles Bradshaw for details of Jack Sach. Andy Renwick, Curator of Photographs at the RAF Museum, and also Tom Cooper who shared a number of photographs from the Albert Grandolini collection.

In Australia: to the ever-patient Lesley Gent of the 77 Sqn RAAF Association and to Wg Cdr Jason Easthope Officer Commanding 77 Sqn RAAF and Ashley Gillett the 77 Sqn house photographer who provided copies of the images held by the unit. Also, many thanks to Wg Cdr Ian Gibson of the Headquarters Information Warfare Directorate RAAF whose help and advice was invaluable. To James Oglethorpe of the 3 Sqn RAAF Association for his advice and to Monica Walsh at the RAAF Museum Point Cook for imagery.

In the USA: Marc Levitt at National Naval Aircraft Museum (US Navy) for photographs and also fellow author Doug Dildy, who shared his own extensive expertise on the KPAAF and CPLAAF.

A special thanks to Krista Strider, Deputy Director/Curator and Brett Stolle Curator/Archivist at The National Museum of the US Air Force, Dayton, Ohio (USAFM) for allowing access to the museum's photographic collection.

In South Africa: Dirk Louw of the South African Korean War Veterans Association (SAKWVA) for providing photographs and material and (through my brother Bob) for arranging for me to meet the late Gen Denis Earp.

In Russia: Gennady Sloutskiy who acted as my contact with authors Yuriy Tepsurkaev and Leonid Krylov and also to fellow author Igor Seidov; all three authors generously shared their research and expertise on the Soviet involvement in Korea.

Finally, to Marcus Cowper at Osprey Publishing for his tremendous support for the project and to my editor, the still indefatigable Jasper Spencer-Smith for all his help, advice and enthusiasm.